So You Want To Be In
Pictures

Val Guest

For Romilla —
Happy days —
Val Guest 2005

So You Want To Be In
Pictures

Val Guest

Reynolds & Hearn Ltd
London

For Yolande
Without whom the best of my life
wouldn't have happened.

First published in 2001 by
Reynolds & Hearn Ltd
61a Priory Road
Kew Gardens
Richmond
Surrey TW9 3DH

A CIP catalogue record for this book is
available from the British Library.

ISBN 1 903111 15 3

Designed by Paul Chamberlain.

Printed and bound in Malta by
Interprint Ltd.

ACKNOWLEDGEMENTS

My thanks to the following people and
organisations:

BAFTA (Los Angeles), the British Film
Institute, Charlie Baker, Ian Crane, John
Herron, Richard Mangan at the Raymond
Mander & Joe Mitchenson Theatre
Collection, Andrew Pixley, Jonathan Rigby,
Adrian Rigelsford, the Royal Opera House,
Charles Russell and Peter Todd.

The following books were valuable references:

Elstree – The British Hollywood by Patricia Warren,
The Film Encyclopedia by Ephraim Katz, *The
History of the Racquet Club of Palm Springs* by Sally
Presley Rippingdale and *World Cinema*.

CONTENTS

PROLOGUE

'Tell it as it was,' said Peter Sellers. 'Not with everyone smelling of roses. We spend half our lives in the crap. The interesting part is how we get out of it. Just tell it as it was.'

That was in 1958, before Pete had become international. In fact, he wasn't sure he'd make it any further than this, his first starring film, *Up the Creek*, which I'd written and was directing for him. We were between shots on a navy frigate off windy Weymouth and I'd shown him a publisher's letter asking me if I'd like to write an autobiography.

I sounded out a few other chums. 'Before you write it,' warned David Niven, 'make a list of your friends and decide how many of them you're prepared to lose. Also, if the book's no good, can you take seeing it on the remainder counter at Foyles?' Producer Carl Foreman's advice was more businesslike. 'Don't pull your punches,' he advised. 'Remember, a good libel suit never hurt sales.'

But the most down-to-earth comment on writing an autobiography came from Cary Grant. 'Don't,' he said simply. 'Unless you feel like an ego trip.' After which I thanked the publishers for asking and told them, 'Thanks, but no thanks.'

So why, you may well ask, am I contemplating it all these years later? I mean, what do I have to tell that's different from anyone else? True, I've been around longer than most of them, but I never played tennis with Garbo, nor wing-dinged with Grable, Bardot, Hayworth or Monroe. Yes, I did fall in love with Jean Simmons when she was 16 and gave her her first speaking part as Margaret Lockwood's tearaway daughter in my film *Give Us the Moon*. I didn't know then that years later, when she was making *Guys and Dolls* in Hollywood with Sinatra and Brando, this deed would bring me one of the nicest and most unexpected surprises of my career. And I did find a youth named Cliff Richard singing in the Soho basement of the 2 i's coffee bar in Old Compton Street, took a chance and paid him £2,000 for his first starring role in *Expresso Bongo*.

Then there was Errol Flynn. Anyone remember him? In olden days we used to frequent the same coffee bar, the Odd Spot in Cranbourne Street. At that time things weren't all that good for either of us, but I managed to loan him five pounds one morning to buy a secondhand sports jacket from Lawrence's in Charing Cross Road. He needed it to wear for his upcoming screen test at Warner's

Teddington Studios. Years later the irrepressible Errol sent me a cheque from Hollywood on which he'd even worked out the interest. I had a bit of trouble cashing it because in those days I didn't have a bank account.

Or I could tell you about that infamous practical joker Alfred Hitchcock, whose office was next door to mine at the old Gainsborough Studios in Islington, where he was making *The Lady Vanishes*. He, too, borrowed money from this struggling screenwriter. It was late Saturday, the banks were closed, he said, and he needed some floating cash. Could I loan him ten pounds and he'd repay it after the weekend. And I did. Came Monday, Tuesday, Wednesday, but no sorely needed ten pounds. Until late Friday afternoon when there was a tap on my office door. It opened to reveal the Gainsborough pageboy. 'Mr Hitchcock says thank you,' he announced, dragging in two heavy sacks filled with ten pounds' worth of farthings. With four of them to the penny and 240 pennies to the pound that made it 9,600 farthings to be exact. Getting them to the bank was another story.

But I retaliated. I heckled my friends for any old, unused keys they had lying around in drawers. I tied a separate tag on all 200 of them. On the tags I wrote: HITCHCOCK – 143 BROMPTON ROAD – FINDER WILL BE REWARDED. Then we dropped them all over London. In buses, trains, parks, greyhound tracks... It was ten days before there was any reaction from Hitch. Then one morning my office door was pushed open and his pink, round face poked around it. 'Just tell me,' he said mournfully. 'How many bloody keys did you drop?'

Amusing, yes, but it's not enough for a book, is it? Well, how about Bette Davis? I once held her hand to calm her tenseness in the firelit lounge of a hotel on the Yorkshire moors where we were filming *Another Man's Poison*, which I had written for her. We were listening to a shortwave broadcast of the Academy Award ceremonies from Los Angeles. Bette had been nominated for *All About Eve*. Having won two Oscars already you'd have thought she'd have been used to it by then. But she sat there, tense and coiled up on the couch, as they announced the winners of earlier categories. And then, on the static-crackling radio we heard: '…and the Award for the best actress goes to … crackle … crackle … Judy Holliday.'

Hysterics? Tears? Tantrums? Not a bit of it. 'Shit,' said the legendary Legend and strode regally to her bedroom. Although this may never be included in the *Oxford Dictionary of Quotations* it may help to humanise that wonderful, feet-on-the-ground lady who became such an intrinsic part of film lore. It may also throw some enlightened light – if there is such a thing – on those crazy, wild, exhausting, frustrating but always exciting days of reels gone by.

I suppose my film life really began in 1932 in the old British International Pictures studios at Elstree. In those days Elstree consisted of little more than a village street, a red phone box at the studio entrance and two cafés, the Grosvenor and the Manx. I was 20 years old and the whole world was out there just waiting to be conquered. I'd been acting small parts on tour in the theatre and at the same time, to eat more regularly, wrote bits and pieces for weekly magazines like *Titbits*, *Everybody's*, *Film Weekly* and *Picturegoer*. One of those pieces was about the internationally known film comedian Lupino Lane.

'Nipper' Lupino Lane (he was about five feet nothing), 'Nip' when you knew him, had gone to Hollywood about the same time as two other English gents, Charles Chaplin and Stan Laurel. They had all ended up making their own comedy shorts for the fabled Mack Sennett stable. Later, moving from shorts to features, Nip Lane starred in such films as Ernst Lubitsch's *The Love Parade* with Jeannette MacDonald and Maurice Chevalier. One day, deciding he was homesick for shepherd's pie and bangers and mash, he bundled up his dollars, returned to England to star in several pictures for BIP and was now beginning to direct them.

So where were we? Oh yes, Nip Lane liked the piece I had written about him, which was lucky.

Even luckier, he asked if I'd like to help him with the screenplay of his new production, *The Maid of the Mountains*, a famous operetta which had already been a great success on the London stage. 'There isn't much money, of course,' said Nip. 'I can't afford to pay you a lot. But I'll help make it up to you by giving you a small part in the film. And I'll tell Weston Drury in Casting to call you whenever there's a crowd scene.'

You see it was ever thus. I'm sure Shakespeare had the same problems. 'Look, Will, you know how it is, they just won't pay royalties...'

So I had a small role in *The Maid of the Mountains* for which I received three pounds ten shillings a day and played actress Pat Patterson's boyfriend. Dear Pat, she survived it well enough to go to Hollywood later where she married Charles Boyer. Much better casting.

In those days the name Elstree had a certain magic about it. They were beginning to call it the British Hollywood and the studio was full of us young, hopeful, ambitious wannabes. There were two young writers, Frank Launder and Sidney Gilliat, who had passed the wannabe bit and now had offices on the so-called 'Minstrel's Gallery' that overlooked the large silent stage. There was someone else with an office up there. Someone aged 33, with the face of a cherub and a propensity for playing naughty schoolboy pranks on the whole studio. The name on his door said: A Hitchcock. All right, so you guessed.

What's more, he had his own gang of star contract 'schoolboys' to help him – two popular light comedians, Bobby Howes (father of Sally Anne) and Sonny Hale, who was married to Jessie Matthews. Plus another ex-comedian turned director, Monty Banks, who later married Gracie Fields. These grown-up 'Dead End Kids', along with sundry other conscripts, made the studio manager's life a constant trauma. This poor, long-suffering man was Joe Grossman. Joe was also chief of the studio fire brigade and was a universally liked five-foot-nothing cockney with a permanent twitch. And the twitch gathered momentum with every complaint about practical jokes.

Occasionally he would call Hitch and the gang together and read them the riot act. Whereupon they would drop their heads abjectly, offer their humble apologies, promise never again and then probably rip the poor man's flies open. A text book case of grown men suffering from delayed adulthood.

Nevertheless, Hitch was already the pride of the studio, his most recent triumph being Elstree's *Blackmail*, England's answer to Warner Bros' first sound feature film *The Singing Fool*. It was Hitch's first talkie production and it has long since gone into the annals of British film history. At the studio they called him 'The Wonder Boy'. Which is not what Joe Grossman called him.

It's fun all these years later to look at the old *Blackmail* poster and its oblique tilt at Hollywood as it proclaimed: SEE AND HEAR IT, OUR MOTHER TONGUE AS IT SHOULD BE SPOKEN. Vive les Brits!

The man responsible for most of BIP's success was studio chief Walter Mycroft. Mycroft was a diminutive hunchback who had once been the *Evening Standard* film critic and had now shown great skills in banding together the studio's production teams. He was a Führer, respected, feared and disliked. I well recall the memorable day after Mycroft had decreed that all lavatories should be repainted. Next morning Joe made an inspection tour of the work, walked into one of the cubicles and recoiled in horror. Scored into the newly painted wall were the words, MYCROFT IS A SHIT. Joe twitched himself into a further spasm as he saw that an arrow had been drawn to within two feet of the floor where it said, I'M NOT!

Painting it out was easy, but how to stop heads rolling if the news got to Mycroft? Fortunately it didn't. Hitch, Bobby, Sonny and Monty all strenuously denied they had anything to do with it but nobody really believed them. Years later both Hitch and Monty swore to me it wasn't them. Honestly, it wasn't them. 'Not that we didn't agree with the message,' said Hitch.

There was an unusual warmth and camaraderie between us wannabes. It seemed we were all wrapped up in the same halcyon dreams as we rabbitted together over pre-studio breakfasts in either the Grosvenor or Manx café which, incidentally, was run by Frank Launder's wife, Ailie. A couple of our wannabes, who picked up a fair amount of 'extra' work, were Michael Wilding and Jimmy Stewart. Not *the* Jimmy Stewart, of course. Our Jimmy finally realised his name would have to go, so he changed it to Stewart Granger. Sometimes these two could actually afford a full egg-bacon-and-sausage breakfast because they'd been elevated to stand-ins.

Another member of the breakfast club was Ronnie, the eager 20-year-old clapperboy, teaboy, messenger and general gopher we'd had on *The Maid of the Mountains*. He didn't change his name but went on to distinguish it by growing into that eminent director Ronald Neame who gave us, among his numerous other films, the memorable *Tunes of Glory*, *The Prime of Miss Jean Brodie* and *The Poseidon Adventure*. And Mickey, that friendly young stills cameraman who nipped in and out of the sets snapping production stills between shots? Did Mickey Powell ever dream he'd end up as Michael Powell, the distinguished producer/director of such classics as *A Matter of Life and Death* and *The Red Shoes*?

Then there was Reginald Truscott-Jones, who for some reason called himself Spike and changed Truscott-Jones to Milland. Spike had gone beyond extra and stand-in work and made a couple of what BIP called Quota Quickies. 'Spike...?' Jimmy Granger had shaken his head in disbelief. 'Sounds like a jazz drummer. How the hell can he ever get that name up in lights?' Well, of course, he didn't. Not until he changed it to Ray Milland.

Heady days? Maybe. But financially tough. I was living in a tiny bed-sit on the top floor of Number 5 Oxford Terrace, off the Edgware Road. Luckily there was a redoubtable Dickensian character called Fred who owned a mobile coffee stall which he parked in the road outside Number 5 every evening. So my coffee and saveloy sandwich dinners were an inexpensive godsend when I got home from Elstree. Every dawn I used to walk along the Edgware Road to Lupino Lane's house in Maida Vale for a lift to the studios in his Daimler.

As it turned out, 1932 was to be a vintage year for me. In quick succession I made four more films with him at Elstree, in which I did the obligatory bit of writing and acting. Not for nothing was British International fondly called 'The Porridge Factory'.

Almost immediately after *The Maid* we launched into *Innocents of Chicago*, a lighthearted romp in which an innocent Englishman got entangled with the Mob. The Englishman was played by Henry Kendall, a great favourite with both the stage and film public. Henry had breezed his way through many successes in both mediums and been hailed as the new Cary Grant. Or, for the benefit of younger readers, the new Hugh Grant. I say this because the year Hugh Grant was hailed as the new Cary Grant, someone asked me, 'Who's Cary Grant?'

You can tell I didn't spend over 50 years in the film business without learning something.

Others in the cast were American actor Bernard Nedell and Margot Grahame. Plus, as a nightclub gangster's moll, Binnie Barnes, a lovely, fun, down-to-earth person who, many years later, was to weave in and out of my life via two husbands. The first: Sam Joseph, whose Joseph's Bookshop was a landmark in Charing Cross Road. Hubby number two was Mike Frankovich, also a landmark for me as the head of Columbia Pictures, for whom I was later to make a couple of films.

Margot Grahame was a well-endowed platinum blonde who eventually went to Hollywood where she was Oscar-nominated for her performance opposite Victor McLaglen in *The Informer*. Nip Lane had venal feelings about Margot and often used me as his messenger. When we were all in the same studio car en route to some location or other, he would lean across and pass me a slip of folded paper. 'Get this from the chemist for me, would you?' The slip usually said something like: 'Tell Margot same place, same time.'

Then there was that great, fun-loving, boisterous young American choreographer who took London by storm in the late 1920s and 30s and had so many West End musicals running it was hard to keep track of them. His name was Ralph Reader and no matter what the show, his dance routines ran away with the reviews. In later years he became involved with the Boy Scout movement and created the famous 'Gang Shows' for which he received a knighthood from the Queen. But in those days Sir Ralph was still just full-of-life Ralph, my good friend and sparring partner. And we had more fun with the parties he threw for his dancers and the girls we flew or drove to football matches around England, Scotland, Ireland and Wales.

At this particular time Ralph had two musicals running in the West End, *Good News* at the Carlton Theatre in the Haymarket and *Hold Everything* at the Palace in Cambridge Circus. One day at the Carlton he invited me to come and see a new routine he'd just put into *Hold Everything*. We grabbed a cab in the Haymarket and were halfway up Shaftesbury Avenue when he suddenly leant across, took me in his arms, kissed me full on the lips and said 'You must know I love you.'

For a long moment I sat in catatonic shock. In those days I was young and incredibly naïve about such things. Later in life I was to meet up with similar highly charged experiences and by then I'd learned the tricks of handling them. But now, facing one of my favourite chums, I felt like Butch Cassidy might have felt had the Sundance Kid suddenly said 'I fancy you.' Or even Stan Laurel learning that Hardy had a crush on him.

'Are you shocked?' asked Ralph, realising my jaw hadn't dropped for nothing. 'No... I mean, yes... I mean...' What the hell did I mean? I remember realising this is how some girls must have felt when I had given them almost the same dialogue. 'I'm sorry, Ralph,' I said eventually, 'but I'm not really into that sort of thing.' Hardly deathless prose and if it had turned up in any of my scripts I'd have fired the writer, but at that time it seemed to cover my point, so to speak.

Poor Ralph, I don't know which of us was more embarrassed. 'I hope it's not going to affect our friendship,' I added lamely. 'Of course it won't,' he said emphatically. And the wonder was that it didn't. Our fun friendship lasted for many years.

Which only goes to show, you never know what's going to happen next. I mean, I once gave Brigitte Bardot a lift back from Pinewood Studios and she never leant over, kissed me full on the lips and said 'You must know I love you.'

Have I been giving out the wrong signals all these years?

CHAPTER ONE

I was 12 before I first learned the truth about my mother. All my father had told me was that she had died when I was three and he and I were living in Calcutta, India, where he was a jute and gunny broker. Yes, I asked the same question and found out that jute was a kind of fibre and gunny was something they used to make sacks.

I don't recall a lot about India except that we had several servants and I was well looked after by an Indian nanny, or ayah, named Ava. It must have been Ava, that gentle lady in the orange sari, who gave me my lifelong taste for curry. She cooked my meals of fruit and vegetables immersed in a warm mixture of creamy yoghurt seasoned with her own curry made up with who knows what exotic herbs and spices. My first comfort food.

Today, whenever my shrewd lady wife, Yolande, wants to feed me healthy food like broccoli, which I hate, all she has to do is give it a taste of curry and I gobble it down.

We returned to London just before the outbreak of World War I and, for some reason that I never fathomed, my father bought a hotel in Lancaster Gate. It was called the Hotel Capitol, where I grew up with a succession of different nannies. It was with one of these ladies that as a four-year-old I had my first fleeting brush with sex. This was Miss Arrowsmith, a very nice lady who happened to have a girlfriend, Miss Hudson, who came and spent the odd steamy afternoon with her while little Val was supposed to be sleeping. All it meant to this child was that the grown-ups were playing games in the adjoining room.

My father was a strange man and sadly I can't honestly say I ever really got to know him. Clean-shaven, portly, prematurely balding, he suffered from a persecution complex. Everyone was against him, nobody could be trusted and they were all out to get his money, not that he had much. Whether this was because of the hotel or in spite of it I never knew. He also lived by the principle that everything could be bought for less. I suppose subconsciously I developed an inner rebellion against all this because I grew up trusting far too many people, believing the best of every three-cardster I came across and couldn't even bargain with an Arab rug-pedlar.

And what an embarrassment this bargaining was for a nine-year-old about to go to his first boarding school. My father had taken me to the boys' clothes department at Selfridges where, in front of several other boys getting fitted for their first school outfits, he bargained unmercifully with the department manager to have the school socks and belt thrown in with the suit. Whether he succeeded or not I never knew, but I do know I wanted to pull the carpet over me and die.

I sat through the same kind of bargaining when Daddy first took me down to meet the Rev Maurice Cowan, headmaster of Seaford College in Sussex, where I was about to be deposited. As this was the associate junior school to Stowe public school, fees were demanded one year in advance. But dear Daddy was able to parley this into one term at a time. Maybe this is why, at school, it was always me who was conscripted to help load the wheelbarrows with grass turfs for the headmaster's new tennis court. Or help pull wooden sleds, loaded with various sized rocks, from the beach at Splash Point to help build a rock mound for a flagpole near the school entrance. Mind you, it did get me off a few classes and Seaford College was a very pleasant spot to push turfs and pull rocks around. And that rock mound is still there today. What's more, I found it actually had the date and my initials carved on it. For posterity, I suppose.

At Seaford, every Saturday morning was letter-writing time, when we all sat at our desks and penned the obligatory note to our parents. After I'd sent a couple of 'Dear Daddy' epistles my father gave me strict instructions that in future I must begin all my letters with: 'My own darling Daddy'. To me all this meant was a few more words to write. I was too young to realise this showed the insecurity he must be feeling about having my love and affection.

But I'm jumping ahead of myself. I'm still at the Hotel Capitol and we still had to get through the Great War. I vividly remember three things about that war. The occasional air-raid siren which I could hear in my small room on the top floor of the hotel, and being taken for a walk one morning in Hyde Park with Miss Arrowsmith during the first Zeppelin raid on London, and watching the enormous German dirigible floating high over our heads. Then there was that 1918 Armistice Day when Miss Arrowmith had taken me down to Miss Hudson's cottage in Bournemouth and we watched the flag-covered British tanks rumble down the cheering High Street.

But perhaps my most impressive memory of that time was back in London, not too long after that, when the two girls took me to the Marble Arch Pavilion to see a film starring Mae Murray and Rudolph Valentino, at which Valentino himself was making a personal appearance. After the show, while the dapper, sleek-haired film star stood in the foyer shaking hands with various notables, Miss Hudson pushed me forward into the line. Valentino smiled, shook my hand, patted me on the head and said, 'Hello, little man.' To me they were deathless words. Not because he was Valentino – had he been Felix the Cat or Charlie Chaplin I might have been more impressed – but because it was the first time I'd been called 'little man'. At that moment I felt myself grow another two inches.

Mae Murray was, of course, one of the most popular silent movie stars of the time. Her famous bee-stung lips and frizzy, curled blonde hair had captivated filmgoers around the world. Funny, the tricks life dreams up for us. For instance, years later when I was 22, I had a love-at-first-sight moment with a redhead called Mae Murray. She was one of the LeRoy Prinz dancers from Paramount Studios, brought over by the still-young Dorchester Hotel, in Park Lane, to launch their famous 'Dorchester Follies'. And I thought she was smashing. At that time I was writing a London column for the now-extinct *Zit's New York Review*, which was a paper similar to *Variety* but without quite as much clout. I chatted up this sparkling redhead at a couple of rehearsals and offered to show her around, starting with Windsor Castle on Sunday. She accepted the offer with enthusiasm. So far I was doing well.

Came Sunday and I arrived at the Mayfair Hotel, where all the girls were staying. 'Please call Miss Mae Murray,' I kidded at the front desk, 'and say her Windsor Castle limousine awaits without.'

Fifteen minutes later there was still no sign of my date so I returned to the front desk. However, before I could open my mouth a voice behind me said, 'Are you the Windsor Castle man?' I turned, and my smile froze in stunned amazement. There she was. Not my dancing redhead but *the* Mae Murray. Glamorously wrapped up for the drive and that frizzy, curled blonde hair still immediately recognisable. In London for a few days and, unbelievably, staying at the same hotel. 'It's darling of them to arrange this for me,' said the bee-stung lips. 'Was it Metro?'

'Well … actually it's my car … and I was … I was about to…' I stammered. I knew this had aleady gone too far to back out. Should I drive them *both* to Windsor? It was like a nightmarish cartoon: 'The Man Who Dated Two Mae Murrays'.

'Is the limo outside?' asked the Lips and glided out through the hotel entrance. Panic. What to do? I raced back to the desk. 'There's another Mae Murray,' I gibbered, 'one of the Dorchester girls.' 'Oh, they're all gone.' 'Gone? Where?' 'Early rehearsal call. They're at the Dorchester.'

Which is how I gave the original Mae Murray a tour of Windsor. She turned out to be a charmer, good fun and a great giggler. 'I'd love to meet the King,' she said as we reached Windsor Castle. 'D'you think he'd like to meet me?' I told her I was sure he would but I didn't have quite enough pull to arrange it. I took her to the Nell Gwynne tearooms for a Devonshire tea and then back to the Mayfair Hotel where she thanked me profusely, gave me a Beverly Hills telephone number and said if I was ever there... Anyway, it ended up giving me a nice piece for my column and getting me nowhere fast with the second Miss M.

Meanwhile, back at the ranch – or rather the Hotel Capitol. It was 1919. The war had been over a year, I was eight years old and my father decided to sell the hotel and buy two houses in Hampstead. Numbers 21 and 32 Winchester Road at Swiss Cottage NW3. The top half of Number 32 was to be our home. The lower half and basement were to be rented out as flats. Number 21 would also be let out on rentals. And the day we moved into Number 32 was to be historic for me. A lady came into our lives who was to be the best thing that could ever have happened to us. My father introduced her to me. 'This is Miss Grey,' he told me, 'and she's going to look after you from now on.'

Violet Grey was of medium height, fair-haired, in her early twenties and had been engaged not only to look after me but to be my father's housekeeper at Number 32. Incredibly, she and I seemed to bond immediately. And all at once I felt there was a mother figure around the house. I am certain that but for her steady, understanding kindness and love in my formative years I would never have made it this far with so few scars. And I'm sure it was her influence that finally made my father decide to allow me to take the bus for the first time and go to Sunday tea with my grandparents, who lived in the Park Royal Hotel at Lancaster Gate. It was to be the first time I had ever met them. They were my mother's parents and up until then their names had barely been mentioned around our house.

On my first school holiday I bussed over to meet them at their hotel for tea. Grandpa was a small, greying man with a beard which partly hid a rather disfigured face. I learned later he had once been in a nasty accident with some lift gates at another hotel. His name was Phineas Emanuel and Granny called him Pinky. Her name was Rose, a small, pleasant woman who, at the end of the afternoon, pressed a two-shilling piece into my hand so I could 'buy an ice-cream and go to the pictures', which is what they called the cinema in those days. One day Grandpa offered to up the ante to two shillings and sixpence if I'd stop biting my nails. So I did. Which shows you what some people will do for money.

Grandpa was a very jolly man who, among other things, had once been a conjuror. Between the Sunday sandwiches and cakes he always entertained me, and the odd people who joined us, with what I found to be mind-boggling magic. One Sunday, just before I returned to Seaford College, there was me, my grandparents and another lady at our teatime session. When the other lady left, Granny put her hand on my knee and asked, 'Did you like that lady who just left?'

'Oh ... yes,' I replied, not really having paid much attention to her. 'She seemed nice.'

'I'm so glad,' said Granny, patting my knee, 'because that was your mother.'

In later film years I might have said: 'What a great line to finish the trailer.' Or in TV times: 'Perfect spot for the commercial!' But the movies were still only silents and they had barely thought of radio, let alone television. For 11 years I had been brought up to believe that my mother was dead and here she had been having tea with me. Was this some awful joke? No, apparently not, because Grandpa was making me promise solemnly, on my Scout's Honour, that I would never ever tell my father about that afternoon meeting.

There have been various moments in my life when I've tried to relive my feelings on that long-ago Sunday afternoon. Shock? No, hardly shock. Puzzlement, yes. Confusion, yes. But most of all a tremendous feeling of guilt. Guilt, because I should have *known* that the lady was my mother. I should have *felt* something. I mean, how can you not know your own mother?

What I did know was that from then on I could never trust my father again. Later I attempted to rationalise his behaviour. Obviously there had been a divorce. By whom and for what was still a mystery about which, in later years, I was often tempted to ask my mother. But it was a precarious cruise we were on and I was always worried about rocking the boat and losing her again. Anyway, a divorce there had been. After which, in my father's mind, the whole episode was dead. So wasn't it simpler to tell the child his mother was dead? I mean, how do you explain divorce to a three-year-old? Outwardly I tried to excuse him. Inwardly, I'm afraid I never forgave him. But I was true to the Scout's Honour I'd given my grandparents. To the day of his death in 1935 my father never knew I had met my 'dead' mother.

This new secret person in my life turned out to be a dark-haired, vital lady who seemed to be multi-talented. She played the violin, wrote short stories for magazines, had a book of poetry published and, under the stage name of Anna Thayer, had starred as principal boy in many pantomimes produced by the eminent London impresario Julian Wylie. She had married again and was now the wife of one Arthur Williams, a civil servant who worked in a government office. He was pleasant enough and friendly, but I always felt he treated me as one might treat someone else's pet. What's more they had a young son of their own called Brennan. Look at me, all of a sudden I have a mother *and* a half-brother!

Mother and I had surreptitious meetings at least once every school holiday. Either for tea in a Lyon's Corner House or in the Regal Cinema at Marble Arch. It was all rather like a younger version of David Lean's *Brief Encounter*. A couple of times she invited me to her basement flat on Abercorn Place in St John's Wood. I often wondered what would happen if she bumped into my father one day. Maybe she had. And maybe he had seen her and simply crossed the street because she was dead. And back I would go to Seaford College wondering if we would ever feel like mother and son, rather than awkward strangers, or at best sympathetic acquaintances.

As colleges went Seaford was one of the better ones. It wasn't their fault that my IQ was only slightly higher than room temperature. I think the most important thing I learned there was how to type. With two fingers. Not that it was one of their classes. I learned surreptitiously. For some reason that I don't remember, I'd been chosen to tell the nightly story once the dormitory lights had been put out and we were meant to be asleep. I suppose that could have been the start of my dreaming up stories. And every night I'd leave them on a cliff-hanger. Came the dawn and I would creep down to the Masters' Common Room where there was an old upright Royal typewriter on which I would learn to pound out my notes for the next night's story. It took me a whole term to learn about back space, capitals, upper and lower case. But then I was only 12. Did Tolstoy start that early?

And we mustn't forget my early college love life. I fell madly in love with one of the school wait-resses. Her name was Lillian and she helped to serve our meals in the big school dining room. Lillian used to smile at me and occasionally gave me a double portion of rhubarb tart. I swore to myself that when I grew up I would marry Lillian. But then I also swore I would marry Vicky, who worked in the Victorian Teashop in the town. Some of the older boys had even taken Vicky out during their Sunday exit passes. 'Bit of all right,' winked Weston major one day, 'but you snotty-nosed little buggers are wast-ing your time.' Even in those early days falling in love had its heartbreaks.

At the end of my fifth year at Seaford, 1927, my father welcomed me home for the Christmas hol-idays and announced that my schooldays were over. Being 15-and-a-half at the time I was mildly sur-prised as I thought this school thing usually went on a bit longer. However, it seemed there was an important company in the City who were prepared to take me on right away as an apprentice. 'An apprentice at what?' I was foolish enough to ask.

'Now don't argue,' said my father. 'You're a very lucky boy. Not many people get a chance like this.' I didn't dare ask 'Like what?' but dear, smiling Miss Grey put her arm round my shoulders and tried to break it to me gently. 'Your father's cousin, Louis, knows a man who is the stepson of the lady who is married to the man who is the head of the Asiatic Petroleum Company.' I remember thinking it sounded like the old song: 'I've danced with a man who's danced with a girl who's danced with the Prince of Wales'.

The man in question turned out to be a Mr Engle and he was, indeed, the president of the AP Co. Which is where I started my working life, one week after my 16th birthday, in the accounts depart-ment. *Me* in the accounts department. Me, who could barely handle his times-table let alone the aggre-gate fuel oil of Australia. My one saviour at the AP Co was a dark-haired young man who sat next to me at the long desk. His name was Norman Aarons and it was to him that I was apprenticed. Dear, patient Norman, it was his ever-watchful eye that spotted all my extra zeros, balanced my compound interests and generally corrected most of my figures. I think it's sad that to this day the Asiatic Petroleum Company doesn't know that but for Norman Aarons in 1928 they would have been several billion dollars in the red. My good chum Norman eventually moved out of accounts and into a syna-gogue, where he became a rabbi. It would be nice to think he didn't make the move because of me.

In retrospect I find it fascinating when I realise it was actually the Asiatic Petroleum Company that propelled me into the entertainment business. Mr Engle and his immediate associates were very keen on sponsoring theatre charity shows at which various stage, screen and variety stars would appear. Anyway, one day Mr Garrett, my department boss, called me over to his desk. Here it comes, I thought, with any luck I'm going to be fired. But no. 'I saw a copy of the *Stage* on your desk,' he said without pre-amble. The *Stage* was the professional theatre paper, but he made it sound as if I'd been caught reading *Lady Chatterley's Lover* in the dorm after lights out. It happened to be an old copy of my mother's that she'd given to me to look at. 'You know anyone in the theatre?' he went on.

'Well, my mother, sir. She was on the stage.'

'Good. I'm going to give you some time off to round up some names for next month's charity show at the Alhambra. It's in Leicester Square; you know it?'

'Yes, sir.'

'All right, go and see the cashier, she'll give you some petty cash. And turn your ledgers over to Aarons.' To me it was like winning the Irish Sweepstake. Of course, looking back, it was a heaven-sent chance for him to get me off Fuel Oil Accounts for a spell. But, just to set the record straight, in spite of unkind department rumours the Australian government had nothing whatsoever to do with it.

That afternoon I practically levitated myself out of the AP building and across that grey St Helen's Court, floated down bustling Bishopsgate and into the Underground, where I boarded however many trains it took me to get to St John's Wood in order to search out my mother. This had to be my lucky day because mother was home. I poured out the gist of my new assignment and within an hour this amazingly on-the-ball lady had arranged several showbusiness introductions for me, typed out copies of the charity's details and given me a lot of useful tips.

'If you're going to approach stars in the theatre do it *after* the show, *never* before. Hand them the details and make sure they know it's for a major charity and not just some Benefit for Retarded Hamsters or something.' This was an old pro talking so I followed her advice to the letter and, surprise surprise, I ended up with a cast that knocked Mr Garrett's eye out. I garnered a young matinée idol and composer called Ivor Novello, who played and sang some of his own compositions; the Gaiety Theatre's star comedian, Leslie Henson, and that smashing, dashing Ella Shields, England's premier male impersonator in top hat, white tie and tails, singing her famous songs, 'I'm Burlington Bertie, I rise at ten-thirty...' and 'The Man who Broke the Bank at Monte Carlo'. There were other stars who might not be remembered today but at that time they were all worthy of oohs and aahs.

The Alhambra had seldom seen such a star charity turnout. Sadly that beautiful theatre is no longer with us, having been demolished to make way for today's Leicester Square Odeon which, incredibly enough, exactly ten years later was to be the scene of another momentous occasion for me. And this one all because of Rita Hayworth. More of which later.

But on that 1928 Alhambra night I stood at the back of of the stalls ooh-ing and aah-ing along with the rest of the audience. And I knew it had changed my life. This was it – the stage. All I wanted to do from then on was to be part of it. I'd be an actor, that's what I'd be. I was sure there was nothing to it. Ralph Richardson said, 'Acting is merely the art of keeping a large group of people from coughing.' And I was idiot enough to believe it. Oh yes, the damage had been done, the die was cast, the seed was sown. Like a circus pony, I'd had the smell of the sawdust and was hooked. The trouble was, my parole was now up and Australia's oil wasn't.

Back I went to my book-keeping bedlam wondering if anyone else could possibly hate their job as much as I did. At least, as it was nearing Christmas, several new theatre shows opened and to cheer me up I went to all of them. Up in the Gods of course, which was what they called the 'gallery', where a seat, if I remember rightly, cost a shilling. I went to the new John van Druten play, *Young Woodley* at the Savoy, with a talented young boy called Frank Lawton and Kathleen O'Regan. Strange how the Funny Finger of Fate crisscrossed our lives so that 32 years later Frank was to be in one of my future wife Yolande's plays, *And Suddenly It's Spring* at the Duke of York's Theatre – and, by then, he was married to a friend of ours, Evelyn Laye. But back in 1928 I simply sat and watched him playing the schoolboy who falls in love with the headmaster's wife and wondered if I would ever be as good an actor.

That was also the year an All-Singing, All-Dancing, All-Talking picture called *Broadway Melody* was pulling in the crowds. The stars were Charles King, Anita Page and Bessie Love. And there goes that Funny Finger again. Twenty-one years later Laurence Olivier brought a young Broadway actress to London to star in his production of Garson Kanin's play *Born Yesterday*. Her name was Yolande Donlan, and who else should be in the cast? Bessie Love.

By Christmas I was glad the year was over. Mentally it had been a somewhat tumultuous one for me. I spent it at home with my father and Miss Grey. Dear, cosy Miss Grey had pulled out all the stops and spent days preparing and cooking us a turkey, chipolatas, stuffing and sprouts followed by Christmas pudding and mince pies. There were just the three of us. It would have been fun to be joined by a few friends or family but I had long ago realised this didn't happen often in our house.

Occasionally odd relatives would pop in and pop out again. Plus, of course, the ubiquitous Uncle Louis who always knew someone who knew a man who knew someone else. Anyway, it was a lovely meal and afterwards I sat at our upright piano and tried to pick out the tunes 'Broadway Melody' and 'Singin' in the Rain'. Yes, that's how long ago that clever Arthur Freed wrote 'Singin' in the Rain' and in that film it was sung by Cliff Edwards, 'Ukulele Ike', backed up by those lovely MGM dancers in glistening raincoats and oilskin hats.

At odd times I tinkled at that piano when no one was around. Miss Grey, bless her, encouraged me, but my old man would often shut me up because 'You'll disturb the downstairs tenant.' In fact I was never allowed to play after seven o'clock at night or before nine o'clock in the morning, and then never for more than a quarter of an hour at a time. I always thought this strange since he had paid for me to have piano lessons at Seaford, even though he stopped them after one term. Either the music teacher told him she was wasting her time or one day he realised the noise he might be in for. Anyway, that one term taught me the basics of music and, lest any new piano pupils should be feeling discouraged, let me say that what I learned in one term at least enabled me to land a contract later as a songwriter with Feldman's, one of London's largest publishers, and write music for various stage shows and films, even though to this day I can hardly tell a crotchet from a quaver. So courage, you learners; if two hands of bananas could do it, you can do it too.

Well, here was 1929 banging on my door. Not long ago, during one of my periodic 'clearing out the crap' sessions, I actually came across my old 1929 diary. Heaven knows why I still had it, unless I'd taken the legendary Sam Goldwyn's advice. 'Good idea, throwing away old files,' he said. 'But be sure you make a copy of everything.' However, this was the original. Glancing through it with curiosity, I suddenly realised how those archaeologists must have felt when they unearthed the Dead Sea Scrolls. Was this really me writing all this guff? Yes, it was me. And here's what I wrote on the obviously historic day of Tuesday 21 May 1929: 'Has anything this good happened before? Today is the day of days – I handed in my resignation!!! – Handed in my resignation!!! Think of it – no more ledgers, no more Current Accounts. I'm free!!! Goodbye APC, goodbye Engle, goodbye Australia – Free!!! Nothing else matters!!!'

As you can see, as far as I was concerned this was obviously on a par with the end of the Great War. Except for one steadying sentence at the bottom of the page which simply asked: 'What do I tell Mr G?' Good question. The Old Man would obviously hit the ceiling. Should I lie and tell him I'd been fired? After all, he'd lied to me. But then Uncle Louis might talk to the man who knew the woman who married the man etc, and then I'd be unfrocked. At least I had the two weeks' notice to work out the best approach to this landmine.

When I got home that night my father was waiting for me in the sitting room. My God, I thought, had someone in the office tipped him off? 'Come in, Valmond,' he said, 'and shut the door.'

All right, so it had to come out sometime: Val is short for Valmond. I understand it was my mother who chose the name after some distant Italian Duke. But in my early youth when people asked my name I found when I said 'Valmond' too many people whistled at me. So I trimmed it to Val.

'Sit down, Valmond,' he said and then, without further preamble, 'It's about Miss Grey.' I relaxed a little; at least it wasn't about me. 'From now on,' he continued, 'I want you to stop calling her Miss Grey and call her Violet.'

'Oh ... I see ... all right,' I frowned. 'I'll do my best, only when you've called someone something for so long – I mean, I might forget now and then...'

'I understand,' he smiled and nodded. 'I know you'll try.' He smiled again and somehow his voice was warmer than I'd remembered it. 'It is rather important. She's a wonderful person and she loves you very much. I'd like you to call her Violet simply because she's now my wife.' He saw my face trying to take it in and put his arm around my shoulder, a gesture that wasn't him at all. 'We were married last week. Didn't tell anyone. Not even family. Registry office. No fuss.'

It was a shock, but a nice one. I loved Miss Grey – sorry, Violet – and the fact she was now one of the family was somehow warmly comforting. 'Now,' said my father in a sudden burst of fatherliness, 'how's the Asiatic Petroleum Company?' Panic. Should I come out with it now, while he was still virtually on his honeymoon, or go the limit of my two weeks' grace? 'Fine,' I said, making one of my instant regret-it-later decisions. Eventually I knew I'd have to do what I always did when seemingly insoluble problems arose. Go to Violet.

She listened to my story quite calmly. 'So you are no longer there after this week?'

'No, Violet.'

She pondered in silence for a moment. 'Did you say your accounting wasn't very good, dear?'

'An understatement.'

'Do you think they might have given you notice one day?'

'I'm sure it was only a matter of time.'

Violet nodded and her big, unblinking eyes looked innocently into mine. 'And that would have embarrassed and upset your father, wouldn't it dear?'

'I suppose so.'

'So maybe you thought it was better to resign before they did it to you, is that it, dear? You felt it was – well, sort of more honourable?' What a woman, what a defence counsel. However, in spite of her help and my mitigating excuses the landmine blew sky high. 'Resigned?' father stormed. 'What sort of gratitude is that? Someone arranges a good job for you and you *resign* from it?'

'I'm just no good at figures,' I offered lamely.

'No good at figures? All that education I paid for and you can't even add up?'

'I can add up, but it's all that compound interest and stuff.'

My father heaved an enormous sigh which seemed to say, What have I done to deserve a moronic son? 'All right,' he said finally, 'what's done is done. But I want you to understand I'm not having a layabout son in the house. And you can't just lounge around town either. So what do you intend to do now?'

I took a deep breath. 'I'd like to try and make a career in the theatre,' I said bravely. The old cliché of 'red rag to a bull' would be quite inadequate to describe the moment. It was more like lighting a thunder flash behind a herd of buffaloes. Of course I'd forgotten that his 'departed' wife had also been on the stage, and that must have affected him even more.

'The *theatre?*' he echoed in a tone that implied he'd have been happier had I said I'd like to try and be a pimp in Piccadilly. 'All right,' he said finally. 'You're 18 and old enough to look after yourself. I'm going to give you one month to get out and find a job.'

That same evening I rushed out to find a telephone and fix a secret liaison with my mother who immediately did her best to talk me out of my harebrained decision. When she found this impossible she waded in and helped me comb the *Stage* to see what, if any, auditions were coming up. In those days the unions weren't wielding their sticks so much and practically anyone could have a go at anything, even non-persons like me.

Saturday 1 June was my last day at the APC. I made my fond farewells trying not to look too happy. 'I'm going on the stage,' I told them airily. Well, I was, eventually – I hoped. 'And I hope you'll all come and see me.'

'What show are you going into?' asked someone.

Good question. 'Ah – can't tell you yet – at the moment the title's a secret.'

'Well, best of luck.'

Which was exactly what I needed plenty of. I took the Underground to Leicester Square and went to one of my West End haunts, a small inexpensive café called the Odd Spot in Cranbourne Street. A cousin of mine, Richard Schulman, had recently opened it up right opposite the London Hippodrome because he was mad about the theatre and hoped that opening in this locale would bring him the theatre crowds. And it had. This was the spot many of us wannabes met up, and the place I first met Errol Flynn.

But Errol wasn't there that night and I poured my heart out to cousin Dick. He thought I'd been very brave and if there was any way he could help, to let him know. I showed him my dog-eared copy of the *Stage* in which I'd circled two upcoming auditions. Did he know anything about them? He didn't. But he'd heard one of his customers talking about an audition, Sunday 10 o'clock at the Poland Street rehearsal rooms. Not a clue what it was for but why not have a go?

I had a go. Early Sunday morning I was first to arrive in that bleak, forbidding rehearsal room. There was a somewhat portly lady, seated at a slightly battered upright piano, who smiled me a good morning. 'Name?' said a man with a clipboard.

'Guest – Val Guest.'

He checked his board. 'Don't see you on the list.'

'No, I was last minute.'

'Okay, well you might as well start off.'

Start off? This was the first audition I'd ever been to and I had only the haziest idea of what it entailed, and this mainly culled from backstage movies. By now other contestants had begun to arrive and were sitting on bentwood chairs around the room watching me. 'Did you bring any music?' asked the clipboard.

'Music? … No…'

'Well, what d'you want to sing? Just tell Doreen and give her the key.' Which was when the full horror dawned on me. They wanted singers. This was an audition for chorus singers. 'All right, darling,' said Doreen, 'what's it going to be?'

My knees trembled, my throat was dry, at least two dozen pairs of eyes were daring me to sing. 'Broadway Melody,' I said off the top of my head. At least I knew the words.

'E flat all right?'

I nodded. Even Z flat would have made little difference. So off we went and at least I got through it on key. There was a moment of silence when I'd finished. I hadn't expected a standing ovation but neither did I expect the curt 'Okay, next' before I was unceremoniously bustled off stage without a word to make way for a balding baritone.

End of first audition. Hey-ho, another milestone.

CHAPTER
TWO

I spent that evening with my current girlfriend, Barbara Dene, who was a dancer in the successful new musical *Merry, Merry*. I realise I haven't chronicled much about my romantic life so far. Maybe because so far my girlfriends had been rather like passing ships in my life. Until Barbara.

There had been redheaded Audrey, one of the APC's cashiers. We saw a few shows together and did some backseat snogging through the *Fox Movietone Follies of 1929*. But our relatively brief romance fell short of being historical. Then there was Sunny Jarman, the blonde American ingenue in the Palace Theatre hit *Hold Everything*. Sunny was 19 and I thought she was a knockout. She wanted to see the famous London markets. So, over the weeks, I took her around Petticoat Lane, the Caledonian Market, Billingsgate, Covent Garden and Portobello Road. After which the poor girl was usually too tired to do much else. Eventually *Hold Everything* ended its run and Sunny returned to America. We corresponded for a year or two and then obviously ran out of things to say.

Going through the recently unearthed Guest Scrolls I see there were quite a few dates with a girl called Chickie, whom I used to pick up at the Garrick Theatre. The terrible thing is I can't remember anything about Chickie. Dear darling Chickie, should you by any chance happen to read this, don't take offence. I promise it isn't because of you, it's my memory.

The trouble with dating girls at that time was that I could never take them home to Winchester Road. It was verboten. So I either had to wait until they invited me to their place, or wing it. And I did quite a bit of winging.

Barbara Dene was different. She was a lovely, fun person, 5'6" with natural blonde hair and a slightly turned-up nose. I first met her on the crowded top deck of a Number 13 bus from Piccadilly. I'd been out on the town somewhere or other, she had just finished her show and was on her way home. We sat next to each other and were soon chatting Theatre. Then she said goodnight and got off at Lords Cricket Ground while I went on to Swiss Cottage.

In bed that night I decided I'd like to see her again. So I devised my devilish plan. I knew the rough time that the Number 13 arrived at the Lords bus stop and, provided she didn't go out on some date, she'd be on it. Next night I was at that bus stop, waiting across the road in the shadow of the St John's

Wood Church cemetery. And there was the bus and, lucky me, there was she, stepping briskly across the road and right into my path. 'Barbara! What a wonderful coincidence!' I explained I'd been visiting and was about to catch that Number 13 back to Swiss Cottage. But now I'd missed it anyway, could I escort her home? It must have been one of my better acting performances because she let me.

She lived just a few minutes away in St Edmund's Terrace and her house was practically at one of the entrances to the park at Primrose Hill. This was to be the first of many after-the-show meetings. Often we would wander on to peaceful Primrose Hill, sit on a couple of park seats under one of the trees and cuddle up. When we knew each other better, she invited me inside. It was Barbara, or Barbie, who first introduced me to Ralph Reader, one night when I went to pick her up at the theatre. Ralph had done the choreography for her show and within a week he had invited both of us to one of his swinging parties, which is how our later friendship began. But on that Sunday night after my first audition, when I told Barbie about my singing début, she sympathised with me and then we both burst out laughing. 'Number One Rule,' she grinned. 'Always check what you're going up for or you could find youself auditioning for *Swan Lake!*' And we collapsed hysterically into each other's arms.

The two auditions from the *Stage* turned out to be a couple more cases of 'Thank you, next please'. One was for a war play and they thought I looked too young, the other was for a producer named Barry O'Brien who wanted a man-about-town type. 'Sorry,' said Mr O'Brien, 'you don't look like you've been about town enough.'

Meanwhile my father's one-month countdown had already ticked off just over a week. I had 22 days left before blast-off. Then two things happened in quick succession. First, dear second-cousin Louis had had another brilliant idea. The place for a healthy, unemployed young man like Valmond was the Royal Air Force. Great career, exciting future. And within 24 hours he'd convinced my Old Man and made an appointment for me to present myself at the RAF building in Whitehall, have my medical and meet the commanding officer. In vain I pleaded with my father to delay any of this until my remaining 22 days were up, but cousin Louis had obviously made a strong case. Probably told him that he knew a man who'd married a girl who'd had it off with both the Wright Brothers and this was the chance of a lifetime.

The second happening was a call from good old first cousin Dick Schulman. 'Val – Friday 2.30 at Dineley's rehearsal rooms, Paddington Street.' My heart pounded and I pressed the receiver close to my ear so that my father wouldn't hear. 'I hear it's a new comedy by Arnold Ridley – you know, man who wrote *The Ghost Train* – it's called *Unholy Orders* and they need several small parts, all ages.' He gave me the telephone number to call, wished me luck and hung up.

'Who was that?' asked my father.

'Dick Schulman.'

"What did he want?"

'Told me about some new orders, for his café.'

The Old Man grunted and returned to his newspaper. I hurried back to my bedroom. Friday? Wasn't that the day I had to report to Whitehall? Frantically I searched for that Air Force appointment letter. Yes, there it was, same Friday. But wait a minute – 10.30 am. Could I have the medical, the interview and still make it across London to Paddington Street by 2.30? Nothing was more certain than I was going to, even if I was halfway through my medical and had to run down Whitehall pulling my pants on.

I pondered long and hard about this new situation. I could defy everyone, skip the Air Force and make sure of the audition. I could say I'd gone there and been failed. But then second cousin Louis might hear it from a man who knew another man who lived with some Air Marshall…

Really, this man was a menace.

Frenetic Friday arrived all too soon. I got to Whitehall at 9 am hoping they might even start my pulse-taking a little earlier only to find at least a dozen other candidates had had the same idea. It was noon before they got to my medical. The usual thing; have you ever suffered from the plague or anything we should know about? Stethoscopes, drop your pants, cup your balls, now cough – then the interview with the Gold Braid. 'Have you got the spirit?' the Braid boomed at me. 'That's what you need, m'boy, the spirit! You want to be a mechanic? A pilot? What d'you want to be, m'boy?'

M'boy wanted to be in Paddington Street by 2.30. And I just made it by the skin of my teeth. The rehearsal room was quite full when I arrived. And right away I recognised the man running the audition. He was a well-known character actor called Aubrey Mather. I'd seen him play comedy butlers and the like on stage and screen. He later went to Hollywood where, after Fred Astaire's *The Gay Divorce*, he became everybody's favourite butler. It appeared he was going to direct the play. I sat on one of the chairs trying hard to sedate my butterflies as I watched a bunch of assorted actors reel off all the things they'd done before. Sitting next to me was a good-looking young man named Alan Keith who said he was there hoping to get the juvenile lead. He'd done quite a lot of acting and had recently returned from New York where he'd played in a show called *The Matriarch* with Mrs Patrick Campbell. Many years later he was to become famous for his *These You Have Loved* music programme on the BBC. Right now he was about to become a trigger to the next part of my life.

'Mr. Guest – Val Guest?' Aubrey Mather was calling my name. My heart, which less than an hour ago had been pronounced okay by the Royal Air Force, was now doing double bongo beats as I walked up to the interview space. Aubrey had a warm, friendly smile and was full of polite charm as he eyed me up and down. 'And what have you done before?'

'Oh, a bit of everything, sir.' Dick Schulman had suggested this tricky answer. It wasn't exactly untrue but if they really pinned me down I'd have to come clean.

Aubrey Mather gave me another quick appraisal and whispered to the man sitting next to him. The man nodded and Mather turned back to me. 'We need a village idiot,' he said with a smile and there was a burst of laughter from the remaining actors. 'Seriously, though,' he went on, 'it's only a small part and he's a bit of a simpleton.' The smile came back. 'Think you could play a village idiot?' The laughter had relaxed me a little. 'I'm perfect casting,' I managed to say, and got the job. I was over the moon. I had my first acting job! In a four-week tryout prior to London. As a village idiot. Were the Gods trying to tell me something?

Racing the good news back to Winchester Road I first broke it to Vi. Violet had long since become Vi. 'Oh, that's wonderful, dear,' she enthused. 'When does it begin?'

'Monday's first rehearsal, open three weeks later up north in New Brighton.'

My father received the news with ill-concealed horror. 'What happened at the Air Force?' he asked.

'Oh I went and did everything. They'll let us know. But isn't this great, about the show?'

'It's good you have some sort of job, but that's no future for you.'

'Dad,' I said earnestly, 'I promise you, one day you're going to see my name in the papers.'

'It's the duty of all respectable people to keep their names out of the papers,' said my father as he went off to collect his rents.

My first day at rehearsals was memorable, worrying and challenging. Memorable because it was the first day of the rest of my life in the entertainment world, worrying because I was the only non-professional in a cast of eight, and challenging because I was diving head first into the deep end of a new profession. Among the seasoned pros in the cast of *Unholy Orders* was a venerable old character actor named Hugh E Wright whom I'd seen in many films; another screen and stage veteran, Patrick Curwen;

Alan Keith, who had won his romantic juvenile lead, plus his leading lady, Joan Harben. Joan would later find acclaim in the BBC's historic wartime radio show, Tommy Handley's *ITMA*, in which she played the beloved Mrs Mopp with her immortal line, 'Can I do you now, sir?' Incidentally, her brother, Philip Harben, eventually found his way into the record books as the popular TV chef who showed us how to make an omelette in one minute flat. You see, eventually we all find our niches in life.

On the very first read-through I was amazed to find that Hugh E Wright and Pat Curwen already knew their lines. Panic. In point of fact I only had six lines in the entire play and to help make my presence worthwhile I was told I would be ASM (Assistant Stage Manager) as well. Blind panic. I was to learn later that whatever went wrong during the run of a show it was always the ASM's fault. In the meantime, the fact that two of the cast already knew their lines didn't seem to faze the others. 'I can't learn mine until I match them with the moves,' said Alan Keith. 'Everyone has a different method.'

Through the years I came across many of these methods. Evelyn Laye, for instance, spoke the whole part onto her tape-recorder, then, with the Stop-Start button, rehearsed the lines with herself on tape. Larry Olivier would go into one of his Notley Abbey rooms and stride up and down booming his lines out loud; Vivien Leigh talked about having that part of the house sound-proofed. Yolande, my very clever wife, would spend hours upon hours studying her script before getting friends or family to cue her through it. I would arrive home from the studios sometimes to find even the furniture had been rearranged to resemble her stage set. And unless you had your wits about you this could be a trifle bewildering. David Niven always used to walk around to learn his lines. Then there was the redoubtable Leo McKern. Dear Leo had the most awesome method of them all. He'd walk onto the set with his script, take one look at the pages and 'click', his mind had photographed it. He could go straight into the scene knowing not only his own lines but everyone else's as well. 'Makes you sick,' said Michael Redgrave one day as I rehearsed them both for my film *Assignment K*, and Leo laughed louder than any of us.

I wish I could remember more about the play *Unholy Orders*. It was a comedy, of course, and took place in a country vicarage. Hugh E Wright was the vicar, Patrick Curwen was a burglar who broke in one night looking for the proceeds of the Church Garden Fête, and I was the housekeeper's dim son, Vincent. Doesn't exactly make you want to besiege the ticket agencies, does it? Still, I'm not really being fair to the talented Arnold Ridley as I don't honestly remember the play's finer points. I do remember there was a large empty safe on stage and that Vincent had been told to clean it out in readiness for the Garden Fête takings. And being the village idiot that he was, the safe door slammed on him and he was locked in. Came night and burglar Pat broke in, worked on the safe's combination and was able to open it only to be confronted by Vincent. Not exactly vintage Hitchcock but good for a laugh. At rehearsals we had trouble with that safe door because it was only made of ply and kept swinging open before Pat had wrestled with the combination. 'You'll have to hold it from the inside,' Aubrey Mather told me. 'Patrick will cue you when to let go.'

'Let go of what? It's flat ply inside.'

'Don't worry,' said Joan, the Stage Manager. 'We'll give you a hook-handle halfway down.' Which is what they did. On opening night in New Brighton I crouched in the safe pulling that hook handle into my stomach waiting for Pat's cue, which was two taps on the door. Tap-tap, there it was. I let go. As he whipped it open the handle got hooked into my trousers and I sprawled out with my fly buttons peppering the stage like hailstones. For a brief moment I was the 'flashing' village idiot. Then, covering myself like Venus de Milo, I turned upstage, said the remaining line back over my shoulder and the Act Two curtain dropped to laughter, not a moment too soon, before Pat Curwen collapsed in hysterics.

My first First Night. But then, if you cast an idiot to play one, these things can happen.

Next day we had a rehearsal call and huddled together backstage in the Green Room to read the reviews. 'Mildly amusing,' said one. 'Not Arnold Ridley's best,' wrote another. To my surprise all of them had accepted my safe door incident as part of the play and one of them even mentioned my name: '... Vincent, competently played by Val Guest ...' My first appearance in print! 'Competently played', which translated means 'Just about got through it.' In New Brighton, of course, we had the usual would-be Bernard Shaw who tagged *Unholy Orders* as 'The play you must not fail to miss.' 'Ride with the punches,' Aubrey Mather advised us as we beavered through more rehearsals. The houses weren't bad and I lost no more fly buttons as Wardrobe had sewn in one of those new-fangled zips.

By the time we arrived at the Theatre Royal Bath, the play was getting most of its laughs and we were a more relaxed company. It was in this beautiful old theatre that I first met Alan Keith's brother, Ivan, little dreaming that within a week of the tour ending Ivan and I would be in partnership as a songwriting team under contract to Feldman's Music Publishers. How can you start a new career as an actor and a month later start a new career as a songwriter? It was about then that I began to realise that in my life anything could happen, and usually did.

This is how it came about. It was between shows and I was sitting in Alan's dressing room strumming a tune on my ukelele. Oh yes, they were very popular in those days, even more so since Cliff Edwards played 'Singin' in the Rain' on his in *Broadway Melody*. Anyway, suddenly I realised someone was standing in the doorway listening to me. 'Hullo,' he grinned. 'I'm Alan's brother Ivan. Is he around?'

'He's gone to fill his thermos. Come in, I'm Val.'

'Oh yes, he mentioned you. Don't stop, that was catchy. What's it from?'

'From me,' I smiled. 'Just making it up as I went along.'

'You write music?'

'I play it. Never learned how to write it down.'

All right, so you're ahead of me. Ivan not only played it but could also write it down. He'd been a cinema violinist and lost his job on the advent of the Talkies and was now helping out in his father's fur business. Not quite the way Rodgers met Hammerstein but we fused immediately. 'I have to warn you,' I told him hesitantly, 'I can only play in the key of F.'

'So what?' said Ivan. 'Irving Berlin can only play in E flat.'

During the next two weeks we raised musical dust and he made piano copies of half a dozen of my melodies. And every free moment I had, even crouching in that safe waiting for Pat's two taps, I worked on the lyrics spinning through my head. By the end of our run Ivan and I had six completed numbers. Now what? Why not my showbiz mother? I told him to grab his fiddle and whisked him off to Abercorn Place. Mother watched in politely disguised astonishment as Ivan unpacked his violin, I sat at the piano and we gave it our all. I even remember three of the titles – 'My Star of Araby', 'Review of the Toytown Soldiers' and 'The Cuban Love Song'. All of which were eventually published; in fact, 'The Cuban Love Song' became bandleader Edmundo Ros' signature tune. Then, of course, there was Lawrence Tibbett, who years later was to have a go with this same title. But we were there first!

My mother, dear sweet Anna Thayer Williams, was wonderful. I think she was glad the songs weren't as bad as she'd expected. She put her arms around both our shoulders. 'They're good,' she said. 'Could possibly make stage production numbers. I'm going to try and get you to Julian.' Julian was Julian Wylie, her old boss, and normally auditioning songwriters getting in to see him had to be at least Gilbert and Sullivan or Ivor Novello. But he must have had a great respect for my mother because he arranged to see us the following afternoon. 'And you don't need to heft that fiddle around,' she smiled at Ivan. 'The piano's good enough for him.'

Up in Wylie's office high above Cambridge Circus, he greeted us from behind a large desk. 'Anna says I ought to hear your stuff,' he said with a businesslike smile and swept his arm towards the concert-sized Bechstein in the corner of the room. 'Fire away.' As I sat at that mighty instrument, hoping my tremble wasn't showing, I wondered fleetingly if maybe Cole Porter had sat at this very piano or even Paderewski. He listened to my playing and singing with his eyes glued to the desk. I finished with 'The Review of the Toytown Soldiers'. There was a moment's silence then he looked up and said, 'That last one might make quite a good scena, but unfortunately I'm not doing any more shows until the end of the year.' I was about to tell him we'd wait as many years as he needed when he continued. 'Feldman's used to that sort of stuff, you ought to let him hear it.'

Oh, fine. 'Let him hear it.' What do I do, just walk into Feldman's and say, 'We've got some of 'this sort of stuff' we'd like you to hear'? But helpful JW was ahead of us. 'I'll call Bert Feldman, see if he can set up an appointment for you.' And he did, right there and then. So far it seemed to be roses, roses all the way!

Two days later we met Bert Feldman in his incredibly bustling four-storey building on Shaftesbury Avenue. Bert was a large man with a mop of grey hair and a bushy grey moustache to match, rather like a warm, huggable Saint Bernard. He listened to my recital with a finger tapping out the beat on his desk diary. When I'd finished he nodded, pressed down his intercom and said into it, 'We'd like some tea, please. Three.' I learned later that the Feldman teas were almost part of the company's folklore. He always entertained his girlfriends, mostly the current music hall stars, with afternoon tea. Not just a cuppa, but silver tray, silver tea-strainer, cutlery, embroidered linen napkins and finger sandwiches. You might say it was his kind of foreplay. Well, in came the tea tray but we obviously didn't rate any finger sandwiches which, to be honest, we could have done with.

'Not bad, not bad at all,' Bert said finally when the secretary had poured the tea and left. 'Would you boys like to work for me?' Like to? From now on I was ready to wash up all the tea trays as well. 'Go and talk to Mr Slevin, he's on the third floor, he'll work something out.'

Neither Ivan nor I could believe our ears. I honestly think that had Bert Feldman been wearing a ring I might have kissed it. But it wasn't quite as dreamy as it sounded. George Slevin, Feldman's business manager, was a dour-faced, steely-eyed Scotsman who gave us the impression he thought his boss must be in the last stage of degeneracy to have done this. However... 'We'll pay you eight pounds a week on account of royalties. D'you understand that? This is not salary. It's on account of royalties hopefully to come. You'll be contracted to Feldman's Music Publishing which means you canna work for anyone else. Right?'

'I presume that's only for songwriting,' I clarified, 'because I'm also an actor.'

'Well, we all have our problems,' said Slevin with an unexpected glint of humour. 'Be here Monday morning, we'll have the papers ready. And bring all your material to Bobby Comber, he's the publishing manager.'

I floated home on a Cloud 13 bus and broke the news to Vi. 'I have a contract — with Feldman's the music publishers!'

'Oh, that's nice, dear,' beamed Vi with her classic gift of understatement. 'I'm sure your father will be pleased.'

Wrong. 'Contracted to a music publisher?' he echoed incredulously. 'What as?'

'A songwriter.'

'How did all this happen?'

Tread carefully, Valmond, watch that landmine. 'Through friends — you know, Alan and Ivan Keith. Feldman liked my numbers and they're going to give us a try. One year with an option.'

'Do they pay you?'

'Eight pounds a week – on account of royalties.'

'So they're not paying you. They're loaning it to you.'

'Well, no – I mean, we don't have to pay it back if there aren't enough royalties…'

'And when does all this start?'

'Monday.'

Vi had joined us, clutching what looked like a long grey envelope. 'Isn't it good news, John?' she beamed at my father. 'The dear boy has a contract.' She handed me the envelope. 'I nearly forgot, dear, this came for you.' Right away I noticed the logo on it, a shield with the legend AD ASTRA. It was the RAF crest. My finger trembled as I slit it open and unfolded the contents. I only needed to read the first word, which said 'Congratulations.'

'What is it?'

'RAF. They've accepted me. Want me to report to Great Missenden Training Centre Monday morning.' My father's face broke into the biggest smile I could remember.

'Well, that really is good news. Now you have a proper career with proper pay and a proper future. This is a proud day for all of us. Violet, put your coat on and I'll take you both out to dinner.'

He took us to the old Swiss Cottage pub on Finchley Road. I don't know how I was able to eat, my stomach was in such a turmoil. For the first time in my life I was about to defy my father. There was no way Monday morning would see me in Great Missenden. I had an appointment in Shaftesbury Avenue and that's where I was going to be. What's more I'd made another giant decision. Before the end of the week I was going to leave home. Looking back now, in fairness to my father, I don't blame him one bit for being testy or short-fused with me. After all, here I was, approaching 19, without a respectable or responsible job, mooning around wanting to be an actor, a songwriter, even at times a writer. In fact, I think he showed remarkable patience. If I'd been my father I'd have slung me out years ago.

As it was, the following morning I broke the news to him that, sadly, His Majesty's Royal Air Force would have to try and win any future wars without my help. That from now on I was going to pursue my own career and in view of this I felt it was time I moved out of the nest. He took it very well. In fact, I'm sure that inwardly he was relieved this recurring problem called Valmond would no longer be on his doorstep.

As for me, I had made my own 'giant leap for mankind'. But whereas Neil Armstrong knew where he was landing, at that moment I didn't have a clue.

CHAPTER THREE

G ood for you, boy,' said Ivan when I phoned him with the news of my imminent move. 'You'll be better off on your own. Meet you at the Corner House for lunch.'

Lyon's Marble Arch Corner House was a popular meeting place in those days. Open 24 hours a day, it was inexpensive and comfortable. In fact, a couple of years later, in the early '30s, it was to become the haunt for after-the-show latenighters. Many's the happy evening I spent there chatting it up with the popular Jack Jackson and his band after their Dorchester Follies show. And I can't count the times I shared kippers and toast there with Will Hay, Larry Adler, Celia Lipton or Wallace Beery's brother Noah, at that time one of Hollywood's favourite film 'heavies' after the original *Beau Geste*. To say nothing of Thelma Todd, in London to make an epic called *You Made Me Love You*, and that clever young film editor, David Lean, to name but a few. As a matter of fact, it was on the night I took my date, Kay Walsh, to our Corner House club that she told me David was dating her too. After which he fell for her, wooed and married her. Ah well, I sighed, que serra serra.

But this lunchtime Ivan and I were sharing a sandwich and poring over the latest copy of *Dalton's Weekly*, which was the accommodation hunter's Bible. 'You don't want to rush into this, boy,' advised Ivan. 'I'd start in a cheap hotel while you sort out the best bedsit deal. And hotels have phones, they take messages.'

Thanks to *Dalton's Weekly* I found Bayswater Court, a small, minus-two-star hotel in St Stephen's Square near Westbourne Grove. And that Sunday I moved in. I had a basement room with a so-called 'kitchenette' comprising a gas ring, a kettle and a cold water tap. When you had to go it was down the passage. For this, my first stately home, I paid 26 shillings and sixpence a week. Which is what Ivan meant by a cheap hotel. The thing I didn't know was that the pair who ran it, Mr and Mrs Smith, were a couple of battling boozers.

That morning had seen an unsettling leavetaking from Winchester Road. Normally, around eight o'clock, Vi and I would have breakfast together in the kitchen. My father, who was never an early riser, would sometimes wander around the house in his nightshirt until noon. But this morning he not only joined us for breakfast but was shaved and dressed as well. Was this a last morning gesture, I remember wondering, or did he have an early appointment?

'I hope it all goes the way you want it,' he said finally after some small talk about the weather and the new price of coal. 'I wish I could help you more, but I can't.' He seemed unusually ill-at-ease. As was I. Suddenly it had become an uncomfortable situation and neither of us was handling it very adroitly. Vi broke what seemed like an eon of silence.

'You will keep in touch, won't you, dear?'

'Of course I will.'

Breakfast was over, my bag already packed, but before I could lift it my father unexpectedly pulled me towards him and hugged me in silence. I hugged him back. Suddenly I felt very sorry for him. His son had let him down. Maybe one day I would make it up to him.

'Anyway, you know where I am,' he said abruptly and hurried out of the kitchen. Vi followed me down to the front door where I hugged and kissed her. 'Take care,' she smiled and pushed two pound notes into my hand. 'Might come in useful, dear, you never know.' She stood on the steps waving good-bye as I lugged my suitcase up to Swiss Cottage Underground station.

Feldman's, 1930. What can I tell you about this cornerstone of English publishers? About that imposing entrance from Shaftesbury Avenue into the thickly carpeted hall with its busts of Chopin, Brahms and Beethoven, a sales counter with Feldman's latest sheet music and songbooks, that grand, carved oak staircase leading up to the first floor. The Professional floor. And what an experience that floor was to this uninitiated rookie. A busy thoroughfare bustling with performers, musicians, singers, dancers, stand-up comedians, all there to hear the newest songs or pick up their band parts. Every demonstration room was banging out a different tune, a dizzying cacophony of showbusiness. The Professional Reception room was at the top of the stairs and presided over by an incredible little red-headed lady, Mrs Elsie Rackham. Elsie sat at a desk facing the door, knew all the stars by their first names, knew which number would be right for their act and had two ace demonstrators to play them.

One of these young men was a tall, good-looking pianist named Ian Stewart. Later he was destined for greatness as the pianist who took over from the legendary Carroll Gibbons with his Savoy Orpheans, and later still would form his own orchestra and become a society favourite for balls, weddings and débutantes' coming out parties. In those days 'coming out' had another meaning. Be that as it may, in his Feldman days Ian was writing out piano copies for me at ten shillings a go.

The other demonstrator was a small, dark-haired ball of energy named Wally Ridley. Wally would sing as well as play the new numbers and given half a chance would have danced them as well. Wally never did anything like forming his own band or playing for those debs' balls. He merely went on to become Walter H Ridley, the all-powerful head record producer for EMI.

Ivan and I were told if we needed a piano we could use Jimmy Kennedy's on the Pro landing. We recognised the name immediately as that of Feldman's top composer-songwriter. Jimmy had a small room with an upright piano, a table and an irrepressible sense of humour; we took to each other immediately. I remember him coming back from Bert Feldman's end of the passage one day with a grin all over his face. 'Just got a great title, straight from the Old Man's office!' he beamed. 'Had one of his harem in there and the door was ajar. As I went by I heard her say, "No, Bert, because I don't like it in the daytime." Whether she meant a drink, a cigarette, or you know what, it's a hell of a title!' 'I don't like it in the daytime?' 'Better,' he grinned. 'How about, "Oh Nicholas, don't be so ridicolas, 'cos I don't like it in the daytime"?'

We laughed with him but didn't really think he was serious. But Jimmy was still laughing when it turned out to be one of Feldman's biggest comedy hits of 1931. Even more so since his boss never did know where the inspiration came from. But I'd hate Jimmy Kennedy fans to think I only remember him for that. There are many standard Kennedy classics still played all over the world today. How about 'Oh, Donna Clara' and 'Red Sails in the Sunset' for starters?

It was always a good show walking up and down the Feldman corridor. All the current musical stars were in an out at some time or other – Florrie Forde, Dorothy Ward, Ella Retford, Ella Sheilds. Even a new star called Anna Neagle floated through one day – something to do with a film called *Goodnight Vienna* she was making with Jack Buchanan at Elstree. And some of these even sang my songs. Feldman had published the three I first played them and our luck was in because they chose 'Cuban Love Song' for their big Blackpool Summer scena. Most publishers used to put on large summer spectaculars to plug their new numbers and sell sheet music, which in those days was a big moneymaker. Some 14 years later I was to write and direct a musical film about all this called *I'll be Your Sweetheart* with a young girl I'd known since her first film part, Margaret Lockwood.

I remember two other regulars who dropped in to the Pro Department whenever they were in town and between variety dates. One always carried a violin case and wanted Wally Ridley to play him every new number on the books. Eventually he was to become far better known as a respected actor than a fiddle-and-patter comic. His name was Ted Ray. The other was a small young man with a ukulele case who was always grinning from ear to ear. 'Don't you ever stop smiling?' Elsie Rackham asked him one day. 'Only when somebody asks me that,' said George Formby and immediately pulled a long, solemn face he was unable to keep for more than a few seconds. At that time neither of us could know that one day I would write 'Let George Do It' for his first Columbia picture. But then I never even knew what was about to happen to me in the next traumatic hour, let alone seven years ahead. Bert Feldman sent for me.

'Can you write a ballet, lad?' he shot at me almost as I entered the door.

'A ballet?'

'Yes, like *Les Sylphides*, that sort of thing.'

'A full-length ballet?' I tried to keep the horror out of my voice.

'No, a 20-minute one. They want to put on a programme of three 20-minute ballets at the Apollo. They already have one by Rimsky-Korsakoff and want a couple of new ones. What about it, lad, can you write a ballet?'

'Of course I can, Bert,' I said without hesitation, wondering how I had the nerve to say it without blinking. But at that age you say yes to everything.

'All right, have a go. It's for Jeavon Brandon Thomas, he's putting it on. You know him?' I didn't, but I certainly knew of his father, now a part of theatre history as the author of *Charley's Aunt*. I left Bert's office as though sleepwalking and headed straight for Jimmy Kennedy's office.

'How do you write a ballet?' I pleaded.

'A ballet? My, my...' After a moment's thought he said, 'I should write a lot of different rhythms, gives the choreographer a chance. Best of luck.' And with this sage-like guidance ringing in my ears I went off to write my first ballet. It took me ten days to complete and was about a little old wizard sitting on top of a tall ladder weaving the cobwebs of life. And that's what I called it, *The Cobwebs of Life*. All right, so it wasn't Prokofiev but at least it would be different from Rimsky-Korsakoff. Anyway, the whole thing turned out to be a bit too complicated for Ivan to make piano parts so I had to pay Ian Stewart to help out and off it went to Jeavon Brandon Thomas.

Meanwhile Alan had told me that our play, *Unholy Orders*, was coming into London and opening at the Ambassadors Theatre. Apparently Arnold Ridley had done copious rewrites and they'd changed the title to *Third Time Lucky*. And that wasn't the only thing they'd changed. They'd changed the village idiot. Ah well, pick yourself up, dust yourself down. Whoever Aubrey Mather had cast I bet he'd never written a ballet.

Two days later Bert Feldman's secretary called me into her office. 'They like the ballet,' she told me.

'They like it?'

'Mr Brandon Thomas wants to meet you this evening, if you're free.'

Free? He couldn't have invited anyone more free. I was to be at his house on Finchley Road, almost opposite the Marlborough Road Underground station, at 6 pm. Next big decision: what to wear? There weren't many options, it simply boiled down to which of my jackets and trousers were the least creased and which of my two pairs of shoes looked better. No matter how much I rubbed and polished those shoes they still looked, shall we say, 'lived in'. So I counted out the coffers, took a deep breath and off I went to buy a new pair that wouldn't leave me lunchless for too long.

Jeavon Brandon Thomas turned out to be a charming man brimming with enthusiasm for his show and life in general. He said he liked my ballet music, was going to use it at the Apollo and had invited his rehearsal pianist along as he wished me to go through the music with her to make sure she knew exactly what I had in mind. And I must say, hearing her play it, the opus sounded at least twice as good as it was.

'Splendid,' said our impresario, 'I think you both deserve one for the road.' But the pianist had another appointment and was on her way while I accepted a glass of pale ale. 'Tell me, Val,' he said, sitting in a chair facing me. 'May I call you Val?'

'Of course.'

'And I'm Jeavon. Tell me, should the choreographer require it would you be agreeable to add the odd bar here and there?'

I was tempted to say I had a whole drawerful of odd bars for anyone that needed them, but I didn't. 'I'd be delighted,' I told him.

'Good, good. Have you been doing this long?'

'Actually, this is my first ballet.'

'Mine, too,' he laughed. 'It's only for a short season and Amy thinks I'm mad. Amy's my sister, she's in the business, too.' His gaze seemed to have shifted to my feet. 'That's a very nice pair of shoes.'

'Oh, these... Yes... They're only Freeman, Hardy and Willis.'

'Do you like shoes?'

'Well... yes...'

'I have quite a collection,' he smiled. 'Like to see them?'

'Well... yes...'

I was beginning to sound like a broken record, but one had to be polite, especially as he'd apparently bought my ballet. He led me to a tall, built-in cupboard just off the drawing room and opened the door to disclose shelf upon shelf of assorted footwear. 'Aren't they beautiful?' I bit my tongue to stop myself saying 'Well, yes...' again. 'Now come back and finish your drink and tell me about you,' he said as we sat facing each other again. I gave him a brief resumé of the Guest music saga to date but somehow he didn't seem to be listening. His eyes were fixed on my feet. Suddenly he snapped out of it. 'Val, would you do me a great favour?'

'If I can, of course.'

'Would you let me kiss your shoes?'

'Do what?'

'I promise I won't touch you, Val – not a finger on you, I swear – just your shoes.'

Well, it didn't take the roof to fall on me to realise Jeavon Brandon Thomas had a thing about shoes. The question was, how would Debrett's 'Perfect Hostess' etiquette book tell one to handle this sort of thing? After all, most of us have our little oddities. I mean, I'm mad about kippers but I don't necessarily want to go around kissing them. And I agreed wholeheartedly with Oscar Wilde when he said that people can do what they like as long as they don't frighten the horses. Then there was the question of the ballet. 'No' might send it flying through the window. But would 'Yes' make me what Barbara Cartland might call 'a cheap little fool'? Was this the flip side of the old casting couch? What would Rimsky-Korsakoff have done?

Finally I crossed my fingers, took a deep breath and said okay. Whereupon Jeavon Brandon Thomas thanked me profusely, kissed my shoes goodnight and I was out on the Finchley Road, back in the real world once more. It was raining hard by the time I reached Bayswater Court and by then my sodden new shoes had lost most of their sex appeal. Approaching the hotel entrance I became aware of an unfamiliar blaze of light coming from my basement area and some sort of commotion going on inside. I hurried down to my room and found the passageway littered with the contents of the room opposite. This was occupied by a young fellow called Brian Elford who had recently lost his job in a bookmakers' office and at the moment was trying to stop the Smiths trashing the rest of his possessions. Needless to say Mr and Mrs Smith were plastered and pugnacious.

'Hey, what's going on?' I shouted above the haranguing.

'You stay out of this,' threatened Smith.

'You've no right to do this to people's belongings,' I shouted back and waded in, helping Brian drag them out of his room and crowd them onto the stairs.

'And he's no right living here without paying!' screamed Mrs S.

'I told you,' insisted Brian breathlessly. 'You'll have your rent this week.'

'We better, or next time this is out in the street,' snapped Mr S as his wife grabbed his arm and dragged him up the stairs.

'Thanks,' Brian said to me. 'Can I buy you a sandwich or something?'

'We'll share one,' I told him. 'I'll go out and get it while you watch your room.'

I must say, this had been quite a day. All part of life's rich tapestry, I kept reminding myself. After our saveloy sandwich I settled down to my rented typewriter to finish a piece I was writing on Paul Robeson, which I was hoping to sell to some magazine. I had been able to augment my weekly Feldman money by selling the odd interview with people like Henry Kendall, Evelyn Laye and Jack Buchanan to various film magazines like *Film Weekly*, *Picturegoer* and *Film Pictorial*. Robeson was appearing at the Ambassadors Theatre, not as a singer but as a straight actor, in Eugene O'Neill's *The Hairy Ape*. I'd found him a warm, kindly man. A couple of years previously I had interviewed him when he was at the Theatre Royal Drury Lane in *Show Boat*. I remember this mountain of a man leading me out across the vast Drury Lane stage and stopping to look out at the darkened auditorium.

'Man, isn't that something?' There was a tinge of awe in his voice. 'This has been the most exciting date of my life. The history out there. And the acoustics – listen!' He boomed out the first eight bars of 'Old Man River'. 'How's that for sound quality? Go on, try it!' Carried away with his enthusiasm I joined him in the next eight bars. 'See what I mean?' he laughed, putting his arm round my shoulder and guiding me to the exit. This was to be a great party-stopper in later years. At the mere mention of the Theatre Royal Drury Lane I would pipe up, 'Drury Lane? Oh yes, great acoustics. I sang there once with Paul Robeson.'

I finished my Robeson piece around two in the morning and fell into an exhausted sleep. I was up again by seven as I'd been told to report to Bert Feldman about the Brandon Thomas meeting and on the way I planned to drop off 'Robeson' at the *Film Weekly* office in the Strand. I always tried to deliver my articles by hand to save on stamps. I had to be an arch improviser to pay my rent and still exist on my four pounds a week. I'd even devised a way to stop buying bottles of ink for my fountain pens; this was before ballpoints. Whenever they ran out I'd go to the local post office to fill them from one of the many inkwells they had scattered around their counters.

As luck would have it the *Film Weekly* editor, Laurence Yglesias, was there when I arrived. 'Hullo,' he greeted me, 'what do we have this time?'

'Paul Robeson.'

'Is he doing a new film?'

'Not yet, but he's talking to Alexander Korda about doing one soon – he won't say what.'

Yglesias nodded. 'Okay, I'll read it. By the way, do you happen to know Lupino Lane?'

'No, but I've met his cousin, Stanley Lupino. Ida's a chum of mine – she's his daughter.'

Yglesias shook his head. 'He's a stage star – Lane's a film star.' I left the Strand with my mind in over-drive. Talk to Ida to ask her father to talk to her uncle... I was beginning to sound like second cousin Louis.

Feldman was delighted to hear the ballet piece had been officially accepted. I didn't tell him I had to pros-titute my shoes in the process, but I was also delighted to know a few more pennies would be coming in to our still rather undernourished royalty account, even though it was only to be a four-week fill-in programme.

Later that afternoon I telephoned Stanley Lupino's Streatham home. My luck was in, Ida answered the phone. 'Ida, darling, are you doing anything tonight? Want to come out and eat somewhere?'

'Val, I'd love to, but I promised Daddy I'd wait for him to get back from the studio.'

'Which studio?'

'Elstree. BIP.'

'You mean he's filming?'

'Yes, his musical, *The Love Race*, with Uncle Nip.'

'Who?'

'Uncle Nip. Lupino Lane, he's directing it. Look, why don't you come over here and if it's not too late we can still go out.' I couldn't believe my ears, or my luck. Filming with Uncle Nip! I took the train to Streatham and almost ran up Leigham Court Road where they lived.

Ida Lupino was a bubbling blonde with a disposition to match. She was 17 and like the rest of us begin-ners finding it tough-going, swimming against the tide most of the time. She was dreaming of one day being accepted as a serious actress instead of a tits-and-arse dolly bird. I'd met her at one of Ralph Reader's par-ties and we'd had several fun dates together since then. I remember how we laughed dreaming up fantasies of the things we'd do if we ever did reach the big time, although sometimes we both had secret moments of doubt. Wouldn't it have been fun to be able to press the Fast Forward button and show her the exciting Hollywood days to come, when she would become not only a star actress but a producer and director as well.

'Don't worry, I'll talk to Daddy,' said Ida when I filled her in about the *Film Weekly* interview. 'I'm sure he'll try and help.'

And sure enough, he did. 'I can't see that's a problem,' said Stanley after we'd finished snacking from the fridge. 'Come and lunch at the studio one day. I'll introduce you. Not this week, it's hectic, we're full of music. Maybe next week. Fix it with Ida.'

When I finally said goodnight I gave her an extra kiss and a big hug. 'That's a thank you for every-thing,' I grinned. 'You want to be my agent?'

'Yes,' she grinned back, 'if I don't get any better offers.'

I went home in a drenching thunderstorm but was happily 'Singin' in the Rain'. Even dreary old Bayswater Court seemed to be shining and glistening like the raincoats on those MGM girls. Until I unlocked my door and switched on the light. It looked as though there'd been a hurricane. The cup-board was open and my clothes had been flung all over the floor. The contents of every drawer had been emptied over them and whatever papers had been on my table were dumped in the waste basket with my typewriter jammed down on top of them. The place was a shambles.

There were no prizes for guessing the culprits. Who else had a key to the room? The bastards had got their own back. The first thing I went to salvage was my typewriter. I prised it gently out of the waste bas-ket to find my worst fears realised. Some of the keys were bent and a couple had actually snapped off. Worse still, this was a machine I'd rented from Selfridges. So what now? It was no good calling the police, what could they do? The Smiths would only deny the accusation and had probably fixed an alibi at their local pub already. No, rise above it, Guest. Tidy it up, pack it up and get the hell out of there by dawn's early light.

Somewhere in the chaos I managed to find the *Dalton's Weekly* in which I had tentatively marked a bedsit in Oxford Terrace – Number 5 Oxford Terrace. Too late to call them at this hour, and certainly not from the hotel. I'd just have to chance the room was still available. It was now close to midnight. Dare I call Ivan? 'Call me anytime, boy,' he'd often said. 'You know me, I read most of the night.' I hurried out to the phone box in the square. At least he was awake. I apologised for the hour, gave him a brief breakdown of the situation and asked if he would help me move in the morning.

My good friend Ivan was at my door by 6 am. By 6.15 we'd cleared the room and were out of Bayswater Court while the malevolent monsters were still in bed with their hangovers. Between us we lugged two suitcases, three carrier bags and the typewriter on and off two buses before depositing it all on the doorstep of Number 5 Oxford Terrace. It was still too early to ring the landlady's doorbell – which is how we first met the unforgettable Fred. I've told you about Fred with the all-night coffee stall outside Number 5. Fred was just going to call it a night, pack up his stall and drive home to bed, but he took pity on us and stayed long enough to make us two cuppas and a corned beef sandwich.

At eight o'clock I rang the bell and was greeted by Miss Jaynes, the landlady or, as she preferred to be called, the proprietress. She was a thin, rather angular lady with a face that could once have been beautiful. Yes, she told me pleasantly, the top room back was still available. For how long would I require it? At the moment, indefinitely. She helped us move my worldly possessions into the narrow hall. 'The rent is 18 shillings and sixpence a week,' she informed me, 'which includes electricity. You have a gas fire and your own meter. Light breakfast is available for an extra two shillings and you leave a note on the hall stand when you want it.'

I made the deal there and then, paid the first week's rent in advance and moved into what was destined to be my home for the next year. It was a small room with a bathroom across the passage. There was a single divan bed under the window which looked out onto the back of the flats in Cambridge Square. I was to learn later this was known to the locals as 'Whores Row' and many times I would glance out and see more than Hitchcock ever showed us in *Rear Window*. In fact one evening the strumpet opposite me burst out onto her small balcony and began to yell 'Murder! Murder!' Not a window went up, not a soul paid any attention. Except Greenhorn Guest. I raced down the stairs, across Edgware Road and into the local police station. 'There's a woman yelling Murder!' I panted. 'Back of Cambridge Square!'

'Top floor?' asked the unimpressed desk sergeant.

'Yes!'

'That'll be Mabel,' he nodded and went back to his reports.

'Well, aren't you going to do something?'

He shrugged. 'We pull her in every now and then. It's the old come-on, sir. "Gimme more money or I'll scream murder." Sometimes she gets it, most times she don't. Anyway, thanks for letting us know.'

One of my earlier fiascos. However, on the night I moved into my new abode all was quiet on the Cambridge front. 'I'd love to see Smith's face when he finds your empty room,' grinned Ivan as he plonked my last suitcase on the bed. 'Do you still owe them anything?'

'Yes, this week's rent.'

'Are you going to pay it?'

'You must be joking! It'll cost more than a week's rent to repair that typewriter!'

Things turned out to be even worse. When I took the typewriter back to Selfridges they said that not only was I liable for the damage but there was no way they would let me rent one again. Okay, how about buying one on the never-never? Yes, but they would need references and a guarantor. I pondered this for a long while and came to the conclusion, loath as I was to accept it, that there was only one other way to spell guarantor – MOTHER. And mother came through with flying colours. She not only guaranteed the deal but made me a gift of the down payment. 'That's for your birthday, Christmas and Easter present as well,' she kidded. 'And may it bring you lots of luck.'

Before the month was through that lucky typewriter was to tap out something that brought in my largest earnings yet. As promised, Ida Lupino had fixed up our lunch at BIP for me to meet Lupino Lane. He was a warm, likeable little man who greeted me with, 'Hullo Val, Ida's told me all about you.'

'Thanks for seeing me, Mr Lane.'

'Everyone calls me Nip so why shouldn't you? Now look, I'm seeing rushes in half an hour, so fire away.' I fired away the questions I'd planned and each one brought forth a steady flow of amusing answers and reminiscences. Half an hour later he shook my hand and got up to leave. 'Nice to meet you, Val. Hope you have enough for the article.'

'I have enough for your life story!' I smiled.

'Then why don't you write that?'

For the moment this stopped me short. Was he making a funny or did he mean it for real? 'Are you joking?' I asked.

'My life story's no joke,' laughed Nip Lane. 'Let's see the interview first. Then maybe we'll talk.'

Once Ida and I were outside the restaurant I let out an exhilarated whoop, grabbed her waist and danced her around the studio drive until a voice said, 'Is this a private dance or can anyone cut in?' Standing watching us was a tall, good-looking young man in his early twenties with angular features and a broad grin.

'I'm just celebrating with my agent,' I laughed.

'I need an agent, too,' he said, 'especially one like that. Would you take another client?'

'Are you an actor?' asked Ida.

'*I* think I am,' he grinned, 'but nobody here does. I'm a stand-in. My name's Rennie, Michael Rennie. Hope to see you in the canteen sometime,' and he hurried back to the set.

It was to be 14 years before I set eyes on Michael Rennie again. The location: Gainsborough Studios in Lime Grove where I was under contract as a writer-director. The year: 1945. The scene: my office, where I was preparing to go on the floor with *I'll Be Your Sweetheart*, my Charing Cross Road film about the music business. There was a tap on my office door one morning and there he was. 'Sorry to bother you,' he apologised, 'but I wondered if there were any small parts I'd be suitable for in your new film?'

We didn't immediately remember each other until he told me what he'd done so far in the business. When the penny dropped we laughed freely about the whole episode. 'Do you still have the same agent?' he asked with a straight face.

I shook my head. 'Didn't make enough out of me. She's now a big star in Hollywood. Listen, how tall are you?'

'Not quite six foot,' he answered quickly and promptly sat down. I found out later he was actually well over six feet but his height had usually gone against him.

'All right, Michael,' I said finally, 'I'm going to test you.' He looked at me blankly. 'Nine o'clock tomorrow morning I'm doing make-up tests with Margaret Lockwood. Get yourself into make-up at seven, we'll give you a bit of script and you can do the test with her.'

'Test me with Margaret Lockwood?' It didn't seem to have sunk in.

'Yes, it's the other lead role. Want to have a go?'

'Well, yes... yes... Thanks a lot...'

Next morning, by the time we'd finished Lockwood's make-up tests there was still no sign of Rennie so I told the assistant director to check his telephone number. In a few minutes he was back. 'He's on his way over now, Guy.'

'Now? He was supposed to be here at seven.'

'He says he thought you were having him on, Guv. He'll be here in 20 minutes at most.'

I tried to explain the situation to Lockwood and she hit the ceiling. 'Now Maggie, darling, relax, it's an honest misunderstanding. He didn't think I was serious.'

'Too bloody bad,' snorted Maggie Lockwood. 'So he can bloody well test with someone else. And you can tell him I *am* serious.' With which she stomped off to her dressing room with me after her.

'Maggie, listen, why don't you just stay and have lunch? I'll buy you lunch. I'll send out to Bertorelli's, get your favourite Italian. I'll even buy you dinner. Now, think how you'd feel if you didn't show up for all that because you didn't think I was serious.' Her large, brown eyes looked at me for a moment, then she burst out laughing. And that's how near Michael Rennie came to *not* getting his first starring part in a movie.

Okay. Fast Rewind. 1931. Oxford Terrace. I sold my Lupino Lane interview to *Film Weekly* and I've already recounted how he liked the piece and gave me a job on his new film as a writer-cum-bit player. What I haven't told you is that he gave me the go-ahead to write his life story and in a mad moment of elation I called the features editor of the *News of the World*, the paper that had been carrying more film biographies that most.

'Yes, we'd certainly be interested in Lupino Lane,' he said. 'Is it a byline?' It took me a while to explain to me what he was talking about. I learned that for a 'By Lupino Lane' story they would pay more than for an 'As told to', and even less for a 'third person' biography. Luckily Nip agreed to an 'As told to' and now all I had to do was tap it out on my lucky typewriter. It took me three weeks, with Nip pitching in every Sunday, and five Sundays later there it was in the paper. I wish I could remember what they paid me for it. All I recall is that it put me on Easy Street for at least a month. I paid two weeks' rent in advance, cleared the slate at Fred's coffee stall and took Ida out to dinner. After all, but for Ida Lupino... Later I was to write two more lifestories, those of Mae West and Marlene Dietrich, but I promise you, all of them were a piece of cake compared to the one I'm trying to write at this moment!

Blinded by this sudden influx of wealth I was now able to lash out for dinner at Fred's coffee stall with the odd steak and kidney pie and maybe, in a mad moment of extravagance, a couple of Chelsea buns as well. I was blissfully unaware of the turbulent bumps, both good and bad, that were shortly to make this year one of the major turning points in my life.

I remember sitting in my top floor back one very cold, damp March night warming my hands over an electric toaster. I'd bought it recently for this very purpose. Electricity was included in the rent, whereas the gas fire ate up shillings in the meter at an alarming rate. And while electric fires were forbidden, Miss Jaynes considered toasters legitimate. So there I sat trying to figure out which way my life was going and why I was messing about with four would-be careers instead of concentrating on one. I wasn't really on a straight line to anywhere, just shooting around in four different directions at once – the theatre, the music, the writing and now the films. Not that I wasn't still composing music for Feldman's, in fact Ivan and I had even completed a full-scale musical comedy called *Let's Go!* which had aroused an enormous amount of no enthusiasm from at least five London managements. Still, we'd had a couple of minor hits and the thing that really excited me was writing a number for the great Ella Shields called 'A Beggar Can Sing the Song of a King', which she not only put in her act but recorded and sang for the rest of her career.

As for the acting, I'd been in a couple of jobs hardly worth mentioning. A small, easily forgettable pantomime at the newly built Embassy Theatre at Swiss Cottage (now the Central School of Speech and Drama) with Sybil Arundel, Helen Goss and Derek Waterlow, plus a short tour in *The Edge of Life* for an actor-manager named Barney Lando in which I played Marc Bois, a French pimp. No one could say I was afraid to stretch my talents. From village idiot to French pimp. I mean, did Olivier do that?

Incidentally, Arnold Ridley's *Third Time Lucky* opened at the Ambassadors and closed a short time later, before I'd plucked up the courage to go and see the new idiot. Poor man, he was now out of work again along with Alan Keith and the rest of them. At least for the moment I was luckier. That's why I wrote so many bits and pieces, I knew I had to earn enough money to be able to earn no money as an actor.

The London theatre scene that year was an exciting one. Evelyn Laye was in Noël Coward's *Bitter Sweet*, having moved over to the Lyceum from His Majesty's to make room for the new JB Priestley musical *The Good Companions*, now installed and packing them in. Paul Robeson was still at the Ambassadors and in April a bombshell from Czechoslovakia burst over London. His name was Francis Lederer, the theatre was the Lyric and the play was *Autumn Crocus*. This handsome, debonair, talented heart-throb from the Continent swept London off its feet. The stage door in Great Windmill Street was besieged by fans at each performance and police had to clear the street continually to let the traffic through. And isn't it fun to think, all these decades later, that Francis and his lovely wife Marion would later become not only our close chums but also our close neighbours in this little desert outpost of the American continent called Palm Springs.

One morning in June 1931 I arrived at Feldman's and walked into my own bombshell.

'Morning, Mr Guest,' said the liftboy.

'Good morning,' I answered jovially.

'There's a letter upstairs for you, sir.'

There was indeed, and Elsie Rackham handed it to me. The envelope was marked 'Val Guest and Ivan Keith'. It was on company notepaper and was from George Slevin. 'From this week on,' it read, 'I must inform you your weekly allowance on account of royalties must stop, for at the moment we see no way in which you can make good your debit, which is large...'

I took the letter back to Ivan who accepted it philosophically. 'Well, boy, it seems I'm back in the fur business.' And it seemed I was now on a single line to the film studios and for the moment Rimsky-Korsakoff and Irving Berlin could relax. I marvelled at how quickly life could turn around and make your mind up for you. I realised that, apart from anything else, if I wanted to live in the manner to which I had become accustomed, which was a mite above the poverty line, I would have to make some extra money. Which meant more articles, more writing, more everything. It was then I devised my nefarious scheme.

At that time various London papers were running a Readers' Letters competition. For instance, the *Evening News* was offering five guineas for the best Great War experience and a guinea for each letter published. Well, if you thought you knew all the legendary battle heroes you should have read some of the experiences I dreamed up for the *Evening News*. Using fictitious names and my friends' addresses, I'm ashamed to say I cleaned up during that two-week competition. This is the first time I've confessed to this sordid stain on my escutcheon and I do so hoping that 60-odd years places me beyond the reach of prosecution. Mind you, many years later I partially redeemed my conscience when the *Evening News/Daily Mail* sponsored the National Youth Theatre. Yolande and I donated a cash prize to be awarded to the best student. The girl who won it was an attractive 19-year-old who, before our award, had decided she couldn't afford to stay in London any longer and was about to return home and become a teacher. Her name was Helen Mirren.

During my last days at Feldman's I took a long overdue look at my suddenly curtailed earning capacity. After adding it up it was crystal clear that of my three, for want of a better word, 'careers', writing had brought me in more than theatre and music combined. So what now, little man? I talked it over with my mother at a hastily summoned Lyons Corner House get-together. As usual she narrowed it down to basics. 'For the theatre you need dedication, for music you need inspiration, for writing you need a typewriter and the determination to use it. Only you can make the choice.'

The logical choice was obvious but I was still loath to burn any bridges behind me. Strangely enough it was a current girlfriend of mine who gave me the most comforting perspective. She was a talented young dancer in a show at the Saville Theatre, which was next door to Feldman's, and her name was Connie Stevens. Connie was blonde, beautiful, ambitious and had a great sense of fun. It happened that on the day of my traumatic letter she had a matinée, so after the performance I picked her up and we walked down to our current favourite tea-shop, next to the Garrick Theatre, where she listened to my tale of woe. She pondered for a moment over her cup of Darjeeling then smiled across at me.

'Well, it could be worse, couldn't it?' she said cheerfully. 'I mean, at least you have a contract to work on *The Maid of the Mountains* script and if that works out, Lupino Lane might give you another one and then maybe you could write in a part for yourself. And, if you're really smart, find a place for some of your music in it, too. Kill three birds with one stone.'

Out of the mouths of babes and sucklings. We laughed and laughed and she even made me feel glad to be through with Feldman's. Happily I was able to do something in return for dear Connie. Not long after that, I talked about her to Stanley Lupino. 'You once did me a favour,' I joked to him, 'now I'm doing one for you. Take a look at a girl called Connie Stevens. She could be an all-dancing, all-singing, all-talking new leading lady for you.' To his credit, Stanley did just that and it wasn't long before he announced her as the new leading lady in his very next musical. All of which launched a successful and starry career for Connie Stevens, under the new name of Sally Gray.

Perhaps one of the most important things that happened to me during the last few months of that year was meeting Edgar Wallace. This incredible character was probably the most prolific and successful thriller writer of our generation. It seemed there was always a new Wallace book on the shelves or being made into plays or films or both. *The Four Just Men, The Case of the Frightened Lady, On the Spot* – his titles went on and on. In fact, the current joke around town was to ask news stands if they had the Edgar Wallace lunchtime edition. I had arranged to interview this legend, hoping to sell the piece to one of the Sunday papers. We met in his Portland Place office. A large, friendly man with an aquiline nose, he smoked interminable cigarettes through a long holder. But the thing that struck me immediately about his office were the four dictaphones spaced about four feet apart in front of the windows. In those days dictaphones were on stands and had changeable wax recording drums. Most offices used them, but not four in a row! 'Couldn't operate without 'em,' smiled Wallace when I mentioned them. His cigarette holder stabbed at them, ticking them off one by one. 'That's for next week's racing article, that one's the new book, that's the new play. Number four's my correspondence.'

What staggered me was how he could work on so many projects at once. 'You have to learn to de-concentrate,' he explained. De-concentrate? And he proceeded to give me a lesson that I was to use all my life. 'Once I've finished my racing piece I sweep my mind for 15 minutes. Clean my shoes, make some tea, empty all the baskets – anything for a clean break. Fifteen minutes, I'm back with a swept mind, ready for the book. Once you've learned the trick it isn't that hard.'

And it wasn't the only thing I picked up that day from Edgar Wallace. He learned that I was writing my first screenplay and sympathised with me. 'Whose story are they butchering this time?' he smiled. When I told him it was *The Maid of the Mountains*, he laughed. 'Oh well, a little butchery might help.'

I'd always heard Wallace was a generous man but I didn't realise how generous until I was about to leave. 'Good luck with your first film script,' he said as we shook hands. 'Have you mastered how to lay it out in scenes and dialogue?'

'Vaguely,' I confessed.

He rummaged through one of his drawers and presented me with a battered screenplay. 'Written for one of my old films,' he said. 'Never know, it might help. Send it back when you're through.'

Sadly I never had a chance to tell him how much that kind deed helped me in writing my script of *The Maid*. By the time I'd finished he'd gone to Hollywood to work on his biggest undertaking yet – a little epic-to-be called *King Kong*. Even sadder, Edgar Wallace died suddenly, without ever knowing what a historic part of cinema history his last film was destined to become.

CHAPTER
FOUR

N ip Lane completed *The Maid* without too many problems and, what was much more exciting, asked me if I would like to work an the script of his next one, *The Milky Way*. This title
was eventually changed to *Innocents of Chicago* because Harold Lloyd had already used the
other one in Hollywood.

BIP, the friendly old 'Porridge Factory', was fast becoming a second home for me. And all those
friendly faces began to feel like relatives. Weston 'Bill' Drury, the casting director, had engaged me for
three pounds ten shillings a day for my small acting part and each evening at the end of shooting I
would take my little green chit along to the payout window and have it cashed for me by one Robert
Clarke. If the name rings a bell it's because this same Robert Clarke became one of the most powerful
moguls in the film business, managing not only Elstree but their entire chain of theatres. However, back
then he was still counting out my three pounds ten for me. In those days the Elstree empire was ruled
by a tough, canny Scot named John Maxwell whose regime, after much share-juggling and financial wiz-
ardry, became known as the Scottish Mafia.

Apart from all this, Hitchcock was having a ball making a thriller called *Number Seventeen* with noted
Shakespearean actor Leon M Lion and an unbelievable model miniature train which took up the whole
of the Silent Stage. In fact, Hitch was so busy playing with this new toy that dear old Joe Grossman
wasn't twitching nearly as much. Except for that unforgettable day when he was showing His Majesty
the King of Greece around the studios. Spruced up in his best Fire Brigade uniform, with medals glistening, Joe ushered the King on to the stage where they were shooting a scene in a French café. 'And
these 'ere, Your Majesty,' he announced, 'are all 'abitats of a French café.' (He pronounced it to rhyme
with 'safe'.) 'Now this 'ere box is on wheels and has the camera in it because we don't want to 'ear anything, and that pole is a 'boom' and the thing on the end is a 'mike', to get the sounds we *do* want to
'ear.' His Majesty was listening attentively when Joe broke off and smiled affably. 'But then I expect this
is all Greek to you.' Of course this story went straight into the annals of Elstree.

Perhaps I should explain that in those 'covered wagon' days of the Talkies the cameras were always
in mobile, soundproofed booths pushed around from place to place with the operator, focus puller and

often the lighting cameraman inside. They were familiarly known as the 'sweat boxes'. As for sound, it was recorded on the floor on large discs and was sometimes absolute hell to synchronise later.

Poor Hitch had a horrendous time with early sound when he was making *Blackmail*. They had engaged the immensely popular Czech actress Anny Ondra as his leading lady. What they had not reckoned with was that the lovely Anny had become famous as a silent film star and whenever she opened her mouth her accent made most of the dialogue unintelligible. It was too expensive and too late to recast so Hitch had to employ British actress Joan Barry to stand behind the camera and speak Anny's lines into a microphone while the lady herself was mouthing them in front of the camera. And that's how *Blackmail* was made. Which had to be the first hesitant step towards post-synching as we know it today. Hitch told me later, 'I never wanted to be a bloody pioneer – it put ten years on me!'

These days, of course, they've brought re-voicing to a fine art. If there's unwanted noise on the original soundtrack you simply whip the artiste into the dubbing theatre for a couple of hours and re-record it. And if for any reason someone has to be re-voiced there are actors and actresses who make a very good living out of being good mimics. The Queen of all these was a young girl called Olive Gregg. Olive could revoice anyone from Marlene Dietrich to Dame Edith Evans, and often did. So when, in one of my own films, I needed to re-record that much-loved character actress Kathleen Harrison and found she was away in Ireland, I immediately called Olive. Only to find that she too was away, in France. Time was of the essence as we had deadlines to meet, so who else could we trust with matching Kathleen's very distinctive voice? It was then I had a wild idea. There was a chum I used whenever possible for re-voicing various small parts that hadn't been very good. He was an up-and-coming name in his own right but these odd jobs were always welcome to swell his piggy bank. His name was Peter Sellers.

'Pete,' I asked him on the phone, 'do you think you could do Kathleen Harrison?'

'You mean physically or phonetically?' he chuckled.

We had him down at the Danziger Studios within the hour and in another hour he had re-done her lines to perfection. There are two tags to this story. Firstly, Kathleen Harrison came to the sneak preview, the trade show and the première and still didn't know that some of her was Peter Sellers. Secondly, the film was called *Up the Creek* and marked the first starring role for, who else? Peter Sellers. 'There I was,' Peter used to joke later, 'up on that screen playing with myself.'

Thanks to Edgar Wallace, the *Innocents of Chicago* screenplay was nowhere near as difficult to write as my first one and, as I've already told you, we went on the floor with the current solid box-office names of Henry Kendall, Margot Grahame, Bernard Nedell, Binnie Barnes and Betty Norton. Bill Drury had cast me as one of the gangsters so I put in a lot of time working on an American accent. This had to be yet another riveting cameo in my repertoire of the demi-monde.

My clock-in time at the studios was too early for the usual lift with Nipper Lane but one of the other gangsters kindly offered to pick me up every morning outside the local cinema at Cricklewood Broadway. His name was Charles Farrell. No, not that one, the English one, who later became a pillar of British Actors Equity. Charlie was a gentle man with the sort of face that got him a lot of work playing heavies. The other three occupants of his small, crowded car were his large Airdale, who chose to sit on a different lap every trip, and Gangster Two, one Cyril Smith, who was later to become a star in his own right in the stage and film classic *Sailor Beware*. Gangster Three was an incredible character named Maurice Beresford. Maurice had a flattened nose, a pushed-in face and an American accent straight out of Damon Runyon, what you might call an inspired piece of casting by Weston Drury. Maurice regaled everybody with endless tales of his days in Chicago where he said he'd been a bodyguard for the notorious 'Legs' Diamond. A likeable enough person, but somehow none of us really believed the gangland tales he told. I remember one day on the set, for a joke, Nip Lane handed him a gun loaded with blanks and asked him to fire a couple. He nearly passed out with fright.

It transpired later that he had never even been to the States. His father was an Irish boxer and Maurice, who now lived in London, was trying to build up his persona. I'm recounting this story as an example of what a fascinating thing human nature is. Here he was hoping to impress us and we would all have been far more impressed had he told us his real story. Acting wasn't his usual profession at all. He was, believe it or not, a composer and lyricist and his professional name was Michael Carr. Everyone into popular music knew Michael Carr as the man who had written a dozen worldwide hits, not least of which was 'South of the Border'. But it would have thrilled him far more to have been 'Legs' Diamond's bodyguard.

Towards the end of our production the normally even-keel atmosphere of BIP was rocked somewhat by a buzz of wild rumours about the British & Dominion Studios next door. Currently leased by producer-director Herbert Wilcox, it was said he had sold out his lease to some European company. Clever snooping by our own Binnie Barnes ferreted out the real details. Apparently Wilcox had merely agreed to sub-lease some B&D stages to three Hungarian brothers who had already made films in Vienna, Germany and France. 'Their names are Alex, Vincent and Zoltán Korda,' explained Binnie, 'and their company is London Films. And you know something else?' she grinned. 'They're all in their thirties and one of them's rather cute.'

Alex Korda was not only 'rather cute', he was the business and creative brain behind his entire organisation. No one could have foreseen the impact, energy and style he and his two brothers would infuse into the British film industry. In less than a year he began shooting the film that was to open the door to world markets and give them a new perspective on British films, *The Private Life of Henry VIII*. Which, Alex admitted later, was no small miracle. The project had been turned down by almost every financial source in town, even though it was a relatively inexpensive production. Then Fate bumped him into a gentleman with the colourful title of Count Toeplitz de Grand Ry and – bingo! – up came the money for a Korda/Toeplitz production. Of course the trade press had a ball with jokey headlines like KORDA IN FOR THE COUNT and TOEPLITZ – COUNT ME IN. But it's hard to top the classic Count story when Carl Laemmle Jr, son of the famous 'Uncle Carl' Laemmle, founder and president of Universal Pictures, was in Paris trying to cook up a joint production deal. He cabled his father: PLEASE WIRE MORE MONEY AM TALKING TO FRENCH COUNT. And Carl Sr's reply was NO MORE MONEY UNTIL YOU LEARN TO SPELL.

It's interesting to note that *Henry VIII*, which became one of the most famous and successful British pictures of all time, had so little British input. As the great Paul Rotha has pointed out, its story, direction, settings and music were all by Continentals. Even the chief make-up creator was brought over from Hollywood. Only the subject and the actors were British, launching a relatively young Robert Donat into starry orbit. Plus, of course, that somewhat larger-than-life character, Charles Laughton, whose Henry was to grab him an Oscar.

I was lucky to achieve quite an entré into the Korda set. To begin with I managed to interview him with two nice pieces in both *Picturegoer* and *Film Weekly*. In later days that would have had to be the *Times* or the *Telegraph* at least, but remember, this was early days and he too was a comparative 'newcomer'. 'Very nice,' smiled Alex Korda when I showed him the spreads. 'From now on you're a welcome guest, Mr Guest.' I took him at his word because the place was a veritable goldmine for interviews and Alex had told his publicity girl to regard me as friend not foe. Which she certainly did. But that's another story.

I'm sure a lot of this favoured treatment was because my old workmate and chum, Binnie Barnes, had put in a good word for me. As luck would have it, Binnie had been cast as Catherine Howard, one of Henry's wives. In fact it was she who introduced me to their imported make-up chief, Jimmy Barker, and we hit it off immediately. But could any of us have guessed that within the month I would be sharing a flat with him in Chiltern Court on Baker Street? And that the flat beneath us would belong to none other than H G Wells, who complained so many times about our parties that eventually we invited him up to join us.

Meanwhile, at B & D studios another small piece of film history was waiting to be made. A gaggle of 'ladies in waiting' were sitting in a corner ready to be called on set and fluttering about the latest production buzz. Actress Maria Korda had arrived on the set and everyone knew that not only was she the ex-Mrs Alexander Korda but that they'd been divorced several years ago. 'Maybe he's behind with the alimony,' joked one of the ladies in waiting, whose full name was Estelle Merle O'Brien Thompson. In her short acting career she had tried several name changes from Estelle Thompson to Queenie Thompson, then Queenie O'Brien and finally Merle O'Brien. Well, not finally because eventually she wound up as Merle Oberon. But right then she was a cheery 22-year-old with a happy 'hullo' for everyone and her current steady date was Frank Joyce, the other half of the heavyweight talent agency Selznick & Joyce.

None of which Maria Korda knew when she told her ex-husband, 'That's the prettiest girl on your entire set.' So Alex tested her, liked what he saw and upgraded her to the small part of Anne Boleyn, the youngest of Henry's wives. It wasn't all that long after that he upgraded her again to become Mrs Alexander Korda. But her biggest upgrade of all was when Alex was knighted and she became Lady Korda. At least it was a switch on the old Boy meets Girl plot. Ex-wife finds ex-husband new girl who marries ex-husband and seven years later also ex-es him. I wonder if they ever compared notes? Then Zoltán Korda married another of the Henry wives, Joan Gardner. I don't know where Vincent ended up in all these royal shenanigans but it wasn't long before the Kordas became known, not unkindly, as 'The Three Elstree Marx Brothers'.

Weston Drury called me back to do another acting job at BIP and this time I, too, had been upgraded to play a newspaper reporter. It was a ghastly comedy called *Toreadors Don't Care* starring their current funny man, Leslie Fuller. One of my recurring nightmares is that some day someone may excavate the archives and find it.

Jimmy Barker dropped over and lunched with me several times at BIP and seemed to know everyone in the place. With Charles Bickford and Raquel Torres shooting *Red Wagon*, Bebe Daniels making *Southern Maid*, and Ben Lyon and Sally Eilers filming *I Spy* it was like old home week for Jimmy. 'Listen,' he said to me one day, 'you're a writer. With all this going on why don't you capitalise on it? Try the American market. Nobody there knows what's happening over here. Write a column, like Walter Winchell.'

'Oh yes, great chance.'

'Why not? Try it out on someone like *Zit's*.'

'What the hell is *Zit's*?'

'*Zit's New York Review*. Same as *Variety* only smaller. Come over tonight, I'll help you write it.'

I spent the next three nights with him at Chiltern Court and between us we got out my first gossip column. Jimmy knew the person to send it to at *Zit's* and off it went. 'If it works,' he grinned, 'I'll be your Elstree stringer and you cover the rest of the town.' And to my unbelievable surprise it did work. Just over a week later I received a letter from Mr Zittel, the owner and publisher, saying he'd like to use the column and could I do one weekly? If yes, please airmail him terms and a photograph. If yes? My own New York column – with a photograph?

Which is how, with the help of Alexander Korda's head make-up man, I landed my first American writing contract. An incredible man, Jimmy Barker. A completely together ball of energy, he lived for his work, loved it and was unsurpassed at it. British leading ladies had never looked as good on the screen as when Jimmy had finished with them. As for me, the moment I finished at Elstree I would race home to Oxford Terrace, have a quick wash and brush-up, maybe a pie and cuppa at Fred's and hie myself down to the West End to see what was cooking for my 'In London' column. Jimmy had advised me that most of the time I should only write about people the Americans would know. So, as a lot of our English names had never been heard of in New York, it rather narrowed the field.

Beatrice Lillie would certainly have been heard of and right then she was doing her nightclub act at the Café de Paris on Coventry Street. This was one of London's top night spots that only booked the best and Bea Lillie *was* the best. She was one of those wonderful performers who appealed not only to the public but to her fellow professionals as well. Her throwaway, sophisticated humour had made her the pros' delight from Broadway to Bombay and all stops between. Later, during World War II, she would help out by travelling to outposts of the British Isles with me to entertain the troops in various shows I had organised. Later still she became a good friend of Yolande and mine, always cheerful, always able to see the funny side of life's more mundane chores. An example was when she thought she'd like to rent a small holiday home in Bermuda. After being showered with brochures and flyers she received a follow-up telegram from a Bermuda Estate Agent which read: HOUSE COMES WITH MAID, SECRETARY AND CHAUFFEUR. Only Bea Lillie could have wired back: AIRMAIL PHOTOGRAPH OF CHAUFFEUR.

Another person in London that year was Fred Astaire. He wasn't the dancing icon we remember so nostalgically today; as yet he had never made a film. But for me it was enough that they knew him in New York! He and his sister Adele had already captured London audiences as the double act who danced their way so gracefully through a couple of West End musicals. Then one fateful day the British aristocracy had stepped in. Lord Charles Cavendish was the bounder in question and he walked up to the dancing couple, tapped Fred on the shoulder, cut in and waltzed Adele out of the theatre to become Lady Cavendish. So now Fred was going solo on stage at the Palace Theatre starring in *The Gay Divorce* with beautiful ex-Ziegfeld girl Claire Luce. All good grist to the columnist's mill. Especially when I learned he was shortly to be tested by MGM.

For one reason or another it seems I spent a lot of the next two columns in and out of Chiltern Court. One evening, when Jimmy was giving me the Elstree scuttlebutt – little gems like Wendy Barrie (who played Jane Seymour) having a bit of slap-and-tickle with Robert Donat, who in turn fancied one of the hairdressers while Charles Laughton was chatting up the clapper boy – Jimmy suddenly poured himself a drink, sank onto the couch and said, 'Can you think of one good reason why you don't move here into Chiltern Court?

'Yes,' I answered promptly. 'Money.'

'Money for what?'

'The rent.'

'Korda pays the rent.'

'You mean move in with you?'

'Why not? There's two bedrooms. Whatever you pay for your current place, throw it in the kitty here for necessities.' It was obviously an offer I couldn't refuse. Back I went to my top floor back, packed my goods and chattels, waved goodbye to Whores Row, bid Miss Jaynes a fond farewell, made sure the slate was clear with dear old Fred and set sail for Baker Street.

I was unpacking at Chiltern Court when the blinding light of reassessment hit me. The moment I came across my old theatre make-up kit – a battered Romeo and Juliet cigar box filled with its sticks of Leichner's Numbers 5 and 9, a bottle of spirit gum and a couple of false sideburns – suddenly it was like seeing a box of relics and I realised that for at least a year I hadn't even thought about the theatre. I'd been to it, written odd songs for it, but thought about it as an actor? Had that really been me with all those dreams of becoming the country's greatest actor? From village idiot to knighted thespian? Right now I seemed to be wrapped up in being a columnist with a smattering of scriptwriting and the occasional bit of film acting.

Somehow or other I'd even managed to do a couple of small films down at Warner Bros' Teddington studios, run by that very nice American, Irving Asher. His wife was even nicer, silent movie star Laura la Plante. One of my never-to-be-remembered performances was in a low-budget boxing picture called *The Bermondsey Kid*, starring Esmond Knight, with me doing my now-famous impersonation of a newspaper reporter.

Errol Flynn was on one of the other stages making a thriller called *Murder in Monte Carlo*. At that time he was with the Northampton Repertory Company so he was having to do frantic commuting between Northampton and Teddington. It was during all this racing around that he caught the eye of Irving Asher when he doubled some fencing scenes in another film. Irving thought he looked quite promising, told Jack Warner and suggested a test. The rest is history and it wasn't long before Errol was at Warners' Burbank studio, shooting his first Hollywood film, *Captain Blood*, with Michael Curtiz at the helm.

But that first day in Chiltern Court, as I finished unpacking, I knew in my heart of hearts that, apart from the extra pennies it might bring in, I couldn't care less if I never acted again. And as if to convince myself of this startling revelation I dropped the battered Romeo and Juliet make-up box into the waste basket. From now on it seemed I was destined to be a writer.

We had a lot of fun at Chiltern Court, quite apart from the occasional weekend parties. Jimmy Barker was a very gregarious person and you never knew who he'd bring back from the studio next. I remember one Friday night he arrived home with, of all people, the local Elstree vicar. A nice cosy little grey-haired man with steel-rimmed spectacles who was perfect casting for the part. 'Can you believe it?' said Jimmy. 'He's never tasted chili con carne, so I promised to make him some.' And he started to do just that. He told me to open a couple of tins we had in the cupboard while he chopped some onions, put three bowls in the oven and before you could say 'Roll 'em' we were sitting down for our 'Dinner for three please, James.' The vicar enjoyed it all immensely and said how much he appreciated the invitation. Eventually Jimmy put him in a taxi and paid his fare back to Elstree, which I can promise you ran well into double figures. But that was Jimmy Barker.

Most weekends odd members of the *Henry VIII* cast dropped in for one reason or another. Merle, to pick up a new eyeliner he'd had flown over for her from Max Factor, or Binnie Barnes for the latest indelible lipstick. Jimmy always had something for everybody. I was disappointed I never saw Charles Laughton. A quote from him would be great for the column because they already knew him over there. He'd recently done a couple of plays on Broadway, the last one as Agatha Christie's Hercule Poirot in *Fatal Alibi* just before he came back to do *Henry*. 'Don't worry, you'll get your quote,' promised Jimmy. 'I'll invite him to our pre-Christmas party.'

We certainly went to a lot of trouble decorating the flat that Christmas, festooning everything with popcorn threaded on string which he told me was an old American custom. And somehow he had talked Wendy Barrie into helping him ornament the Christmas tree and it looked great. Wendy was a nice girl and she also went to Hollywood on the strength of her performance in *Henry VIII*. She did quite a few pictures there but then went and screwed up everything by getting engaged to one of gangland's most notorious hoodlums, Bugsy Siegel. For some reason Tinseltown's own hoodlums didn't approve of this and her career seemed to fade away. But she was a great Christmas tree dresser.

Our party was on a Saturday night early in December and Jimmy had invited the rest of his make-up department and our new friend the Elstree vicar, who was dying to meet the great Charles Laughton, Merle and boyfriend Frank Joyce, Wendy, Binnie and Georges Périnal, Korda's French director of photography. Laughton was the last to arrive, full of apologies. 'So sorry, darlings, my chauffeur's just become a father and...' He broke off, beaming at all the decorations, and roared, 'Christ, a fucking Christmas tree!' Of course everybody laughed and I glanced nervously at our little vicar. He, too, had mustered a smile, which is tough to do when you're trying to keep a stiff upper lip. Anyway, I'd just had my first Laughton quote, although I doubted very much whether *Zit's* were avant-garde enough to use it.

And talking of *Zit's*, I must say I got an enormous kick when two of America's best known columnists, Walter Winchell and Sidney Skolsky, lifted pieces out of my column. Winchell grabbed a couple of gossip items and not only credited me with them but sent me a copy via *Zit's*. It was my first contact with the famed Winchell and was the prelude to my actually working for him during World War II. Skolsky had borrowed a piece I'd written about a Mayfair shirtmaker who was so fed up with the number of overdue accounts that he put a printed card in his window which read: ON THE BACK OF THIS CARD ARE THE NAMES OF ALL OVERDUE ACCOUNTS. NEXT MONDAY THE CARD WILL BE TURNED AROUND.

Within a few days most of his bills were settled.

CHAPTER
FIVE

O n one of my periodic visits to Winchester Road to see Vi and my father I told him I was
writing a column for an American newspaper. 'Why not an English newspaper?' was his first
reaction. Reasonable question, so I attempted to explain it, but I don't really think it got
through to him. Even at the ripe old age of 22 I still found it difficult to make a contact there. Vi, as
always, was affectionate and enthusiastic.

At this time I was seeing my mother once or twice a month for lunch or tea. She, too, was a
warm, understanding and generous person. So why did I have such difficulty accepting the fact that
she was also my mother?

'This could open all kinds of doors for you,' she told me when she heard the news. As usual she
was right. The first door it opened was at the Grosvenor House where I had arranged an interview with
one Billy Wilkerson, owner and publisher of the *Hollywood Reporter*. This made him a powerful person
in Hollywood because the *Reporter* was widely regarded as the Bible of the film industry. A small man,
wearing a grey suit and a purple shirt, he was passing through London on a short vacation to play the
tables in Cannes and Monte Carlo. But it seemed all he could talk about was his paper, of which he
was inordinately proud, and how his wife, Edith, wrote their 'Rambling Around' gossip column. 'Best
in town,' he enthused. 'Leaves Louella [Parsons] and Hedda [Hopper] standing.'

He boasted about his editor, Frank Pope, and how brilliant he was when he was sober and sometimes
even better when he wasn't. As none of this seemed to be much good to me for *Zit's* I was getting a little fidgety when he suddenly announced that he was aware of my column and asked how tied I was to
Zittel. I told him it was a monthly agreement at which he got to his feet and said, 'Okay, let's have lunch.'

Over our Grosvenor House lunch he told me his London correspondent, John Paddy Carstairs (who
was also an assistant cameraman and son of stage actor Nelson Keys), was leaving them to become a
screenwriter and possible director. 'So the job's open. D'you want it?' The offer was so unexpected it
caught me with a mouthful of Dover sole and I mumbled something inaudible while I tried not to choke.
'We need a London piece every two weeks,' he continued, 'plus usual news coverage, starting next month.'

Which is the rather undramatic way I became London correspondent for the *Hollywood Reporter*. And what a job it turned out to be. The bit Billy Wilkerson hadn't told me was that I was also expected to drum up UK advertising for his paper. Every so often I would get a Western Union cable saying things like HAVE EVERYONE WISH ME HAPPY BIRTHDAY and round the studios I would go. Some people didn't care if Billy ever had another birthday, but others believed it was politic to take a page every now and then. Alex Korda was always very good to me in this way, so were BIP and Herbert Wilcox. But it wasn't always as easy as that. There were people who couldn't wait to take a page in the *Reporter* and then couldn't wait to find ways of not paying for it. But I was green enough not to know about this.

Gregory Ratoff was one of these. Gregory was a larger than life personality who was one of the best known character actors in Hollywood. His thick Russian accent was never out of work and always out of money. His trouble was gambling. In fact, in his poker games with Darryl Zanuck, he lost so much that Zanuck had to keep him working in order to get some of it back. Gregory had come to London to appear in a British film at the same time as another distinguished old-timer, Richard Bennett. They had put Bennett in a flat on Half Moon Street and Ratoff into the Dorchester Hotel. I let them get settled in for a few weeks before convincing Bennett to take a half page telling everyone about his new British film. Then I called on Ratoff to try and sell him some space. His first question was, 'Has Bennett taken any?'

'Yes, half a page.'

'Then I'll take a full page,' he said imperiously.

Elated by my success I cabled the *Reporter*: FOUR AND A HALF PAGES COPY FOLLOWING KORDA BIP WILCOX RATOFF AND BENNETT. Almost by return came the reply: TELL RATOFF NO MONEY NO PAGE.

When he received me in his Dorchester suite Ratoff had just summoned all the floor staff to come and see him. Once the valet, the floor waiter, the chambermaid and the shoe polisher were assembled in front of him he beamed at them benignly and said, 'My friends, thees week no teeps. Instead I geeve you the winner of the Grand National.' Only Ratoff could dream up something like that. Sadly for everyone the horse didn't win. When I called on him the following week to pick up his full page money he had just rung the bell for the valet to have his dinner jacket pressed. Ten minutes later, without warning, the door was flung open and there stood the valet. 'What d'ya want now?' he snapped.

Richard Bennett had different problems: his famous daughters, Joan and Constance. 'They've no time for their poor old father,' he cried to me one evening when I called on him in Half Moon Street. He appeared to have had a tipple or two and was becoming maudlin about it. 'Raised 'em, cared for 'em, taught 'em their trade, what do they care? Don't even answer the old man's calls. They'll be sorry when I'm gone. Serve 'em right if I died tonight. They'd feel guilty as hell. I'd like to make 'em feel guilty as hell. Maybe I'll poison myself, that would teach 'em.' He launched off into the bathroom and came back with a bottle of iodine in his hand. 'Serve 'em right,' he said, trying to uncork it. By now I was getting worried. 'Mr Bennett... please... wait a minute...' I tried to take the bottle from him but he pushed me aside. 'You can tell 'em they drove me to it.' At which point the cork came out and splattered iodine all over him. He looked down at the mess on his chest and in a voice full of impatience said, 'For Chrissakes, a clean shirt!'

Charles Farrell (the American one) and Ralph Bellamy were much more fun. They, too, had checked into the Dorchester. Farrell had come over to make a film called *Falling in Love* with English actress Mary Lawson and his buddy Ralph had come to see the sights and keep him company for a couple of weeks. And what was the sight they wanted to see first? 'Rotten Row,' said Ralph promptly.

'We've heard on Sunday mornings the place to be is in Hyde Park watching the riders,' added Charlie.

The Rotten Row, at the Hyde Park Corner end of the park, was the starting and finishing place for all the Sunday horseback riders and in those days was popular as a morning promenade for people in their Sunday best. But I must say I didn't expect them to know it, let alone want to go to it. 'Well, if you like I'll take you there next Sunday,' I offered.

'Not until you've taken us shopping,' smiled Ralph Bellamy. 'We need the right hats.'

'Derby hats,' added Farrell. 'You people call them bowlers. We need some bowler hats and umbrellas, so we look real British.'

I took them to Dunne's, the hatters in Piccadilly, where they were fitted with two black bowlers and a couple of umbrellas. That Sunday morning Charles Farrell and Ralph Bellamy, two highly paid international film stars, were happy as sandboys parading at Rotten Row in their black bowlers and swinging their furled umbrellas. Needless to say, no one recognised them, which made them even happier.

Working for Billy Wilkerson wasn't all roses, it had its moments of deadly nightshade, too. To start with, Billy was almost always short of cash. Whether this was the fault of the casinos or because one of his hobbies was to open new restaurants I don't know. He already owned one of the 'in' night spots in Hollywood, the Vendome, where it was almost a 'must' to be seen eating at least once a week. Suddenly he had decided to open a new one, the Trocadero on Sunset Boulevard. However, his suppliers considered it too much of a gamble and were giving him a hard time. But Billy, being the courageous Covered Wagon type that he was, decided to go ahead anyway and launched a brilliant promotion in the *Reporter* suggesting that anyone who wasn't at this historic opening could never face their grandchildren again. Within no time his restaurant-to-be had a sold-out opening-night-to-be. He also had his suppliers.

The Trocadero opened in a blaze of glory and soon became an intrinsic part of the Hollywood scene. You had to admire someone who pulled off successes by the skin of his teeth. But I didn't admire him when it became the skin of *my* teeth. Suddenly my pay cheques stopped arriving, but the cablegrams didn't. Messages like SELL ELSTREE SPACE UPCOMING PRODUCTIONS STOP or WHY NO WILCOX AD. I even received one telling me to ARRANGE BIRTHDAY GREETINGS RIN-TIN-TIN JR. And one day, when the great South African leader General Jan Smuts came to England and there was some talk about a possible film co-production deal, I received the following: GET INTERVIEW WITH SMUTS STOP. At that time my salary was three weeks behind so I cabled back, SMUTS NUTS WIRE MONEY. I got my money so Billy got his interview.

One week I had a brainwave and sought out the manager of the Grosvenor House in Park Lane. I showed him a copy of the *Reporter* and told him everyone who mattered in the film business read it, so how about the Grosvenor House taking space in it? He skimmed through the paper and asked, 'How much?'

'Depends,' I answered tantalisingly. 'Could be as little as nothing. We might be able to give you a quarter of a page every week in return for an office here. That way you'd get the ad in once a week and the editorial page would say 'London Office: Grosvenor House, Park Lane, London' every day.'

It was obviously one of my Academy Award performances because he fell for it and from then on I ran Billy's London office from a room in Grosvenor House. Flushed with success I suffered another brainstorm. How about a British *Hollywood Reporter*? Run it once a month inside the *Reporter* proper. I could do all the book, theatre and film reviews as well as local production news. Again Wilkerson bought the idea. With one proviso – 'You do it for the same dough.' And I did it for less, without realising that this decision would soon change, not only my career, but the rest of my life.

Writing the column was the easiest part of it. There was so much good copy around at that time. For instance, Marlene Dietrich was at Elstree playing Catherine the Great in *The Scarlet Empress* opposite Douglas Fairbanks Jr, and their film romance had spilled off the screen into the Mayfair Hotel where Marlene was staying. The Mayfair is not the easiest hotel to slip in and out of unnoticed and, although Doug always swore he never used the fire escape, there are witnesses who swear he did. I was to come into close contact with Doug years later when I wrote and directed the film *Mr Drake's Duck* for him and Yolande, by which time he was playing footsie with Princess Margaret, more of which later.

Noël Coward was also in town, back from a New York stint in his play *Private Lives*. Noël was a perfectionist and 'good' just wasn't good enough for him. When impressario Harold Fielding put on a musical version of *Gone With the Wind* at Drury Lane, Coward went to the dress rehearsal, at which a precocious child actress sang and tapped her way into a frenetic ovation from family and friends.

'Any suggestions how to make it better?' asked Fielding after the show.

'Yes,' said Noël Coward without hesitation. 'Cut half the second act and the child's throat.'

The British *Hollywood Reporter* was being well received and all was peaceful until my fourth edition hit the news-stands. That was when the doo-dah hit the fan and started the countdown to my future. The cause was one of my smart-alec film reviews. It was for a Hollywood picture called *Chandu the Magician*, starring Edmund Lowe and directed by Marcel Varnel. In the brashness of youth I had said: 'If I couldn't write a better film than this with one hand tied behind my back I'd give up the business.' When Varnel read it he called Wilkerson, whom he knew, and told him, 'If your reviewer is so clever let him write my next.'

Wilkerson in turn called me. 'You made the challenge, he's taken you up.'

'Oh, come on, Billy, that wasn't a challenge, that was me trying to be funny...'

'Listen, you can't make the paper look goddam stupid. Either do it or get off the pot. Go see him.'

'For God's sake, I'm in London!'

'So is he. He's at Elstree.' And down went the phone.

It took me some moments to collect my scattered wits and then I checked the studios. Marcel Varnel was indeed in town at BIP, where he'd come over to shoot a picture called *Freedom of the Seas*. I took a deep breath, called his secretary, made an appointment to see him, and off I went to the studio, hat in hand. Marcel turned out to be a small, cheery, chubby, slightly balding Frenchman with merry, twinkling eyes. I apologised for what I'd said in the review, told him it was just one of those trying-to-be-clever cracks and that of course I couldn't write his next.

'I'm not so sure. I like your column – it has bite,' he said, completely flooring me. 'My next movie is a comedy and the dialogue needs some bite. Roger Burford's writing the script, you know him?' I'd heard of him, he was already an established screenwriter. 'I think you two together might make a good team. You have an agent?' An agent? This was really ha-ha time. I debated whether to say I was currently between agents but he seemed like a no-crap sort of person so I told the truth. 'Never mind,' he twinkled, 'we'll work something out. Let's have lunch tomorrow.'

And that, wild as it seems, was the way it happened. I know it sounds rather like the flip side of that scene in *42nd Street* when the chorus girl is told, 'You're going to go out there a dancer and come back a star!' I didn't exactly come back a star but I did get to partner my first top screenwriter. As for Roger Burford, it was the only time we worked together but he taught me more about screenwriting in four weeks that I could have learned in a dozen 'How to Write' courses. I stayed on to script 17 more comedies for Marcel, all the way from Will Hay's *Oh, Mr Porter!* through the unforgettable Crazy Gang and on to George Formby. Marcel also took me on the floor with him in all these productions as general dogsbody and gag man, which allowed me to learn my eventual trade as a director.

Our first picture was called *Monkey Business* with Hollywood actress June Clyde and a popular romantic light comedian, Gene Gerrard. There was also a young acrobat-cum-actor making his first appearance on the screen, Richard Hearne, who was hidden in an orang outan skin for the entire picture playing the monkey of the title. Poor Dickie Hearne, apart from the billing no one even knew he was in it. Luckily it didn't stop him going on to have a successful career, not the least of which was to be immortalised as television's 'Mr Pastry'.

For me the most memorable thing about that production was something the unit came to refer to as 'The Laugh'. We first heard it the day there was a crowd call of about two dozen extras for a theatre audience. Suddenly, during one of our shooting breaks, this husky, infectious laugh echoed across the stage and was stifled quickly as though the person realised it was too loud. It was the sort of laugh that raised an involuntary smile when you heard it. On the second crowd day 'The Laugh' was still with us and started Marcel laughing too. Whereupon he instructed his First Assistant to see who owned it.

It turned out to belong to an attractive young blonde called Patricia Watson, who at night was a dancer at the Gaiety Theatre in the current Leslie Henson hit *Seeing Stars*. She was both horrified and embarrassed at being identified as 'The Laugh'. 'Oh, how awful,' she winced, 'my terrible laugh... I'm so sorry... Did I spoil anything?' Told 'No' – and not to worry as everyone thought it was a rather good laugh and at times could be very useful – she slunk back into the crowd. I thought she looked great and when the First Assistant told me he'd offered her a lift to Elstree station to catch her train to the West End, I offered to relieve him of the chore.

'You must be joking,' he grinned. 'This is the best date I've had all year.'

As we had the crowd for three more days I vowed that tomorrow, to hell with Elstree station, I'd offer to drive her all the way to the Gaiety. However, she seemed the sort of girl who might easily say no to a stranger so somehow I had to make it an offer she couldn't refuse. Conniving cad that I was, I stayed in that evening working out my dialogue. The following morning, while they were relighting the set, purposely by mistake I stumbled on my prey at the tea trolley. 'Hullo and good morning,' I smiled.

'Hullo,' she smiled back.

'Listen, is it true you're in *Seeing Stars* at the Gaiety?'

'Yes, I am.'

'Well, what a coincidence! I have a ticket for it tonight. Hey, as I have to drive to the theatre anyway when we finish shooting, how about me giving you a lift?' I turned on a bit of the old schmooze. 'It has to be quicker and more comfortable than the train.'

She looked at me for a moment, then out came 'The Laugh'. 'I don't believe it,' she said.

'That I'm offering you a lift?'

'No, that you're going to the show.'

'I'll be at the stage door afterwards, to prove it.'

It worked. As soon as I'd dropped her off I raced around to the Gaiety box-office and was lucky enough to buy a return in the Upper Circle. It was a great show. Leslie Henson, as always, was a very funny man and of the 12 dancers I only had eyes for 'The Laugh'. After the show I took up my stand at the stage door in the Aldwych. Get me, a Stage Door Johnnie at, of all places, the Gaiety! This is where it all started in the Victorian and Edwardian days, when the aristocracy and the landed gentry came a-courting the famous Gaiety Girls. But they usually arrived with bouquets and diamonds. All I had was a ticket stub to show her I'd really been there. And why do I recount the saga of this contrived studio date? Because it turned out to be one of those important 'little-did-I-know' moments in my life. To start with, little did I know, or even dream, that this time next year 'The Laugh' would become my wife. How's that for a trailer?

Apart from which, the rest of that year seemed to be all go. My friend Jimmy Barker returned to Hollywood and I moved out of Chiltern Court into a comfortable room with bath at the newly built Mount Royal block at Marble Arch. It was a fun place in those early days, mainly because as yet there were only eight of us living there and we had that vast building to ourselves. We used to meet up at odd hours in the clubby coffee bar at the top of the marble entrance stairs.

We, the 'Magnificent Eight', were a widely assorted group. There was a young Larry Adler, staying there with his father. The year before, the great C B Cochran had brought him over from America for his revue *Streamline* at the Palace Theatre and Larry was now doing a number of variety dates. I remember one night in the coffee bar when a proud Daddy Adler showed us the snapshots he'd taken of Larry's billing outside the Streatham Hill Theatre. 'My boy's going places,' he predicted. And he was right.

On the fourth floor there was a 27-year-old film editor named David Lean. This was a great year for David. Having slogged his way up from tea boy at the old Gaumont Studios, to clapper boy and messenger and then into the cutting rooms where he helped to edit newsreel footage, he had just begun editing features. Another member of the coffee club was Will Hay, then a top music hall act as headmaster to an unruly bunch of schoolboys. But he hadn't yet hit the screen and become one of Britain's major box-office stars. At that time neither Bill Hay nor I had the slightest idea that over the next four years we would make eight films together. Then there was Bob Wyler, a nice little man who lived in the shadow of his famous brother, director William Wyler, and that fun American comedienne Norah Williams. We never met number eight in the coffee bar. He always nodded pleasantly at the odd times we saw him coming up those marble stairs with his glamorous girlfriend. His name was Max Aitken and he was the son of press baron Max Beaverbrook. I don't blame him for not wasting his time in the coffee bar when he could go upstairs with this cool, sophisticated society lady who went by the fascinating name of Toto.

Of course the place filled up in no time. Cornel Wilde and his wife Jean Wallace moved in, as did Noah Beery, one of Hollywood's favourite screen tough guys and brother of Wallace. Noah spent a lot of time showing everyone the contents of a match box he carried around in his pocket. 'It's desert soap,' he explained. 'I process it from desert lava. Best cleaning power and full of skin vitamins.' He sounded rather like a fatherly snake oil salesman as he told us what a boon to the world this would be once he'd got it launched onto the market. To the best of my knowledge dear old Noah was unsuccessful in his second career. Later still, some of the more adventurous Dorchester Girls also moved into the Mount Royal, causing some of the unkinder taxi-drivers to rename it the Royal Mount. This was highly libellous and, as they were quick to tell you, was only meant as a funny.

Which reminds me of the story about one of our favorite Soho restaurants, the Venezia in Great Chapel Street. It was a small, popular, family-owned Italian eating place run by Luigi Rienzo, a wonderful character who bustled around serving and cooking while constantly worrying about the fact that several prostitutes had rented rooms above his restaurant. His problem was that the upstairs customers always had to pass the waiting room of his downstairs customers. It never worried any of us; in fact, many Venezia regulars fondly and jokingly referred to the place as 'the brothel'. One day, years later, Robert Mitchum was in town on his way to the Cannes Film Festival and craved some good Italian food. 'Okay,' I told him, 'we'll take you to the brothel. Best spaghetti in town.'

'The where?' he asked. Laughingly we explained the reason it was known as that but its real name was the Venezia. So we dined there and, after the usual great meal, Mitchum promised Rienzo he'd be coming back. A few days later I bumped into Mitch and he asked, 'Where the hell was that restaurant?'

'The Venezia, Great Chapel Street.'

'The Venezia,' he laughed. 'I asked the cab driver to take me to the brothel in Great Chapel Street and he asked me "Which one?"'

At times during that first year at the Mount Royal I almost wished I still had my column. There was so much good copy flying around. Marcel asked me to come out to see him at Elstree where he was making *Dance Band* with Buddy Rogers and our old workmate June Clyde. On the next stage they were shooting *Blossom Time* with Richard Tauber singing 'You Are My Heart's Delight'. And Richard had apparently found his own heart's delight in British actress Diana Napier. In fact, according to the unit, he was having his heart's delight almost between choruses. However, in fairness to Richard, he did make an honest woman out of her and they were actually married during this production.

The Tauber film was a big hit for BIP, unlike their other 'greatest yet' production, *Abdul the Damned*. For this epic they had flown over MGM's Nils Asther, European megastar Fritz Kortner and thrown in our own Adrienne Ames. Sadly, when *Abdul the Damned* hit the screens the critics labelled it 'Abdamned the Dull'.

Next door at British and Dominion my friend Doug Jr was making *Mimi* with Gertrude Lawrence. And if you thought *La Bohème* was a heavy romance it was small fry compared to the Doug and Gertie story. Gertie Lawrence was being her usual scatty self on the set, playing practical jokes on everyone. Which would have appealed to Doug, who was into all sorts of parlour tricks himself, like sending a pair of mechanical false teeth clacking across the table or having you sit on whoopie cushions. Later that year their romance progressed into doing a play together, *Moonlight is Silver*, at the Queens Theatre and, would you believe it, those damned cushions were even in his dressing room.

The assignment Marcel Varnel had called me for turned out to be a new musical with a Vivian Ellis score and the bubbling, all-singing all-dancing Frances Day as the star. He was going to shoot the picture at Beaconsfield Studios which, he jokingly warned me, meant getting up an hour earlier as it was a much longer drive than Elstree. Frankly I would have driven even further to work with Frances Day. I'd seen her in so many hit stage musicals and thought she was great, with that trademark mop of wild blonde hair and that divine streak of mischief that seemed to keep everything around her sparkling. When Cole Porter, who was a friend of hers, first heard her sing his 'D'Lovely' he insisted that from then on it had to be her signature tune. And so it was for the rest of her life; from the cabarets to the war zones of World War II, 'D'Lovely' meant Frances Day.

As for *Public Nuisance No 1*, it was a lighthearted, frothy piece of nonsense probably only remembered by Vivian Ellis buffs for Frances singing his much-loved ditty 'Me and my Dog Are Lost in the Fog'. But for me it was memorable for three other things. Firstly, it was my courting time with Pat Watson who was still in the Henson show. Talk about fighting the odds. Every night I sent a car to pick her up at the Gaiety stage door and drive her down to Beaconsfield to join me at the Saracen's Head where I was staying. Poor girl, it was a good 45-minute drive after doing her show and for what? A midnight meal of cold leftovers in the hotel restaurant under the one remaining light, followed by a day on the set of a film she wasn't part of, topped by that long ride back to London for the evening performance. I don't know how our romance survived it, but so far it seemed to be doing all right.

Then there was Marcel. He sprung the next unforgettable surprise of my life. We were coming out of the projection room having viewed the previous day's work when he said suddenly, 'What would you say to me putting you under personal contract?' My mouth opened but nothing came out. 'It would simply mean you can't write any film I don't direct and I won't direct any script you haven't worked on.' The only sound I could make was a series of stunned frog noises to let him know I agreed. And that's how our seven-year, 17-film partnership began.

And last but by no means least, it was memorable because of Frances Day. I'd stumbled into one of those lucky occasions when two people jell from the start, not sexually but emotionally, and we became close friends, buddies and playmates through the ups and downs of many years. I shall always be grateful to this d'lovely lady who seemed to know everyone everywhere and opened so many doors for me, eventually becoming my son David's godmother.

One of the nicest doors she opened for me was the one to the South of France. On the last day of shooting she buttonholed me during the lunch break. 'Next Saturday I'm off to Cap d'Antibes,' she said. 'Ever been to the South of France?' I told her the furthest I'd travelled since babyhood was New Brighton. 'Okay,' smiled Frances, 'want to come with me? It'll be fun. I've lots of friends down there and I'm going on my own.'

'Sounds great,' I laughed, 'but I can't afford all that.'

'You might be surprised,' she twinkled mischievously. 'To start with, the head of British Airways is a fan of mine and I can get you a real knockout rate. As for Antibes, André Seller who owns Hôtel du Cap is a very old friend and he'll fix you a room for less than you'd pay here at the Saracen.'

That night I reported the whole conversation to Pat. 'What a fantastic offer,' she enthused. 'You've said yes of course.'

'Not yet. I wasn't too sure about it.'

'Are you out of your mind? Look, firstly you deserve a break and secondly she can turn out to be a very useful lady.' Good old Pat, unselfish and far-seeing at the same time.

'If I went it would only be for a week. You sure you wouldn't mind?'

'Mind?' she joked. 'It'll give me a chance to catch up on some of my old flames.'

Marcel said it was all right with him if I went on the Monday instead of the Saturday as he wanted me to see the rough cut with him that weekend. Which meant I would get there two days after Frances. 'Great,' she enthused when I explained things. 'Now here's what you do. When you arrive in Nice don't let anyone talk you into a taxi. Look for the Carlton Hotel shuttle bus which will give you a free ride into Cannes. You should arrive at the hotel around five, five-thirty. Leave your bags with the concierge and if he asks tell him you're waiting for your friend. Then go out and sit on the terrace, order something to drink and I'll drive over and pick you up between six and six-thirty.'

Which is how I made my first historic trip to the South of France. Everything went according to plan and there I sat on the magnificent Carlton Terrace, sipping my coffee and surveying the magical scene of the Croisette and the blue Mediterranean beyond. It was all so laid-back compared to London. The pedestrians ambled, even the traffic seemed to amble, in fact one of the cars almost came to a stop at the foot of the terrace steps and the occupants waved in my direction. Could this be Frances? No, the car moved on. Ten minutes later another car slowed up and waved at me. This time I waved back. Perhaps Frances had told her friends I'd be there. A third car actually stopped and the smiling driver got out and came up the terrace steps towards me, hand outstretched. 'Welcome to Cannes,' he said. I got up to shake the hand and it walked right past me. I turned to find Noël Coward had been sitting at the table behind me. As he rose to leave Coward smiled, patted me on the shoulder and said, 'I thought you handled it very, very well.'

CHAPTER
SIX

In March 1936 Pat and I were married upstairs in the registry office of the Marylebone Town Hall. I don't think her family were too happy about this although they all showed up smiling for the ceremony.

There was her mother, Scott or Scotty, a pleasantly outspoken lady who felt her lovely daughter could have done much better. Always charming and nice-as-pie to me, she would sometimes ask Pat, 'Are you still going out with Crippen?' Apart from the fact that both the notorious murderer Dr Crippen and I had dark hair and moustaches I couldn't see the likeness, unless she felt I might easily poison my wife and bury her in the cellar as he had done. Then there was Jackie, Pat's very attractive teenage sister, who, with my help, became a showgirl in Robert Nesbitt's new West End musical. With this showcase it wasn't long before Jackie herself got married, to Derek Blyth who just happened to be the head man of Gilbey's Gin. This was much more in Scotty's line. Lastly there was Pat's stepfather, Charlie. Charlie was a likeable barrel of a man who owned and ran a fish and chip shop in Streatham. Somehow I don't think he ever really forgave me for not holding the wedding reception there.

We moved out of the Mount Royal and into a rather elegant block of flats around the corner, Number 15 Portman Square. There was no time for a honeymoon as we were both working like lunatics. Pat was rehearsing for the new Leslie Henson show, *Swing Along*, which was going into the Gaiety with the same cast and dancers as before, and Marcel had just signed a contract with Gainsborough Pictures which included me. I was to get £25 a week and bring their number of staff writers up to four, the other three being my old pals Frank Launder and Sidney Gilliat as well as another newcomer to the fold, George Marriott Edgar.

George was quite a bit older than any of us and had a venerable history of comedy to his credit. The popular musical comedy *Jill Darling!*, with Frances Day, for whom he wrote the book, had clocked up its second year at the Saville Theatre, apart from which he had written many other books for successful musicals and pantomimes. Perhaps he was best known for writing the classic monologues that helped to make Stanley Holloway famous. The mutinous Crimean soldier ('Sam, Sam, pick up tha musket, Sam') and the Tower of London Ghost ('With his head tucked underneath his arm, he walked the Bloody Tower'). George Marriott Edgar was a great find for a studio about to launch into a big programme of comedy productions.

The overall boss of Gainsborough Pictures was Maurice Ostrer who, for some reason, was known to one and all as Bill. Bill was the business side of operations but the presiding genius in charge of production was Ted Black. Ted, the younger brother of the all-powerful theatre impresario George Black, had an incredible knack of picking and handling people and subjects. From thrillers to comedy to historical dramas, from Hitchcock to Varnel and Walter Forde, as well as Robert Stevenson and Carol Reed, Ted was at home with all of them and, what's more, he earned their respect.

So there was I, the new boy at Gainsborough Studios in Poole Street, Islington, still trying to catch my breath, when Ted Black suddenly decided that George Edgar and I were going to be his new comedy writing team. Whereupon he gave us an office on the production floor and told us to start thinking about scripts for a stage comedian he'd just contracted called Will Hay. Later on, he added, he was also thinking of signing up brother George's popular bunch of comics at the Palladium, the Crazy Gang, and we'd be writing for them too. And as if that wasn't daunting enough, this was when I discovered the office next door to us belonged to one Alfred Hitchcock. 'Just remember your Boy Scout's motto,' I warned George, 'and "Be Prepared".'

I was also prepared for this unbelievable stroke of writing luck to be no more than a temporary state of euphoria for me and that after two or, at best, three finished screenplays Ted Black would come up with another comedy scribbler to take my place. Twenty-two pictures and nine years later I was still there. Through seven Will Hays, four Crazy Gangs, five musicals and half a dozen other assorted films, Gainsborough became my second home. What's more, everyone who worked there became my second family. And there were always old friends dropping in to join in the family fun. People like 'Sexy Rexie' Harrison, Paul von Henreid (who decided to drop the von before World War II), and lovely Lilli Palmer who came into my office one day and flung herself into my arms crying her eyes out because the Ostrers had taken up her contract and she wanted to go to Hollywood.

Then there was the amiable Boris Karloff, dear old Uncle Boris, who couldn't wait to finish shooting so he could scamper off to Lords and watch the cricket. And the young Michael Redgrave, called in by Hitch for his first screen test to see if he was right for *The Lady Vanishes*. Michael, who had chosen the balcony scene from Noël Coward's *Private Lives*, was doing the test with his wife, the lovely Rachel Kempson. After the first couple of takes he got a mild attack of hiccups and pretty soon he also got an attack of the giggles. Which meant that Rachel got them too and the more they tried to contain things the worse they got. By Take Ten the whole unit were at it and Noël's balcony scene had become hysterical. 'Maybe we should just rewrite the character,' quipped Hitch. Later, as we all know, Michael got the part that began his film career.

And we mustn't forget one of our more distinguished members, that great old English gentleman, George Arliss, who was fondly referred to around the studio as Gramps. Not in his hearing, I hasten to add. Gramps, or rather Mr Arliss, had gone to Hollywood and become a film icon, winning the Academy Award for playing Disraeli in a picture of the same name. Ted Black had brought him home to star in Russell Thorndyke's classic period smuggling story *Doctor Syn*, to be directed by Roy William Neill. I had no hand in the writing of this film but Ted thought it might be good experience for me to sit in on the first Arliss script conference.

With almost Victorian courtesy and a streak of genteel steel, this 69-year-old actor was a fascinating character. He knew exactly what he wanted and usually got it. One of the clauses in his contract stipulated that, come what may, when it reached four o'clock he would retire to his dressing room where he and his wife Florence would partake of afternoon tea. Of course the unit loved this because, unless

Roy Neill could find a way to shoot around Gramps, they all stopped for tea.

That script conference was indeed an experience. I sat quietly at the back of Ted Black's office listening to him discuss suggestions with Roy Neill, Mr Arliss and his business manager Rufus le Mair, who was perfect casting for a Hollywood business manager, and Frank Launder, our story editor. The only concern Arliss seemed to have about the film was that since it was a historical drama all departments should do their research most thoroughly. 'It would be nice to have all the details correct,' he said finally, 'to make absolutely sure that we do not have any anachronisms in this picture.'

'No anachronisms,' insisted Rufus le Mair firmly. 'So Casting should be instructed not to call any.' Somehow everyone kept a straight face and George Arliss rose with the ghost of a twinkle. 'I am sure we can rely on you, gentlemen,' he said, 'and now, if you will excuse us, it's teatime.'

Our first and only conference with the Crazy Gang was a different story. It was, in two words, disconbobulated chaos. Perhaps I should explain. The Crazy Gang was comprised of three variety acts, all stars in their own right: Flanagan & Allen, Nervo & Knox and Naughton & Gold. In a stroke of genius George Black had banded them together as the Crazy Gang and launched them at the London Palladium in a wild musical extravaganza called *O-Kay for Sound*, which had become the sensational hit of the season. Ted had bought the film rights, signed up the Gang and thought it might be a good idea to invite them to a conference as they might have some ideas of their own to feed into the screenplay we were about to write.

They all arrived at the studio smack on time and were bubbling over at the prospect of making their first feature film. When coffee had been passed around Ted sat behind his desk, gave them his best fatherly smile and said, 'Before George and Val start on their script we wondered if you boys have any specific business or routines you'd like them to try and work in.' Imagine saying that to six comics? Before you could say 'Action!' they were going through every routine they'd worked in every theatre across the country.

'Hey, what about our slow-motion wrestling?' asked Jimmy Nervo.

'Yes, film it in a real ring!' enthused Teddy Knox, and before we knew it they were all rearranging us and Ted's office into a wrestling ring. I must say we laughed to see them both wrestling in slow-motion, then Bud Flanagan chipped in.

'I know, I know, we could do the train rumble!'

'Yes,' explained Chesney Allen, 'you write us living in a house next to the main line and every time a train goes by the place shakes and we have to hold everything down.'

'Look out!' shouted Bud suddenly, checking his watch, 'here comes the 10.20! CLACKERTY-CLACK, CLACKERTY-CLACK, CLACKERTY-CLACK...' And as Bud made train noises the rest of them rattled Ted's furniture, shaking his bookcase while Charlie Naughton and Jimmy Gold lifted the top of his desk, swaying it back and forth as the coffee slopped over his blotter. Once the 10.20 had gone through, Ted Black rose to his feet, smiled a trifle wanly and said, 'Want to hear my idea?'

'Yes,' they chorused.

'Why don't we break for an early lunch,' he said. And we did, leaving his long-suffering secretary to straighten out the shambles of the first and last Crazy Gang script conference.

The only other problem we had writing those scripts was keeping track of six comics. We'd be skating along merrily and on a casual check-back find we'd left one of them out and that Charlie Naughton hadn't said anything for eight pages. So back we'd go and write him in. Eventually we kept a chart and every time one of them spoke we ticked the list. Like Hitchcock, the Gang turned out to be incurable pranksters. I came on the set one morning wearing a new sports shirt I'd bought the day before.

'Well, get you!' said Bud. 'Aren't we looking natty today. Where did you find that?'

'Simpson's sale,' I told him. They all gathered around me to study it closer. Teddy Knox ran his fingers over it.

'Not very good material,' he pronounced. 'This stuff tears easily you know.'

'It doesn't,' I laughed. 'It's textured linen.'

'It's textured linen...' Teddy winked at the others and grasping one side of my collar he gave an almighty tug which literally ripped the shirt in half. Then Jimmy Nervo did the same with the other collar and I stood there in a gale of laughter and a ribboned shirt.

'Looks like Simpson's did you,' grinned Jimmy. 'Don't worry, we'll buy you a better quality one.'

'In the meantime,' smiled the wardrobe mistress, 'you'd better go to Wardrobe and borrow something.'

Ten minutes later I was back on set wearing a very nice silk beach top. 'You won't tear this one,' I smiled at Teddy. 'This one is special.'

'He says it's special,' grinned Teddy, his eyes gleaming.

'Yes, it's guaranteed not to tear.'

This was too much for him. Still grinning and egged on by the others, he came over to me and felt the material. 'Want to bet?' he asked and then tore it into spaghetti-like shreds. When the laughter had subsided he put his hand on my shoulder. 'Don't worry,' he smiled, 'we'll get another one for Wardrobe.'

'It doesn't belong to Wardrobe,' I told him. 'It's yours. From the cupboard in your dressing room.'

The explosion of laughter from the rest of the set and the other members of the Gang finally broke up Teddy, too, as he checked the tattered shirt and grabbed my hand. 'A nice bit of touché,' was all he could say. I'd won my spurs and, just like Hitch, they never tried anything on me again. But I must tell you they bought me not one but six wonderful shirts that I could certainly never have afforded.

That Gainsborough decade holds a kaleidoscope of many fond and happy memories for me, some major some minor. Like Graham, the cheeky, chubby studio pageboy who earned 12/6d a week until Ted Black decided to put him in a film and he emerged as Graham Moffatt, the fat boy in Gainsborough's classic trio of Will Hay, Harbottle and Albert. And of course, Hay himself, the master of blustering, bumbling inefficiency with comic timing which for me surpassed everyone but Jack Benny. It's interesting to recall that Benny himself once went into print saying that the two British comedians he most admired and had learned from were Will Hay and Alastair Sim. How lucky I was to have worked with and written for both of them.

Bill Hay was anything but a bumbling inefficient. He was a highly intelligent man whose abiding hobby was astronomy. Not only had he built his own observatory in the garden of the small house he'd bought on Hendon Way, he also caused an astronomical sensation by discovering a new white spot on Saturn through his homemade telescope. The *Daily Mirror's* front page headline trumpeted: COMEDIAN'S BIG DISCOVERY ON PLANET – WILL HAY BEATS AMERICA. He then wrote a book about it, after which the Royal Astronomical Society made him a Fellow and to Bill this was a greater thrill than winning the Irish Sweepstake or getting knighted.

A private, friendly soul, he had a quiet sense of fun but this didn't stop his hypochondria. There seemed to be something or other wrong with him every time you met. 'I think I may have fractured my tibia,' he said as he limped onto location one morning. We were shooting *Oh, Mr Porter!* just outside Basingstoke on a disused piece of railway line that they were pulling up behind us as we filmed. He hobbled manfully over the sleepers and got through the day's work without any hold-ups. Came wrap-up time we were all delighted to witness the miraculous cure when he walked briskly to his car.

To be fair he never gave us a moment's problem with his assorted 'complaints' and it always gave the unit a few smiles. I remember once, while filming *Old Bones of the River*, we were night shooting on location at Shepperton. The Art Department had built us a native village on the banks of the river with a hundred extras and a herd of goats, smelling as only a herd of goats can smell. We were cold, damp and miserable when one of the camera crew had an idea to cheer us up. Why didn't we run a sweepstake on what Bill Hay's complaint was that night. On separate bits of paper they wrote everything he'd suffered from that month, put them in a hat and charged five shillings a draw. Needless to say, since Bill had complained of 'back pains' for the past week the gaffer who drew the paper marked BACK was jubilant. He even refused an offer of two pounds for it. Then came a moment of panic. Bill Hay arrived in time to see the end of the draw.

'Hullo,' he said breezily. 'Can I buy a ticket? What is it, a raffle?'

'Oh, it wouldn't interest you, Guv,' said our quick thinking First Assistant, 'it's tickets for the Union Dance.' Then he asked the vital question. 'How d'you feel tonight, sir?'

Twenty hands clutched twenty bits of paper.

'Oh, I feel fine,' said Will Hay. 'Although my foot seems to be acting up again...' He never saw one of the Props behind him, grinning from ear to ear and waving the bit of paper with FOOT on it. All in good fun and I'm sure Bill would have taken it well had he found out.

Always popular with the crew, at times he could be unexpectedly thoughtful. I was the recipient of one of these moments on the completion of *Porter*. It was the second film I'd made with him and throughout both productions I had squatted around the stage on boxes or property hampers and had had my backside booted out of other peoples' chairs. A week after we'd finished shooting there was a knock on our office door. 'Oh, no,' I sighed, 'not Hitch again!' But it wasn't Hitch, it was Bill Hay's personal secretary, Peggy Bradford, and she leaned a large brown paper package against our wall. 'From Bill,' she smiled. Inside all the brown paper I found a brand new canvas chair with my name beautifully painted on the back of it. Taped to one of the arms was a note which read: FOR VAL – YOU'VE EARNED IT! BILL HAY.

That chair stayed with me on every production through the rest of my career, in Africa, Germany, Austria, Belgium, Beirut, the Canary Islands, Italy and France. A lot of famous bottoms have sat on it and it's now a genuine antique. In 1990, after I'd retired from directing, they even persuaded me to put it up for auction at Sotheby's. Telling myself it was silly to be nostalgic about it, I agreed. But when I finally saw the picture of my chair in the Sotheby's catalogue I couldn't go through with it. Hurriedly I withdrew it and presented it instead to the National Film Theatre's Museum of the Moving Image on the South Bank, where it now rests surrounded by stills of some of the more illustrious bottoms sitting in it.

Also, in those early days of what is sometimes lightly referred to as my 'Gainsborough Period', there was this very pretty young stage actress Ted Black had signed up to groom for eventual stardom. Her name was Margaret Lockwood and they had just cast her to play opposite George Arliss in *Doctor Syn*. Maggie Lockwood was a delightful young person with a great sense of fun but probably the most unworldly 21-year-old any of us had ever encountered. Born in India, where her father was in the Colonial Office, she'd apparently been sent to England for her schooling and had been brought up by a couple of aunts in Norwood. Her ignorance of the facts of life was so astounding that at first we all thought she was joking.

No way. One evening when she'd finished shooting she went out to her car, parked with the rest in Poole Street, to find the local 'Dead End Kids' had done what they did to all our cars if we didn't pay them now and then to wash them – scrawled a four-letter word in the soot and dust of her rear window. The following morning Maggie arrived on set as usual all bright-eyed and bushy tailed and recounted the incident to Jack Cox, Gainsborough's senior lighting cameraman, and asked him what the word meant. After a moment of stunned silence he told her, 'It's an Indian word for love, dear.' Of course, the story flashed around an amused but incredulous studio. A few days later I was summoned to Bill Ostrer's office.

'Margaret Lockwood,' he started without preamble. 'Is she really that innocent?'

'Well,' I replied, when I'd got over the unexpectedness of the subject, 'let's say she's led a rather sheltered life in Upper Norwood.'

'Then we have to broaden her life, open her up. I mean, we're hoping to make something of her, she can't be that unsophisticated. Take her around, show her the outside world.'

'Who, me?'

'Yes, you've been around. Theatre, newspapers, music and all that. Just take her around.'

'But Bill, I'm a married man!'

'So what?' he smiled. 'I'm not asking you to deflower her, just take her around.'

'Such as where?'

'I don't know,' he shrugged. 'Anywhere – show her something that isn't Upper Norwood. Perhaps you could start with Olympia.'

I couldn't believe my ears. Olympia was holding the Bertram Mills annual Circus and Fun Fair. This would help to sophisticate her? 'Bill, if you don't mind...'

'Look,' he sighed patiently, 'you're doing it for Gainsborough. Right? And don't worry, I'll explain to Pat.' And that, straight out of *Alice in Wonderland*, was the reason Maggie Lockwood and I found ourselves circling on the Olympia ferris wheel having spent a fun-filled afternoon seeing the circus, doing the side shows, bumping the dodgems and braving the Ghost Train. I can't think what it taught her about life unless, like me, she learned that everything is twice as much fun when the studio is paying for it.

Maggie and I became firm friends and, more importantly, she dispelled all Bill Ostrer's fears by becoming Britain's Number One film star, to say nothing of being the first one from Upper Norwood. Later I wrote and directed two films for her, one of which was called *Give Us the Moon*, and thereby hangs a tale. In the story, which we adapted from a Caryl Brahms novel, Maggie had to have a tearaway teenage daughter. After I'd tested half a dozen girls and not been really happy with any of them, Bill Ostrer summoned me to his office and told me no more testing, just pick one of the six and get on with it. On my way back to the projection theatre I passed the open door of the casting office waiting room and sitting inside was the most adorable looking teenager I'd ever seen. The lady with her was obviously her mother and asked if I was Mr Drury the casting director. I told her I wasn't but asked the girl what she'd done before. Before she could answer, mother chipped in with the information that she'd done a couple of very small parts in two very small films I wouldn't have heard about.

'What's your name?' I asked the girl.

'Jean,' she said with a faintly drama school accent.

'Could you read a bit of script for me?'

'I'll try,' she smiled.

I showed her a page in the script I was carrying, let her read it to herself then read it with her and knew immediately that this was the girl for my tearaway teenager. I grabbed her hand. 'Come with me,' I said, telling mother I'd bring her right back. Down the corridor I marched her, straight into Ostrer's office. 'This is the girl I want to use,' I told him.

'I said no more tests.'

'I'll take her without a test.'

He shrugged. 'It's your responsibilty.'

And that's how Jean Simmons began her screen career. At the end of her first day's shooting, her mother waylaid me. 'When will everyone see the work Jean did today?' she asked and I told her we always saw the 'rushes' at lunchtime. 'May I have a word with you after that?' she asked. I told her of course and thought no more about it. The following afternoon there was Mrs Simmons again.

'Were you happy with Jean's work?' she asked.

'Very happy. She's doing a great job.'

'And the producers?'

'They're happy, too.'

'Then I have to tell you something, Mr Guest.' She was obviously ill at ease. 'I lied to you. Jean's never done any acting before. There were no two pictures.' Poor Mother Simmons had been living with her guilty secret since the day we met in that casting office. I comforted her by saying that at some time or other we'd all told fibs to get jobs and told her just to relax and enjoy her lovely daughter's new career. As for Jean, she surprised us all with her professionalism. When we came to her crying scene I told her not to worry, make-up would supply some glycerine tears. 'Oh, I can cry if you want me to,' she said brightly. And she did, magnificently.

Later, during a lighting break, I sat with her on the set's prop staircase and we talked about acting, life in general, her ambitions and how she hoped she'd live up to my faith in her. 'Listen,' I joked, 'one day you' re going to be a big star and I won't be able to afford you.'

'Well, if I am,' she smiled, 'I'll always work for you for half!' Laughingly we shook hands on the deal.

As you know, she did become a big star and, as I had predicted, far too expensive for our modest budgets. But what you don't know is that almost ten years later I was trying to cast one of my films and needed an English star name for the female lead. Someone suggested Jean Simmons, who was currently making *Guys and Dolls* with Frank Sinatra and Marlon Brando. Great idea but a wild one. Off went a cable to her agents: PLEASE ADVISE PRICE AND AVAILABILITY JEAN SIMMONS. Back came the reply: SIMMONS AVAILABLE SEPTEMBER PRICE $500,000. I sat up half the night with my production manager and accountant trying to see where we could prune our budget to make this amount possible. But next day came another cable which simply said: CORRECTION $250,000. My 'tearaway teenager' had grown into a lovely, lovely lady with a long, long memory. There aren't many like our Jean. As it happened, one small thing got in the way of us working together again. She became pregnant.

And what of the rest of my pals in the Gainsborough 'family'? Well, there was a young, wide-awake assistant in the Production Department by the name of Roy Baker. Years later he would extend his name to Roy Ward Baker and become the respected director of such films as *Inferno*, *A Night to Remember* and Dirk Bogarde's *The Singer Not the Song*, which he also produced.

'Elegant, worldly, gentle, intelligent' is the way the *World Film Encyclopedia* describes Lilli Palmer and I couldn't have put it better, except perhaps to add that she was also loaded with sex appeal and nobody had to take Lilli to Olympia. Back in our Gainsborough days she was a sexy 22-year-old who'd just had her contract renewed and the world was ahead of her. So why was she so unhappy? 'This studio will never take me seriously,' she kept telling me. 'Their publicity's always calling me a sex-pot. I don't want to be known as a sex-pot, I want to be known as a serious actress!' It was to be ten more hard-working years before Hollywood agreed with her, cast her opposite Gary Cooper in *Cloak and Dagger* and gave her international stardom. But right then she was still Gainsborough's own registered sex-pot and there was worse news to come. George and I had written another film for Will Hay called *Good Morning Boys*. It was about him taking a group of schoolboys to the Louvre in Paris and getting involved in a plot to steal the Mona Lisa. One member of the robbers was a sexy French cabaret singer. And guess who Ted Black chose to cast in that part?

'Don't worry, Lilli,' I said, trying to cheer her up. 'We'll put in a scene where you sing a song, that'll open up another side for you.'

'They'd never get a song written for me.'

'They won't have to, I'll write it for you.'

And I did. A piece of musical genius called 'Love is Just a Racket and You're a Racketeer of Love'. It never made the top ten but it did give Lilli a chance to show she wasn't just any old sex-pot, she was also a singing sex-pot.

CHAPTER
SEVEN

The thirties and forties also held some of my life's more traumatic moments.

One day my mother suffered a burst appendix. Nothing really scary and normally you'd be whisked into hospital, whip out the offending organ, pour in a jar of penicillin and you'd be back home before you knew it. But not Mother. I learned later she was a hard and fast dyed-in-the-wool Christian Scientist and would have none of this. Faith could heal everything, she said. It wasn't long before septicaemia set in and there was nothing anyone could do but go to the funeral. To make it all even sadder, I knew nothing about any of this until I rang her up one day and was told by someone on the other end of the line, 'Oh, hadn't you heard, she was buried last week.'

Not long afterwards my father died suddenly of coronary thrombosis at the not unreasonable age, for those days, of 69. Vi called me one evening to break the news.

'Would you like to see him, dear?' she asked.

To my eternal regret I said, 'I think I'd rather not, Vi... I'd like to remember him as he was...'

'Of course, dear,' said that perpetually understanding lady.

My father had left her a small amount of money, which was all he had, and the two Winchester Road houses which she decided to sell. The estate agent who had originally sold them to my father had become a close friend of theirs and it was to him Vi turned in her hour of need. His name was Will Richardson, a gentle, kindly man who was now a tower of strength for her and sold the properties reasonably quickly. This gave her enough capital to get on with her life. Which she did. In fact, less than a year later Vi and Will Richardson got married. But by then I'd learned to expect the unexpected.

Pat had quit dancing in shows and we rented a small weekend bungalow on the beach at Shoreham-on-Sea. 'Bungalow' is perhaps too grand a description, it was actually two converted railway carriages placed side by side on the beach, about 12 feet apart with a roof over them, making a central sitting room. There was quite a colony of these on the beach and it made a fun place to drive down to for weekends. In the bungalow next to us were a couple who were always good company, Harold and Nikki James. Harold was part of a bookmaking firm and went by the professional name of Wilson. But on our second summer at the bungalow there was no longer any Nikki. They'd been divorced. Harold was now on his own and becoming an increasingly significant part of our lives both in Shoreham and London. I didn't realise it then but this was a big trauma in the making, because less than ten years later Harold James/Wilson was to be a quite large factor in the break-up of my marriage.

And then, of course, the other spot of bother was the rumble of war reverberating around Europe. Daily we would hear and read about some unspeakable bounder named Adolf Hitler who was marching across other peoples' frontiers without being invited and how His Majesty's Government were taking a dim view of this. So one day Prime Minister Mr Neville Chamberlain hopped on a plane to Munich and shook a British finger at the beastly Adolf, who not only agreed never to do it again but also to put that in writing. Whereupon Mr Neville flew back waving that famous piece of paper that promised us 'Peace in our Time' and the whole country heaved a sigh of relief.

This was the second historic announcement I'd heard that year. The first one was made by Patricia Watson Guest when I returned home from the studio one evening. 'You have nine months to get into training,' she laughed. 'You're going to be a father.'

Well, this sounded like true immortality in the making and even Grandma-to-be Scotty Watson was so overjoyed she never once asked, 'And when is little Crippen arriving?' Sure enough, nine months later, on 31 January 1939, my greatest co-production to date, David Val Guest, had his opening night. That's when we decided to move out of the hurly-burly of Portman Square to quieter Hampstead, where I rented a larger flat in Lyndhurst Road. And we weren't the only ones moving. All sorts of new and exciting things were cooking at Gainsborough. It seemed their parent company, Gaumont British, had virtually gone bust and the Ostrers were now moving all of us from Islington to the larger studios at Shepherds Bush in an effort to pull things together.

But just as we were all settling in, that awful Adolf was on the move again, goosestepping into Poland. And suddenly we had declared war on Germany. Even as Chamberlain was telling us this on the radio, the first air raid sirens wailed out across London. No one was quite ready for this sort of thing so it was just as well it turned out to be a false alarm. It seemed an over-zealous coastal watchdog had spotted a flock of seagulls zooming in on Dover, mistook them for a fleet of Heinkel bombers and pressed every button he had.

After that first attack of the collywobbles it was football and cricket as usual and they called it 'the Phoney War' because nothing at all happened except that lots of people made lots of money selling blackout material, sticky tape to keep our windows from shattering, flashlights and batteries. Some of our Gainsborough gang went into part-time training as Air Raid Wardens and the Production Department drew up a rota which had four of us at a time doing a night's duty on the roof as Fire Watchers. The whole thing was looked upon as a bit of a giggle and a chance to play poker up there, until that June when the first real air raid took the giggle out of everything.

But at the moment we were still having fun at Lime Grove Studios sorting out our new offices, dressing rooms, typing pools and music department. The latter was headed by a vital, energised little man, Louis Levy, who had previously conducted one of the country's best-known broadcasting and show bands. He had been the little genius who orchestrated and recorded the 'Love is Just a Racket' number I wrote for Lilli. He would later do the same for the three musicals I wrote and directed for Gainsborough. It was Louis who introduced me to the American composer Manning Sherwin who, among his many other hits, had written the now almost legendary 'A Nightingale Sang in Berkeley Square'. He told me his lyric writer had been Eric Maschwitz, but Eric was about to become a lieutenant colonel in the British Intelligence Corps, which had left Manning without a lyricist. 'I think you two should get together,' suggested Louis.

Slightly awed at following in the footsteps of the talented Maschwitz, I replied rather hesitantly,

'Well, I'm game if Manning is. We can at least see if it works.' It did work. Within four months we'd done scores for two London revues, Firth Shephard's *Sitting Pretty* followed by *Shephard's Pie* at the Prince's. Thanks to my friend Louis Levy who 'married' us, Manning and I turned out six West End musicals and five Gainsborough films in our six years together before he returned to America to get properly married.

I have a montage of wartime memories from those Lime Grove Studios. Between the firewatching, the sirens, the bombs and the all-clears, our Gainsborough army beavered away: James Mason, Robert Donat, Carol Reed, Maggie Lockwood, Rex Harrison, Phyllis Calvert, Johnny Mills, Paul Henreid, Michael Redgrave, Stewart Granger. (Oh yes, Jimmy Granger was now a name to be reckoned with.) As Goldwyn might have put it, we'd passed a lot of water since those old BIP days.

There were often nights when we all slept in our offices and dressing rooms in case roads were impassable next morning. Inevitably this led to some interesting room-sharing. In fact, Carol suggested that every 6 am the studio should ring a bell which meant 'Everyone back to their own rooms.' One heavy call day the production office asked if I'd mind someone sharing my room. I accepted with alacrity only to find I spent the night with that respected actor Cyril Cusack. In later years he became a friend and part of my film 'stock company'. I often used to kid people he only got the part because he slept with me.

'You know if you're smart,' Jimmy Granger advised me one day in the canteen, 'you'll join something part-time. The auxiliary police, warden, fire brigade, anything. There's less chance then of being shipped across the Channel.'

It was a kind thought, but what he didn't know was that we writers had already been told we were in a semi-reserved job since the Ministry of Information would be needing us later for propaganda purposes. Still, I thought maybe I should make an extra gesture toward the War Effort so I joined the AFS, the Auxiliary Fire Service. Had I known it I might have been better off being shipped across the Channel!

Twice a week I went for a couple of hours' Fire Drill Training – how to hold a hose, enter a burning building, give victims the fireman's lift. Towards the end of this latter course we were taken to a four-storey schoolhouse in St Paul's Yard, where the instructors positioned extension ladders against the building and told us to pick a partner and carry him up to the roof. Guest, being the smart one, grabbed the smallest man there, one Nobby Clarke, who was about 5'3". With a lot of luck and positive thought I 'lifted' him to the roof. And just as we were congratulating ourselves the instructor yelled, 'All right, now switch partners.' Even now I break into a cold sweat thinking about it. Somehow Nobby managed it, grunt by grunt, with me hanging over his shoulder, head down, frantically grabbing the side of the ladder whenever I could find it.

At the studio Carol Reed was shooting *Night Train to Munich* with Rex Harrison, Margaret Lockwood and Paul Henreid. It was always fun to visit Carol's sets and with these three characters on the picture even more so. Maggie Lockwood had recently thrown caution to the winds and become a Mrs Rupert W Leon, which had brought lots of ribbing from her two co-stars because in an unguarded moment she mentioned that she and Rupert slept in separate rooms. This became a daily game for Rex and Paul who insisted they couldn't work until they knew who knocked on whose door the night before. As for sexy Rexy, this time his loins were stirring for my old friend Lilli Palmer who, he swore, was the one person he couldn't live without. To prove it he eventually made her the second Mrs Harrison. Poor Lilli, how could she know she'd be followed by another four couldn't-live-withouts?

The year was 1940. Quite a year by any standards with the war in Europe, the fall of France, Dunkirk, the aerial Battle of Britain and, just around the corner, the Blitz. Our daily lunchtime chatter ranged from Winston Churchill becoming our new Prime Minister, all the way to how we could beg, borrow or steal more rationed petrol coupons for our cars. Incidentally, I remember one night in the Savoy Grill when I sat at a table next to Sir Winston and the great man actually leaned across and spoke to me. What he said was, 'May we borrow your pepper? Ours seems to have run out.' But at least I felt I had been touched by history. Even more so when, years later, we were the proud owners of a brown poodle called Figaro, who was the grandson of Winston's famous dog Rufus.

Towards the end of the *Night Train* shooting Paul Henreid was not his usual lighthearted self. He confided to us that for the first time, with all the carnage in Europe, he felt uneasy being a foreigner in England. The authorities were already rounding up sundry aliens for so-called security reasons and packing them off to internment camps. The week before they had picked up one of variety's best known clown acts, the Cairoli Brothers, and bundled them off to a camp in the Isle of Man. Even more of a shock, Luigi, the Savoy Grill's almost legendary maitre d'hôtel, was sent to join them. So fame was no guarantee you'd be left alone.

Paul, born in Trieste, had come to London from the Max Reinhardt Theatre in Vienna and in those volatile days anyone from that part of the world with an accent could be regarded with a degree of suspicion. He had already arranged that at the end of *Night Train* he would emigrate to America, if he was still free to do so. 'All it needs is for someone to check I once had a 'von' in my name,' he smiled, trying to make light of the situation.

That's when five of us — Carol, Rex, Maggie, Frank Launder and myself — cooked up our harebrained scheme to try and outwit the Home Office and MI5 should they decide to call on him. We'd checked out that usually, to save undue attention, they picked up people when they returned from work. As Paul had only five more shooting days, we told him he could stay with each of us on a different night so that no one would know where he was on any given evening. Of course, the whole plot was pretty ludicrous because they could just as well have sent a troop of Household Cavalry to pick him up at the studio, but at least it made him laugh and cheer up to know everyone was on his side. The one evening he did spend with us at our new Hampstead home Pat had cooked a splendid three-course dinner and, in the other room, young David Guest squawled throughout the meal. Except for the food, an evening in the internment camp might have been better for Paul.

One other memory of that night, apart from the inevitable air raid sirens, is that when it came to after-dinner smoke time I put a couple of cigarettes in my mouth, lit them both and handed one to Pat. It was something I'd done so often I thought nothing of it. But Paul laughed and seemed impressed. 'Well, well,' he joked, 'that's quite a trick. No wonder he charmed all the girls!' They never came to intern Paul and off he went to the US, becoming a citizen and carving himself a great film career. PS: his second Hollywood picture was *Now Voyager* with Bette Davis and it contained a memorable balcony scene in which he put two cigarettes in his mouth, lit them both and handed one to Bette. Now I wonder who thought up that trick — the writers, director Irving Rapper or Bette? Of course it just might have been Paul Henreid.

August 23rd was the night the full fury of the German Blitz exploded on us and suddenly our lives were re-evaluated. Somehow, in spite of the devastation and sleepless nights, people managed to get to work in the morning, skirting the bomb craters and rubble. That's when we members of the Auxiliary Fire Service were warned we'd be used as back-up units during particularly heavy raids. Never was a country so woefully unprepared for a war. We had too few ships, too few planes and too little ammunition. So you can imagine how much 'too little' we had in the Fire Brigade.

Our unit, sleeping on mattresses on the floor of St Paul's School, consisted of 24 people. Between us we boasted one regular fire engine and six manual trailer pumps latched on to the back of six commandeered London taxis. The day we discovered a seventh pump we lashed it to the back of my old Graham car. To misquote Churchill, 'Never in the field of human conflict was so much needed by so many.' And don't think being in a reserved profession kept me away from the London docks, with half the city alight from incendiaries dropped by the first wave to guide the bombers in. 'Douse the fires before they get here,' was the order. With our jet power? It was like using soda syphons to put out the flames of Hell. One thing we learned, somehow one had to try and keep a sense of humour. We almost lost it that night when the bombers finally came in and dropped their load. The whole riverline seemed to be burning as a dozen of us clutched our hoses, turning them on whatever we could reach. On the far bank other units were waging the same battle. And as if that wasn't enough a long barge to our right suddenly burst into flames, slipping its hawser.

'Shit! Anyone order a bloody barge?' quipped our chief and for the moment it broke the tension. 'We've enough problems this side,' he snapped, swinging his hose on it. We joined in laughing as we pushed it across river to the other bank. In a few moments a stream from their hoses sent it back to us. For some brief minutes of relaxation we played ping-pong with it, waiting for it to sink. But it didn't, because the next time it reached their bank it blew up. No one had known it was an ammunition barge. There was no time to dwell on this; we were too busy trying to stay alive and too numb at the thought of how close we'd been to losing that ping-pong game. With bombs still bursting and ack-ack thundering I was never more terrified in my life. Silently I started to pray. 'Dear God, if I ever come out of this alive I'll never worry about anything again...' I can't tell you how often in later life it's helped me to recall that moment.

It wasn't always quite as hairy as that. Even the Blitz had its lighter moments. Like the lovely lady caught in her bath on the third floor when the outside wall collapsed exposing her to the street, followed by our stampede of volunteers willing to risk life and limb to give her a fireman's lift down. Then there was the night they hit a lady of the night's house in Shepherd's Market, catching an errant Prince with his pants down. This royal spouse of a European queen-to-be came careering downstairs hugging his uniform jacket yelling 'I'm not here! I'm not here!' and ran down unlit Curzon Street, abandoning his parked Lamborghini. 'Your car, sir!' yelled a fireman. 'What about the car...?' 'Lose it!' screamed His Royal Highness, struggling into his jacket and disappearing into a blacked-out Berkeley Square.

Perhaps the memory that gives me the biggest smile is the night they bombed De La Rue, the printers. We were all flat out on our mattresses grabbing some desperately needed sleep when the alarm went off. 'De La Rue's been hit!' shouted the duty man through the door. 'Bunhill Row EC4. Get to work!' Grumbling and sleepy-eyed, we rolled over searching for boots and belts. Until someone said, 'De La Rue? Blimey, aren't they the blokes who print the banknotes?' Never in the field of human conflict had a fire unit kitted itself, manned appliances and 'got to work' quicker than we did that night.

De La Rue was a mess, as were most of the cratered streets around it. There were smoke and flames everywhere and the massive printing presses had crashed through all floors. It needed men of super-human courage and considerable daring to enter that building where more machinery might come down any moment. Or simply men with the urge to look for banknotes. I have to tell you, besides getting the fire contained and extricating a nightwatchman and two security guards, we climbed unclimbable staircases in almost pitch blackness, circled the edges of floorless rooms and attempted leaps for which stuntmen are paid fortunes. Furthermore, men have won the Victoria Cross, Légion d'Honneur and Purple Heart for less than we did that night to stuff tunics and boots with banknotes we could only feel in the darkness. Came the dawn and begrimed, pooped out, our uniforms bulging with contraband currency, we returned to our mattresses in St Paul's School and for the first time saw our haul in the light. They were dollar bills printed for the Northern Bank of China. The denominations ran in the thousands. Wow! What a holiday this would be when all the war crap was over!

'The next move,' said one of the smart ones, 'is to find what they're worth on the exchange.'

'Better be bloody careful there,' said an even smarter one, 'because this comes under the heading of looting.'

You've never seen so much currency swept under so many mattresses so fast as the chief poked his head around the door. 'Nice work, lads,' he said. 'Turn in and get some kip.'

As luck would have it Nobby Clarke's elder brother worked in the currency kiosk at Charing Cross station so Nobby took one of the slightly charred notes to start some undercover enquiries. For the rest of the week we waited with bated breath until one day he turned up for duty with the answer. 'Are you ready for this?' he asked, holding up one of the $1000 bills. 'First of all there's two thousand of these to the shilling. Second of all,' he added, pointing to the corner of the note, 'none of them have been numbered yet.'

Suddenly I knew how people had felt in the 1929 Stock Market crash. All at once you've lost a fortune. And that wasn't the end of our problems. How to get rid of them? Put them in a bag and throw them into the rubbish bins? Much too dicey. What was the possible sentence for looting? A firing squad? Or at best the Tower of London? Someone suggested tossing the bag out of a moving car onto Hampstead Heath. Hullo firing squad! Finally it was decided to burn the lot in the school grate. So one night plumes of Chinese banknote smoke spiralled out of the St Paul's School chimney. It looked almost as if the Vatican had elected a new Pope.

CHAPTER
EIGHT

During those early Fire Brigade days Gainsborough were very good to me and continued to pay my salary. For my part I grabbed every possible moment of Leave to turn up at the studio and join my poor, long-suffering writing partner, George Marriott Edgar, on our current screenplay assignment. Most of the time I was little more than a walking zombie. And if there's anything worse than a walking zombie it's a typing zombie, especially for George who was always the long-hand writer while I was the two-fingered typist of our partnership.

When, one day in the studio canteen, I fell asleep between the soup and the spam fritters, Ted Black took pity on us and arranged for a girl from the typing pool to help out. Her name was Edna and being fairly new to the game she found it as difficult to take script and dialogue dictation as we did to give it. We were so used to pounding out scenes in rough and seeing them right there on paper that this way seemed to take double the time. Poor Edna, she tried her best though. I remember one day dictating the line 'The Captain picks up the speaking tube and bawls to the Mate.' When it came back in script form, she'd typed 'The Captain picks up the speaking tube. CAPTAIN: Balls to the Mate.' It wasn't long before George and I decided that maybe even a typing zombie was better than this, so a relieved and happy Edna was returned to the Pool.

Somewhere along the line I had managed to move the Guest family away from the bombs and out into a small house I'd rented in Sunningdale, not far from Ascot racecourse. Surely, I reasoned, even a no-class schweinhund like Hitler wouldn't be cad enough to bomb Ascot. And somehow, between sleeping on school floors and studio dressing rooms, I actually managed to spend the odd night down there with Pat and David. Harold James was still a constant visitor, as was Pat's sister Jackie, so it was comforting to know she wasn't on her own just because I was absent.

And absent I was, quite a lot. The Blitz, the fires and the Battle of Britain continued and so did production at the studio in spite of several near-misses all around it in Shepherds Bush. Some nights, before extra-heavy shooting days, the dressing rooms might be filled with various Gainsborough glamour ladies – Phyllis Calvert, Margaret Lockwood, Patricia Roc, Carole Lynne (later to become Lady Bernard Delfont), Linden Travers, and a gaggle of young actresses groomed by the Rank Charm School.

These included a smashing young nympho who went on to become the leading lady of many British films and a couple of Hollywood ones. Out of respect for her hardworking, still-in-the-business family I won't identify her other than to say that the studio, with a certain degree of fondness, would point her out as being the original good time that was had by all. One of these being our own studio manager who got lucky with her one night during a midnight bombing raid and they had what we'll delicately call a 'bonking session' in her dressing-room shower. But in the middle of it the poor man got unlucky, slipped on the wet tiles and, trying to break his fall, broke his wrist. At his next canteen appearance he carried his plastered arm with great panache, telling us how he'd fallen off a ladder nailing up some loose boarding. Somehow we all kept straight faces because First Aid had already blown his cover and we knew it wasn't loose boarding but loose bonking.

Needless to say none of the beautiful ladies named above were part of this Shepherds Bush dolce vita. They were all solid, hardworking pros who only stayed on if they were worried about driving home during an alert or getting back for a seven o'clock make-up call. Except one of them. She was all those things but stayed one night just for the hell of it. She was a lovely person, a lovely looker and a lovely actress. She was also married. So was I and both of us should have known better. But we grabbed onto that oh-so-easy wartime excuse – with death and destruction so close who knows if we're here tomorrow? We'd become friendly during the preceding weeks when she was working on one of the films George and I had written. Afterwards we realised we were dicing with another kind of emotional death and were never extramarital together again. 'I think we were good for each other at that moment,' she said simply when we talked about it later and we remained good friends through the many troubled years ahead.

Perhaps the second stupidest thing I did at that time was to confess my brief encounter to Harold James, because he immediately passed it on to Pat who, understandably, blew her top. I think it was then that this village idiot began to get the message that friend Harold was less a friend to me than to Pat. Anyway, in the words of the old song, what can you say after you say you're sorry? Eventually Pat was extremely generous and forgiving and emotions seemed to get back to normal until I suggested that Harold should become a lesser part of our lives. The temperature dropped several degrees. 'Because he's done something you don't like,' said Pat, 'you want to banish him. You've done something I don't like but I'm not banishing you, am I?' End of argument.

But it wasn't all bad news. At the studio the incredible Ted Black had achieved the impossible. He'd petitioned the Home Office to honour my 'reserved profession' status as he needed his comedy writers to help keep up public morale. In view of this, he said, they should release me from any further fire-fighting duties. And they did. Suddenly I was free, alive and 29! You can't imagine the sudden burst of youthful energy this galvanised in me. The script George and I had been writing between bombs was finally finished for Marcel to take on the floor with Bebe Daniels and Ben Lyon. It was called *Hi Gang!* and was loosely based on their smash hit radio show of the same name.

Manning Sherwin and I finished the score of a new Firth Shephard revue called *Fun and Games* which opened at the Prince's, while Ted Black loaned me out to brother George who teamed me up with author James Hadley Chase to dream up a gangster musical we called *Get a Load of This* for the London Hippodrome. Since our show took place in a Chicago nightclub, George Black removed many of the theatre seats replacing them with tables to give the illusion of a club. It's interesting to note that years later when the Hippodrome became the Talk of the Town they used the same idea. Perhaps my most endearing memory of *Get a Load of This* was one of our show's cabaret acts, a cute little six-year-old girl who stood there twisting a handkerchief as she sang and brought the house down every night while father Ted accompanied her on the piano. His full name was Ted Andrews and hers, of course, was Julie.

And as if all this leaping around wasn't enough we gave up our rented cottage in Sunningdale and bought an attractive country house in Virginia Water called Gorse Hill Manor, which would be the Guest citadel for the rest of the war. London was 30-odd miles away but I drove to the studio and back every day, with the exception of Thursdays when I stayed there overnight to do my obligatory studio firewatching. And don't think those Thursday nights weren't viewed with a certain amount of suspicion at Gorse Hill Manor. Which was reasonable enough, I suppose, in view of what had happened, except that I was slightly worried because Pat wasn't really that sort of a person and I had the uneasy feeling someone somewhere was stirring it up. Was it Scotty mum-in-law saying 'I wouldn't trust Crippen an inch!'? Or maybe Harold James with a solicitous 'I'd hate you to be hurt again, Pat.'

Then one day, out of an all-clear sky, came another of those career-swinging moments that seem to have peppered my life. The Ministry of Information appoached me through the studio to write them a propaganda short. Nothing as rousing as 'Once more into the breach, my friends...' but a simple message to remind people not to spread colds and germs to their fellow workers as it interfered with the War Effort. Not a very world-shattering assignment, until I learned through the grapevine they'd already asked six other writers to have a go and turned down their results. Well, this is when the Guest histri- onics came out. How dare they ask me seventh in line! Okay, I'd accept their apology and write what they wanted – on one condition. Even recalling this gives me a touch of the vapours at the thought of my youthful arrogance. Who the hell did I think I was to lay down conditions? But I did and, what's more, they accepted. The condition? That if they took my work they'd let me direct it as well.

So I sat up all night writing a ten-minute short to go with the stirring slogan COUGHS AND SNEEZES SPREAD DISEASES. It was called *The Nose Has It!*, wherein the Minister of Health was to lecture on various types of noses. Except that the Minister himself had a running one and his assistant had one bunged up with 'flu. So the last-minute replacement was the Minister's assistant's assistant, who was played by the popular new Gainsborough comedian, Arthur Askey. In an illustrated lecture he demonstrated the danger of nasal germ warfare on Britain's war effort. For example, he pointed out that snub noses sneezed their ammunition upwards, whereupon the camera followed the imaginary germs racing across the ceiling, hitting the next wall and down onto an unsuspecting group of munition work- ers. Similarly, the aquiline nose trajectory was downwards and along the floor of buses, Underground trains, restaurants and offices. Etc etc...

Not exactly Oscar material and I'm sure someone like Graham Greene could have done a lot bet- ter but at least it made them laugh. What's more they put it into the programme at the Leicester Square Odeon for the press show of the Rita Hayworth/Victor Mature film, *My Gal Sal*. Sadly the main fea- ture received rather poor reviews; in fact, that doyen of film critics, Jympson Harman, went as far as to write in the *Evening News*: 'As far as I'm concerned the best thing on the programme is the MOI short.' And – bingo – I'd become a director!

'Congratulations,' said Bill Ostrer as he read the *Evening News* cutting I'd pushed across his desk. 'Never know,' he smiled, 'you could become the MOI's favourite filmmaker.'

'I'd much rather be Gainsborough's,' I blurted out.

He looked up in surprise. 'What's that mean?'

'Would you let me direct a feature for Gainsborough?'

After a moment's thought he pushed the cutting back to me. 'Take it to Ted,' he grinned. 'He's the one who makes the tough decisions.'

Ted Black was unexpectedly amenable. 'Don't see why not. You've had a lot of good groundwork with Marcel. Okay, find the right subject and we'll have a go.'

'I have the right subject, Ted. At least, it isn't written yet but I have the idea and it won't take that long. It's a musical.'

'A *musical?*' He stared at me in disbelief. 'My God, can't you pick something simple to start with?'

'Will you let me show you, Ted?'

He sighed, spread his arms in despair then nodded. 'All right, show me.'

I practically levitated back to my office which was almost opposite the main stage where Carol Reed was shooting *Kipps* with his current girlfriend, Diana Wynyard, and Michael Redgrave. As it happened they were the first people I bumped into coming out for their lunch break. 'I'm going to direct!' I burbled hysterically. 'They're going to let me direct!'

'Well, thanks for the warning,' laughed Carol.

'Good for you,' smiled Diana. 'Can I be in it?'

Carol took my arm, 'Come on, we'll celebrate. I'll treat you to a spartan Gainsborough wartime lunch!' Which he did, and we were joined by Alastair Sim who was shooting *Cottage to Let* on the next stage. He had one of his cast with him, a 16-year-old lad with a mop of black curly hair, large eyes and a smile to match. Alastair introduced him as his protégé, a young cockney kid he'd seen somewhere, thought had promise and taken under his wing. His name, the lad told us, was George Cole and this was his first film. 'Perfect,' said Carol. 'We'll make it a double celebration. Dare we have some wine?'

And we did. Incidentally, some years later, when that young lad was an old man in his thirties, I was to make a couple of films with George and he'd more than lived up to all Alastair's predictions. However, my celebration lunch turned out to be somewhat premature since the script and score of *Miss London Ltd* wasn't ready to show Ted Black until almost two years later! The problem being that work on this project could only be done in my spare time and there wasn't much of that as Ted kept us all jumping around the clock working on comedies for their new box-office draw, Arthur Askey. One of these being a remake of Arnold Ridley's *The Ghost Train*, which brought back distant memories of his play *Third Time Lucky* and my historic performance in it as the village idiot. Ted also shipped me out again to big brother George.

'I'm planning another revue,' George Black told me. '*Strike a New Note* at the Prince of Wales. Bringing in a new comedian, Sid Field. He's a very funny man, see if you can come up with some sketches for him.' Which is how I came to meet that warm comic genius, Sid Field, another of those rare performers who was a pros' favourite – like Bea Lillie and, later, another beloved funnyman, Frankie Howerd. George Black had a happy flair for spotting touring talent and launching them into West End stardom. I remember someone else he introduced to London. 'Go and see Tommy Trinder,' he told me one day. 'Needs some new material for the next Palladium show.'

'What I'd like from you, Val,' said Trinder the first time I met him, 'are some new, well-thought-out ad libs.' You know the sort of thing. Someone in the audience arrives late. 'Hullo,' the joking Tommy would greet them. 'We started without you, I hope that's all right. I'll give you a quick run-down of the show so far.' And no one was better at these ad libs than Tommy; in fact, they became his trademark.

Meanwhile Gainsborough was still a teeming ant-hill of activity. Carol Reed was post-synching *The Young Mr Pitt* which he'd just finished shooting with Robert Donat, who had now become an international name since those *Henry VIII* days of 'Robert Who?' Eric Portman and Johnny Mills were bustling in and out of a submarine making *We Dive at Dawn*. On Stage 2 screenwriter Leslie Arliss, son of the redoubtable George Arliss, had also talked Ted Black into letting him direct his own screenplay of *The Man in Grey*, a costume drama with Maggie Lockwood, Phyllis Calvert, Stewart Granger and James Mason. Not a bad cast for your first directorial job. What's more they'd given him the fabulous Arthur Crabtree as his lighting cameraman. Arthur had lit my MOI short and had been a tower of strength.

And as if there weren't enough things jumping, Diana Wynyard and Carol decided they were going to get married, which of course called for another studio lunch celebration. It wasn't long before Sexy

Rexy, never one to be outdone, announced that at long last he was going to make an honest woman of Lilli Palmer. Those were the days when the customary studio Chianti magically changed to Champers and it seemed that apart from the escalating horrors of the nightly Blitz there was love and contentment all around us. Except on Stage 2.

The rumblings first started in the make-up department, which is where most studio rumblings begin. In those early dawn hours, sitting in the make-up chair looking at your half-awake self in the mirror, that's the time most performers drop their defences and let it all hang out. It seemed there was a mutiny brewing on *The Man in Grey* set. They weren't happy with their director and were feeling more and more insecure, which is the last thing any actor wants to feel. Unluckily for poor Leslie Arliss, he had no previous experience of working on the floor and was relying so much on Arthur Crabtree to help him out camera-wise that the actors felt they weren't getting any direction.

It was the morning after a particularly noisy night of bombing that tempers finally exploded on Stage 2. James Mason, the quietly humorous intellectual Jimmy Mason, had actually hauled off and bashed his director, sending him spinning across the set. The studio walls trembled at the news. 'I'm afraid he asked for it,' Granger filled me in later. 'Arliss was trying to assert his authority and of course we all knew he didn't have any. James had been up all night with the bombing and simply lost his cool.'

Leslie was unhurt and there were apologies all round while Ted Black had a secret meeting with Arthur Crabtree and asked him to keep things on a diplomatic and steady course from behind the camera. A long-faced Arthur slipped into my office after shooting one day. 'I'm virtually directing this picture,' he grumbled, 'and I'm only paid to be the bloody cameraman. Should I ask for more money?'

'Either that or tell them that if you help them out now they should do something for you later, like give you your own picture to direct.'

Which he did. And they did. And that's how lighting cameraman Arthur Crabtree became the much-heralded director of Gainsborough's *Madonna of the Seven Moons* and many more hits. As for Jimmy Mason, he received a lot of good-natured ribbing and for a while was known as 'Basher' Mason, which he took with his usual good humour. In fact, Jimmy had more than a sense of humour, he also had a sense of fun, and that's not always the same thing. I remember how fascinated he was with my cuttings book of newspaper and magazine misprints. At that time I was an avid collector of these bloopers and I recall the one that tickled him most was the headline streamer in a Johannesburg paper which proclaimed: CENTENARY OF EMILE ZOLA, THAT GRAND OLD MAN OF FRENCH LETTERS.

One day towards the end of *The Man in Grey*, Jimmy and I happened to meet up in the corridor. 'Just the man I want!' he said, grinning from ear to ear. 'Have I got one for you!' Grabbing my arm he almost dragged me to his dressing room where he searched for his wallet and produced a cutting he'd torn from a Hollywood trade paper. 'Top this one!' he laughed. The heading, in bold block type, reported: GARBO MAKES RARE PUBIC APPEARANCE.

But for me perhaps the most memorable event of that year was George Edgar and I finally finishing the script of *Miss London Ltd*. Manning Sherwin and I had completed the score and to top it all Ted Black had read it, heard it and given me the go-ahead to direct it in the New Year. Wow! I was far too nervous to throw a celebration lunch in the canteen although veteran director Walter Forde insisted on buying me one. Walter was in the middle of shooting *ITMA* ('It's That Man Again'), the wildly popular wartime radio show starring comedian Tommy Handley.

'Got any girls in your show?' asked Walter.

'Quite a lot. It's about an Escort Service for troops on leave.'

'You should take a look at a redhead on our set. There are three of them doubling a vocal for the Greene Sisters.' The Greene Sisters were currently a top singing group who'd recorded a number for the film, but the-powers-that-be had decided they weren't photogenic enough so casting had signed up three dolly birds to mime the song for them. 'There's a lot of personality there,' said Walter. 'And if you want adjectives,' he grinned, 'I'd describe her as 'regally feisty'.' So off I went to the *ITMA* set and watched those three girls leaning on the back of an upright piano swinging, tapping and mouthing the Greene Sisters' vocal. Walter was right, the one you looked at was the redhead in the middle. He introduced us between takes and we arranged to meet for lunch in the canteen next day.

Her name, she told me over the meal, was really Joan Summerfield but she'd changed it to Jean Carr. She'd been a dancer at the legendary Windmill Theatre and, finding that there was already a well-known actress called Jane Carr, she'd 'changed hers again to Jean Kent. And how right Walter had been with that 'regally feisty' bit. I well remember as we sat in the restaurant for our first meal she cast her eyes around the room, taking in the lunching Maggie Lockwood, Phyllis Calvert and Dulcie Gray. 'They ought to turn that lot out to pasture and give some of us newcomers a break,' she said imperiously.

That was the 22-year-old Jean Kent. Well, 'that lot' weren't turned out but I did write a small cameo for her in *Miss London Ltd* as a door-to-door salesgirl trying to peddle encyclopedias. And it apparently did the trick because not long after the film was finished Gainsborough put her under contract and la Kent was on her queenly way to stardom.

We were also able to launch another newcomer in the film. She was a cheerfully tubby teenager with the voice of a young Sophie Tucker and would later, together with Vera Lynn, become the Forces' Favourite as well as a big recording star. Her name was Anne Shelton and she sang three of the film's songs for us, taking one of them into the Top Ten. This was a featherweight number called 'Wrap Yourself in Cotton-Wool – and Save Yourself for Me'. Strange, the things that sometimes happen to lyrics. In this case, when it crossed the Atlantic, no one in America had the slightest idea what cotton-wool was. They, of course, simply called the stuff cotton. So every time it was recorded for us in the US it became 'Wrap Yourself in Cellophane'.

And while we're on the subject of lyrics, it was around this time, when Manning and I were contracted to music publishers Francis Day & Hunter, that Fred and Eddie Day called me to their Charing Cross Road office. "Rum and Coca-Cola," said Eddie without preamble. 'The song's number one in the American charts but we have a lyric problem. Firstly we'd like some extra choruses and secondly the BBC won't broadcast it here because it advertises Coca-Cola.'

Just to fill in the background to all this, the legendary Andrews Sisters had already recorded 'Rum and Coca-Cola' and made an enormous hit of it, even though at that time it had never been played on American radio. The reason? Believe it or not, in those days you couldn't mention any kind of drink on their airwaves. So the Andrews Sisters had managed to top the charts for weeks simply by having their disc played on juke boxes throughout the States. The whole set-up was again straight out of *Alice in Wonderland*, with American radio saying 'No Rum', the BBC saying 'No Coca-Cola', and 'Rum and Coca-Cola' being the season's runaway top-seller. Anyway, the combined genius of our brains went to work and solved the BBC's problem, so that in England, at least on the air, it was retitled 'Rum and Limonado'. The sacrifices some of us have to make for Art.

In the euphoria of completing my first full-length picture and finding everyone still happy and talking to me, I careered on like a runaway train, writing and directing two more that year, one of them being the Jean Simmons début, *Give Us the Moon*. My world was so full of film I was almost impervious to life's slightly more historic happenings. Little things like 6 June – D-Day – when our troops finally invaded Europe. Or the sudden arrival of Hitler's secret weapon, the V2 rockets, the Flying Bombs. You could hear the buzz of their engines, see the flames coming out of their tails and pretty soon learned that from the moment their engines cut out you had less than 60 seconds to hit the ground and pray. So why did none of this worry me nearly as much as whether Louis Levy would have our music playbacks ready for next week's shooting? Because my youthful priorities were hopelessly screwed up, and I was about to learn this the hard way. September 8th was the date the first V2 exploded on London. I remember it well because it was also the night my marriage exploded.

With the somewhat useless attribute of hindsight I can see now how a large portion of the blame was mine. My almost maniacal involvement with writing and directing three pictures in a row had relegated my family to second place in my life. Added to this hazard, Pat and I had decided, at the suggestion of our 'friend' Harold, that with the pressure of production and the additional possibility of me having to drive back to Virgina Water during a Blitz, I should stay up in London and come home weekends. To this end I rented a small, inexpensive two-room flat where I shacked up during shooting. All was well until one night, when I drove the car into my usual overnight garage, the attendant tapped on my window. I lowered it and he leaned in. 'In case you weren't aware of it, sir,' he said with a knowing wink, 'you're being tailed.'

'Tailed?'

'Kind of private eye type,' he grinned. 'Been asking who you come in with and things.'

I walked back to the flat, my mind spinning. Tailed? By whom? Who in the world would be interested in my comings and goings? Or were they interested in whoever they thought I might be with? I glanced over my shoulder. There was no one following, unless he'd ducked out of sight. Suddenly I felt I was part of some awful B-movie.

Around midnight I sat bolt upright in bed, instantly wide awake as a thought struck me. Scrambling into my pants, I slung a coat over the rest of me and raced back to the garage. 'This private eye type,' I fired at the startled garage man. 'Describe him.' He did. And it was a pretty good identikit of one Harold James. What a Machiavellian bastard, I seethed, and I was even angrier knowing I'd have to bottle it up until the weekend. That Friday, 8 September, I wrapped up shooting half an hour early, aimed my car at Virginia Water and homed-in like the second flying bomb of the day.

It wasn't a happy weekend with two people, who thought they were reasonably mature, acting like a couple of battling adolescents. Pat insisted she knew nothing about me being followed, only that it seemed she had no husband any more, just someone who dropped in weekends and spent most of them working on what he was going to do when he got back to the studio. There are probably statistics somewhere on how many marriages have been broken by how many careers. Part of our trouble, I suppose, was that we were both unable to handle the situation with any degree of grown-up compromise. Mind you, it didn't help to have a cuckoo-in-the-nest doing his best to stir things up behind the scenes. Anyway, that weekend, in a burst of youthful foot-stamping, I gave an ultimatum. From then on either the cuckoo was banished from our lives or I was. And that's when our marriage became a statistic.

It was Pat, with more than a little outside prompting, who decided it would be better if we separated for a while, play it by ear and try to remain good friends. For the moment young David Guest, now five years old and going to Virginia Water High School, would simply be told Daddy was away, working hard – which happened to be the truth. So there it was: 8 September, that sadly historic date on which Hitler's first V.2 exploded and my first marriage did likewise. Although, in retrospect (to use another word for hindsight), I'm afraid it wasn't as unexpected as it should have been.

I moved back to London and a slightly larger flat over a garage in Devonshire Mews behind the London Clinic. Once again in a man-on-my-own world, I plunged into another year of even more hectic work. Between the All Clears and the next sirens I made Margaret Lockwood's *I'll Be Your Sweetheart*, the musical that launched Michael Rennie into co-stardom. Meanwhile, Manning and I had written some numbers for a Robert Nesbitt extravaganza called *The Night and The Music* at the Coliseum, where we happened to be rehearsing when Churchill declared Victory in Europe – VE night – whereupon our entire cast stopped dancing at the Coliseum to go dancing with the rest of London in Trafalgar Square.

Another of that year's memorable moments for me was the night Jack Hylton summoned me to his office above Her Majesty's Theatre. 'I'm doing a new revue with Will Hay, Nervo & Knox and some other acts,' he said. 'You've worked with most of them. We have to open at the Theatre Royal Brighton in two weeks. Can you do it for me?'

'In *two weeks*? ' I gasped. 'My God, you better let me read the book.'

'Oh, you'll have to write that,' said Hylton.

Believe it or not the curtain did go up in two weeks even though we still hadn't dress-rehearsed the second act. So, on opening night, I sat in the stalls with a concealed mike close to my mouth still prompting the actors as the show proceeded. 'Don't forget the scrim... take down the floats... close tabs after the coda... stage left spot...' The audience didn't even notice. Even more miraculously, the show, *For Crying Out Loud*, came to the Stoll Theatre in London where it ran for over 300 performances. Which only goes to show that if you're young and foolhardy enough not to think of the sheer impossibility of a task it sometimes becomes possible.

With no more family weekends at Virginia Water I tried to compensate by rounding up a bunch of card-playing chums and instigating a Sunday poker game at my Devonshire Mews flat. Some of my regulars included Michael Rennie, Frances Day with her current beau, Anthony Beauchamp (the number one society photographer who had lensed most of the Royal Family), bandleader Billy Ternent and Maggie Lockwood with husband Rupert, who now and then held alternate games at their flat in Dolphin Square. We had an ever-percolating pot of coffee, a boiling tea-kettle and whatever goodies had been uncovered through our various fans on the ever-growing Black Market. Don't forget, it was the height of rationing in England. Everything from food to clothes was on coupons and each day was a trial of instant genius, discovering under which counter one might get eggs, butter, meat or the extra petrol coupons. As well as my tea and coffee, I usually had a couple of bottles of plonk standing by, plonk being the blanket name for any run-of-the-mill domestic wines still obtainable. Mind you, at times, when the spoils of foraging had been slightly more rewarding, it might even be a case of real Beaujolais that had 'fallen off the back of a PX truck'.

Perhaps one of the cheeriest persons around our table was Noël Holland. Noël was young, good-looking and one of the toppest top people in the mighty Gillette Razor Corporation on the Great West Road. And when they launched their popular 'Good mornings begin with Gillette' slogan it wasn't long before the gang changed it to 'Good mornings begin with Noël Holland'. A sentiment eventually shared by our friend, actress Greta Gynt, who went ahead and married him.

And I mustn't forget our lively off-and-on drop-ins who became known fondly as 'The Serving Wenches'. Whenever they had nothing better to do on a Sunday evening these d'lovelies would show up for a few giggles as they refilled percolators, kettles, cups and glasses for us. I recall three of them in particular. There was Michael's current girlfriend, Olga, a strikingly statuesque, dark-eyed beauty who was immediately labelled 'Olga the Beautiful Spy'. Then there was Patricia Owens. Twenty years old, cute and quietly ambitious, Pat Owens was working as a manicurist at Benthall's in Kingston when she showed up for my *Miss London Ltd* audition. I cast her as one of our three singing porters in the Waterloo Station number. Eventually she was whisked off to Hollywood where, among other films, she made *Sayonara* with Marlon Brando and *Island in the Sun* with Harry Belafonte. Not a bad follow-up for a singing porter.

Our third 'Serving Wench' was a girl I'd met through her sister, Kim, in a George Black revue. 'I've found a six-foot knockout,' George Black grinned at me one day. 'Kim Kendall. I'm going to make her

Below: As a gangster in
Innocents of Chicago (1932).

Below: Val Guest in his first stage role, as
Vincent the village idiot in Arnold Ridley's
Unholy Orders – New Brighton, 1930.

Bottom: Pat Patterson, Val Guest, Hal
Walters, Florence Vie, Betty Stockfield
and Harry Welchman in the 1932
musical *Maid of the Mountains.*

Opposite: With Marcel Varnel on the set of
Good Morning, Boys!, Gainsborough Studios, 1936.

Left: On the set of
Convict 99 (1938) with
Will Hay (seated). Back
row: Moore Marriott, Val
Guest, Marriott Edgar
and Graham Moffatt.

Below: Comparing
waistlines on the set of
Hey! Hey! USA! (1938).
Left to right: Will Hay,
Val Guest, Edgar
Kennedy, Marriott Edgar
and Marcel Varnel.

Above: The first Royal Command Film Performance, held at the Empire, Leicester Square, in 1946. From left to right: Bessie Love, Laurence Olivier, Vivien Leigh, Valerie Hobson (shaking hands with Queen Elizabeth), Rosmund John, Sally Gray, Their Majesties, Val Guest and RC Bromhead, president of the CTBF.

Right: Fishing with Margaret Lockwood on the set of *Give Us the Moon* in 1944.

Above: The first picture ever taken of Yolande Donlan and Val Guest, on the set of *Just William's Luck* (1947).

Left: *Murder at the Windmill* (1949): Diana Decker and Val Guest with some of the glamorous dancers on the Windmill Theatre stage.

Above: *The Body Said No* (1950): Yolande Donlan shows Michael Rennie and Val Guest where she received the blow on the head that delayed filming by a week.

Right: Reginald Beckwith, Peter Butterworth, Yolande Donlan and Dirk Bogarde in *Penny Princess* (1952).

Below: Val and Yolande, about to board a plane to
Tangier. While on holiday Val read the scripts for the
BBC's series *The Quatermass Experiment*.

Below: Yolande and Brian Donlevy at
the première of *Quatermass 2* in 1957.

Bottom: Camera operator Len Harris,
production manager Don Weeks, VG
and Brian Donlevy, shooting
Quatermass 2 in summer 1956.

Following page: Directing Peter
Cushing and Forrest Tucker on the
Pinewood Studios snowscapes created
for *The Abominable Snowman* in 1957.

the compère of my new Palladium show. Write some material for her.' Which I did. Kim was a third generation member of that well-known show-business family, the Kendalls. And George was right. She was indeed a six-foot knockout and she became an instant success as the West End's newest MC. Her younger sister's name was Kay and, whereas Pat Owens was quietly ambitious, Kay Kendall was noisily so. The sky was the limit for Kay. She'd danced in the chorus at the Palladium when she was 13, said a few lines in a film or two and now, at 19, she and Kim had tried out a sister act on the halls without much success. 'Material wasn't good enough,' she told me bluntly one day as we lazed around the Great Fosters swimming pool.

Great Fosters was a famous old Elizabethan mansion in Egham, now a hotel at which the rich and famous stayed. Incidentally, it was later to be the setting for some unforgettable moments I spent with Bette Davis. But at the moment it was just Kay and I discussing the career she was battling to launch. 'It's only a suggestion,' I offered tentatively, 'but why don't I try and write an act for you two?'

Her merry laughter rippled across the pool. 'Are you joking? We couldn't even afford your typing paper!'

'You don't have to afford me. You can pay me something any week you work. And if you don't work, we're all in trouble!' I wrote them a new act, but sadly it still wasn't good enough to launch the Kendall Sisters as a bookable proposition. Which, as it turned out, was just as well for both of them.

Another card-playing member of our motley Sunday get-togethers was a new RAF pal I'd met up with, Leonard Cheshire, or, to give him his full title, Group Captain Leonard Cheshire DFC and DSO with two bars. And, as if that wasn't enough for one war, he flew another 100 death-defying bombing raids into Nazi Germany for which he was awarded the Victoria Cross. Leonard had a quiet, wicked sense of humour and was an enthusiastic part of our card sessions. One Sunday when he didn't turn up, we thought he might be ill so I called his home. No reply. The following weekend, with still no sight nor sound of him, we concluded he'd been whisked off again on active duty. It was a while before we saw Leonard again and learned why he hadn't shown up that Sunday for poker. He'd only been on a flying mission over Japan, as Britain's official observer with the B-29 Bomber that dropped the 9000lb atom bomb on Nagasaki. Slightly higher stakes than our quiet little Sunday games.

When he eventually rejoined us, his VC, DSO and DFC now had an OM on the end. The Queen had awarded him her Order of Merit. Dear Leonard, who never seemed to stop doing things, would later dream up the historic Cheshire Foundation for the Relief of Suffering and receive a knighthood for it. But Her Majesty the Queen hadn't finished with him yet and Sir Leonard's final achievment was to end up as Lord Cheshire of Woodhall. How's that for a poker partner? But in those early Devonshire Mews days his most unexpected achievement was to do a sudden double-loop for American stage actress Constance Binney. And Connie, being no fool, charmed Leonard out of all future poker games and married him.

All of which, had I known it, could have been that funny finger of Fate staging a dress rehearsal for what Laurence Olivier had in store for me less than 18 months later when he brought another American actress to London. She was to star in his own Garrick Theatre production of Garson Kanin's Broadway smash *Born Yesterday*. Her name was Yolande Donlan and she would turn out to be not only double-loop but triple-loop material. And my looping-the-loop performance would turn out to be a lot bumpier than Leonard's.

CHAPTER NINE

David Guest was now six years old and had moved out of Virginia Water High into Cranleigh School in Surrey. I still made sporadic visits to Gorse Hill Manor although Pat and I were then leading completely separate lives on the amicable understanding that there would be no divorce unless either of us found a serious need for one.

This was also the year of another family break-up – our Gainsborough family. After being ten years with the same studio all us old-timers were pretty gloomy to learn that not only was our much-loved Ted Black leaving us and going to MGM, but the whole Ostrer regime was bowing out, too, leaving writer-producer Sydney Box and family to take over our home in Lime Grove. And since Sydney had a writer-wife Muriel, a sister-producer Betty with her producer-husband Peter Thomas, whose brother Ralph was also a director, and they were all dabbling in writing scripts as well, it soon became obvious there weren't enough offices for all of them and all of us. So, as contracts expired, off into the wide blue yonder went the old Gainsborough alumni. In the words of that old wartime refrain, it was 'Toodle-oo, Cheerio, Chin-Chin', and a brand new era was about to burst over my unsuspecting head.

1946 was destined to become the year jokingly referred to as my 'By Royal Appointment' year. The year King George VI shook my hand and, unexpectedly, noticed a small purple swelling that was forming on the back of it. 'That looks like a boil,' smiled His Majesty sympathetically.

'Yes, sir.'

'I had one, too,' he nodded. 'Not much fun, are they?'

'No, sir.' I wish I could record some more momentuous dialogue for this historic meeting, but at least it was comforting to know that the King and I had something in common – even if it was only a boil. Moments later his radiant Queen, Elizabeth, grasped the same hand, not quite as carefully.

'It was a lovely show,' she beamed at me.

'Thank you, Ma'am,' I beamed back, trying desperately not to wince.

The occasion was the very first Royal Command Film Performance at the Empire Theatre, Leicester Square. Every year there had been, and still is, a Royal Command Variety Show at which all the top variety stars, singers and comedy acts are summoned to appear before the Royal Family. This year the

Powers that Be of the cinema world had decided it was time to put on their own Command Show and Buckingham Palace had agreed they could do so in November. The film chosen to be world-premièred on this royal first was the Michael Powell-Emeric Pressburger production *A Matter of Life and Death*. All this was broken to me in a telephone call from Reginald Bromhead, president of the Cinematograph Trade Benevolent Fund, before the official announcement.

'It's going to be a historic night,' he enthused. 'And the Board have asked me to see if you would consider collaborating with Michael Powell to help devise some kind of stage presentation for the occasion? That is, of course, if you're free.' Free? I was not only free but stunned and overawed as well. Yes, yes, yes, I'd be honoured, I told him when I'd regained my breath. It was several weeks before the enormity of my decision dawned on me, as did the unexpected weightiness of this royal load.

Up until then it had been a reasonably normal sort of working year and exciting in a completely different way. Early in January my agent, the redoubtable Christopher Mann, called to say that the Rank Organisation were about to launch Sid Field onto the screen in a big-scale musical called *London Town*, which they planned to make with Hollywood director Wesley Ruggles. 'I think I've made a deal for you there,' said Chris.

'As what?'

'General Script Doctor – watching over the Sid Field material. Ruggles would like to lunch today at Shepperton.'

Wesley ('call me Wes') Ruggles was a doyen of movie makers. He'd first entered films as a Keystone Kop, he told me, thereafter supporting most of the early comics from Chaplin onwards. Later, of course, as a director he became part of Hollywood history, from his epic *Cimarron* all the way to Mae West's *I'm No Angel*. He'd covered it all but, he confessed over lunch, he'd never before come across the kind of warm, gentle, throwaway humour at which Sid Field excelled. 'Aside from your agent,' he grinned, 'both George Black and Sid gave you a good CV. Want to watch points for me?'

Which is how I came to be involved in what was to be one of Rank's costliest disappointments. It was Ruggles' first non-American film produced by his own company, Wesley Ruggles Productions for J Arthur Rank. The story had been conceived by him with a screenplay by Hollywood writers Elliot Paul and Siegfried Herzig. To be honest, the script didn't bear much resemblance to the London Town I knew, but any of my tentative queries were usually met with answers like, 'This way Americans will understand it.' However, being producer as well as director, Wes had assembled such a dazzling array of production talent it was hard not to be excited.

For the music he had signed two of America's foremost songsmiths, Jimmy Van Heusen and Johnny Burke, plus Sinatra's arranger and musical director, the great Salvador 'Toots' Camarata. Then, for good measure, he contracted the formidable Agnes de Mille to do the choreography with top English dance director, Freddie Carpenter. What a dream package for anyone making a musical. And how sad that somewhere along the line that dream went astray. Maybe it was because they tried so hard to please both the English and American markets that *London Town* ended up sinking in mid-Atlantic. It just wasn't a good enough picture and it opened in London to very lukewarm reviews. Which only goes to show, you can have all the finest ingredients in the kitchen but, without the right chef, bang go your three stars. In America they released it as *My Heart Goes Crazy* with even less success. Later they cut the picture down to little more than some of the musical numbers and Sid Field's classic routines. This version went the rounds of various show-business parties and was eventually put out as a programme filler.

Incidentally, one of the film's best musical moments was the Van Heusen & Burke number 'Any Wind that Blows', about which the critics were almost unanimous: it was a personal song-and-dance triumph for a young newcomer whose presence, they said, was one of the brighter things in the picture. This was a girl I had persuaded Wes to audition. After which he tested her, liked what he saw, decided to make her one of his two leading ladies (the other was Greta Gynt), and her career was on its way. For me, it was one of the more gratifying things about *London Town*, if only because her name was Kay Kendall.

As for poor Wes Ruggles, the financial failure of this film seemed to bring his career to an abrupt end. Suddenly Wesley Ruggles Productions ceased to operate and to the best of my knowledge he never made another picture. The last I heard of him he had returned to his home in Santa Monica where sadly, almost forgotten by filmdom, he died at the age of 83.

From the problems of *London Town* to the problems of the first Royal Command Film Performance was another giant leap for me, but somehow in this case the problems seemed to be a worthwhile challenge. I walked into the first one the morning I was summoned to the Empire Leicester Square, to meet the CTBF Board and Michael Powell regarding the proposed stage show. After a cheery exchange with Mickey Powell things got down to the nitty-gritty.

'So far we've received a heartening response to our invitations,' beamed Reginal Bromhead. 'Vivien Leigh and Laurence Olivier have accepted. So have Deborah Kerr, Anna Neagle and...' He clicked his fingers. 'Who's that feller, just won the Academy Award... You know, *Lost Weekend...*'

'Ray Milland?'

'That's him – he's coming from California.' He checked the list in front of him. 'So are Joan Bennett, Pat O'Brien, Stewart Granger, Maria Montez, Walter Wanger and Anton Walbrook. The latest home 'yesses' are Ralph Richardson, Mai Zetterling, Michael Redgrave, John Mills, Diana Wynyard ....'

'Wait a minute, wait a minute,' cut in Mickey Powell. 'You're not seriously suggesting all these people take part in the stage show?'

'Well, we thought it would give us a particularly memorable occasion,' said Mr Bromhead.

'It would give you a particularly memorable headache,' answered Mickey. 'You can't ask that lot to be part of a stage show. It'd be chaos. Besides, they wouldn't do it. Line them up in the foyer after the film and present them to the Royals, fine. But on stage? Forget it.'

'You're suggesting no stage show?'

'They're coming to see a film,' shrugged Mickey 'But if you feel you need a stage show, make it just that. Book some acts. Anyway, it's not my department, I make films. If Val wants to have a go that's up to him.' He glanced at his watch. 'Look, you'll have to excuse me, I'm due at the labs any minute. And don't worry about your show print, I'll see you have it well in advance.' On his way to the door Michael Powell patted my shoulder. 'Good luck,' he said.

Six pairs of eyes did a slow 'pan' back to me. 'And how do you feel about that?' asked Mr. Bromhead.

My silence was deafening. Come on, Guest, pull yourself together. Finally I said, 'Well, I could ask them... I mean, if they'd agree to be part of a stage show... I'd have to dream up something for them to do, of course...'

'Does that mean you will?'

There were six beaming smiles telling me this was an offer I daren't refuse. So I didn't. I drove home with my mind in overdrive. There had to be a theme, some theme I could hang those names on. They'd given me a list of acceptances so far and as there were a frightening 36 of them it was obvious I couldn't use that many. Whittling it down, I realised I had at least a dozen chums on that list, among whom was Will Hay. And since he was the one with the most stage experience I decided to use him as a sounding board and called him that evening.

'Bill, they've asked me to put on the Command Film show. I know you're coming, but would you do something on stage for me as well?'

'You mean my act?'

'No, no. It could be an intro, or a commentary, I don't know yet. Would you do it for me?'

'Yes, sure,' said Will Hay. 'But commentary on what? Do I have to swot up cinema history or something?'

Wow! He'd hit it in one! Cinema history – do a virtual cavalcade of the movies! And that's what we'd call it: 'Cavalcade of the Movies'. Bright and early next morning I telephoned the British Film Institute Archives. Could they round up early film clips from the Keystone era, Chaplin and onwards? They could. And what if I needed some excerpts from past Academy Award material? Given enough warning, they said, it shouldn't be too difficult. And I was away on a dream! I'd present clips of movie highlights through the years, where possible using films in which our attending stars appeared. Then maybe, just maybe, I could get them up to introduce the clips in person. Anyway, I'd have a damn good try.

Within days the BFI had come up with the Keystone Kops, plus a print of an early Chaplin short called *The Champ*. Great stuff, but what now? That evening they had a rehearsal screening of the chosen film, *A Matter of Life and Death*, in which a pilot (David Niven), whose brain is damaged bailing out of his plane, has visions he's actually been to Heaven, where a celestial guide, in the person of actor Marius Goring, shows him around. Suddenly all my bells were ringing. Why couldn't this same celestial guide kick off my Cavalcade, wearing his actual film costume? Happily both Michael Powell and Marius gave the idea their blessing and for our opening the resplendently celestial Marius guided us safely through the Keystone Kops era to Will Hay, who finished our comedy section with Chaplin.

Moving on to the sound era, MGM came up with a reel of the first full-length, all-talking, all-singing, all-dancing Academy Award-winning musical, *Broadway Melody*. At this moment I think my own celestial guide was watching over me because who should drop into London that week but the star of that very film, Bessie Love. And she even agreed to appear and talk about it. Meanwhile I had chased up a clip from the Noël Coward epic, *Cavalcade*, in which Diana Wynyard's performance had been nominated for an Oscar. Whereupon, shamelessly pleading the 'old pal's act', I asked Diana if by any chance she would step up and do the memorable toast scene from that film? To my surprise and delight the darling, lovely Mrs Carol Reed said she would.

Another personage to be present on that big night was celebrated Greek actress Katina Paxinou and incredibly, still heady from my Wynyard achievement, I talked this formidable lady into reciting passages from her Oscar-winning performance as Pilar in the Hemingway classic, *For Whom the Bell Tolls*, after we'd shown a clip. Slowly this was growing into quite a show and with one more spurt of bravado, after Paramount had supplied a reel of Ray Milland's *The Lost Weekend*, I called Ray in Beverly Hills. 'He's on location,' said the PR man who answered the phone. 'I'll give him your message but I ought to warn you, he doesn't like getting up and doing things.' Two days later a Western Union cable arrived for me at the Empire. It read: HATE BEING EXHIBITED BUT FOR DEAR OLD ELSTREE WHAT DO YOU WANT OF ME NOW QUERY EXCLAMATION. Came the night, we screened part of his Academy Award performance as the tortured and struggling alcoholic, after which Ray came on and joked about some of the problems in shooting it, not least of which was that all the whisky he drank in the film was cold tea and he was now off tea for life.

Somehow I managed to persuade our other stars to introduce yet more stars and for the Finale brought all 36 of them on stage to Edward Elgar's rousing arrangement of 'God Save the King', sung by a choir led by the popular Frank Titterton and accompanied by my old chum Louis Levy with his ever-popular Concert Orchestra.

And that, roughly speaking, is how the first Royal Command Film Performance came into being.

Rehearsing it wasn't easy because half the people hadn't arrived in the country yet and the other half were only available sporadically. So most of the time we were working with stand-ins and I must say I was most grateful for all my early 'Just get on with it' training with George Black and Jack Hylton. And then, of course, there was security. With royalty involved, the whole building was vetted from roof to cellar, not once but several times during the week of the event. 'It only needs one nut to leave a parcel,' explained a laconic gentleman from MI5.

Protocol for the royal evening was rehearsed almost as much as the show. Firstly, it was stressed that once the curtain came down no one, but no one, must leave their seats until the King, the Queen and the two royal princesses had left the auditorium. Whereupon everyone on stage should hurry to the Promenade Foyer and await their presentation to the royals. Furthermore, it was decided the person who should perform the desperate feat of attempting to remember all 36 names, as he led Their Majesties down the line introducing them, should be the man whose fault it all was. Me.

Our first Hollywood contingent came in on the Queen Mary and I trained down to Southampton to greet them. However, it was days before the rest of our overseas guests flew in. The evening of the royal event was Friday 1 November and it wasn't until 11.30 pm the night before that I was finally able to get everyone on stage for what was laughingly called my dress rehearsal. There they all were, bundled up in overcoats and furs, trying to keep warm in the late night chill of winter in London on the Empire stage.

'I'll need someone to guide me on,' said Joan Bennett unexpectedly. 'I can't see without my glasses and I never wear them in public.'

'I'll guide you on,' said Hollywood production mogul, Walter Wanger, who also happened to be her husband.

'Where's the Royal Box?' asked Pat O'Brien. 'Don't we have to bow to it?' I explained it was customary but not obligatory to do so and that the box was in the centre of the Royal Circle. I also tipped off the foreigners that one should never speak to Royalty until spoken to. I thought it safer to do this just in case we had any kind of friendly 'Nice to meet you, George' or 'Hi, Your Majesty' type of socialising.

During my 89 gnarled years of 'kicking the gong around', there have been relatively few nights indelibly inscribed on my memory. The evening of Friday 1 November 1946 is one of them. What's more, any long-time residents of Leicester Square will remember it too, because not since VE night had there been such a milling mob of people there. And whereas the police had been ready for VE night, they were not expecting the thousands who massed in the square to cheer the royal party and the British and Hollywood stars. British International Studio manager, the redoubtable Joe Grossman, was there with his staff of six nursing sisters and 12 ambulancemen who treated 80 casualties, of which three were taken to hospital. Then, according to a report in *To-Day's Cinema*, 'Only with the greatest difficulty could a passage be made for the royal cars, which, due to the enormous traffic jam, arrived some 12 minutes late.' Royalty arriving 12 minutes late? People have been sent to the Tower of London for less.

And inside the theatre, far from the madding crowd? Miraculously the evening went off without a single hitch. Even Joan Bennett reached the footlights without a falter. The film was, of course, magnificent, the stage show seemed to please the fans and the final curtain fell to long and enthusiastic applause. I sat in the front row of the Royal Circle, basking in my dream world, watching the royal party leave their flower-bedecked box, the young Princess Elizabeth and Princess Margaret following their parents, making their way towards the Promenade Foyer.

It was then that something pressed my panic button. The foyer! My God, I had to be up there before them, ready for the presentations! I should have left long before the end of the show! Bounding up the nearest aisle, I was halfway up it before I was grabbed by two security men. 'I'm part of the show!' I babbled breathlessly. 'I should be up in the Promenade!' Tearing myself free, I leaped up the remaining steps into the foyer only to come skidding to a halt right behind the two princesses. They were following the King and Queen towards the top of the presentation line, where I was supposed to be. There was only one way to get there, between the two princesses. Streaking through the narrow gap I almost sent the young Elizabeth flying.

'Oh dear, so sorry!' I gasped to my future Queen and raced to the top of the line just in time to present Maria Montez to His Majesty King George VI. I'll never know how I remembered all those names, but I did, and at the end of the line it was my turn to be presented to Their Majesties by CTBF President Reginald Bromhead. Which was when His Majesty and I had that riveting conversation about my boil.

A MEMORABLE EVENING, trumpeted the press next morning and as far as I was concerned that neatly summed it up. Later, I was presented with a magnificent parchment scroll bearing the Royal Coat of Arms and inscribed with the signature of every one of my valiant cast. Today it hangs in a place of honour on the wall of our so-called 'Trophy Room', or what Yolande often refers to as our 'Graceland'. Thus ended my Royal Year and somehow the event has always seemed to be a fitting finish to what I think of as Part One of my life. With 1947, Part Two was about to burst on me like a Monte Carlo Fireworks Gala. Dazzling, colourful and completely unpredictable.

And just for nostalgia's sake, as well as for the records, I'd like to end this chapter with my Royal Cast List. Quite apart from any possible interest to historians, fans, or the mildly curious, you might, who knows, even recognise some names of parents, grandparents or great grandparents amongst them. Here then is a page from the programme.

ROYAL COMMAND FILM PERFORMANCE
EMPIRE THEATRE, LONDON
8 PM, FRIDAY NOVEMBER 1ST 1946

BESSIE LOVE	WILLIAM EYTHE
MARIA MONTEZ	SALLY GRAY
ALF CJELLIN	NAUNTON WAYNE
ROSAMOND JOHN	REGINALD GARDINER
DIANA WYNYARD	LAURENCE OLIVIER
STEWART GRANGER	RALPH RICHARDSON
VIVIEN LEIGH	ANTON WALBROOK
SID FIELD	WALTER WANGER
DOROTHY MALONE	JEAN KENT
PAT O'BRIEN	BUD FLANAGAN
MICHAEL REDGRAVE	MAI ZETTERLING
DEBORAH KERR	ANTHONY KIMMINS
WILL HAY	VALERIE HOBSON
JOAN BENNETT	JOHN MILLS
RAY MILLAND	MARGARET LOCKWOOD
KIM HUNTER	PATRICIA ROC
ROGER LIVESEY	ANNA NEAGLE
MARIUS GORING	GERRY WILMOT

CHAPTER
TEN

It was Laurence Olivier who caused 1947's earliest theatrical firework display. With his newly formed Laurence Olivier Productions, he launched into his first managerial venture with Garson Kanin's *Born Yesterday* at the Garrick Theatre. And even producer-director Larry O couldn't have envisaged the impact his production would have on that first night audience. When the final curtain fell on the evening of Thursday 22 January, the audience rose to their feet with a storm of applause, shouting 'Bravo!' and throwing their programmes into the air. People lucky enough to have been there that night said they had never seen a London opening like it. After the cast had taken their umpteenth curtain call Olivier himself walked onto the stage. Acknowledging the cheers, he took his leading lady by the hand, led the surprised girl down to the footlights and introduced her as 'My enchanting new star from America...'

Overnight, Yolande Donlan had become part of London's theatre history. The play, a smash, ran for the best part of a year. So why did it take six months before I even met the girl with whom I was destined to share the rest of my life? Because, as usual, I was in the throes of one of my 'complete immersion' periods. It was a common complaint with me when I was either dreaming up, writing, or trying to promote films which, with any luck, I might direct. It was then that the outside world seemed extraneous and I tried to brush it aside.

Mind you, I was vaguely aware that a 'dumb blonde' had made a resounding hit in some play or other; how could one not be aware of it with all that newspaper coverage? I also noted that she looked quite a dish. But more than that? Niente. It took its place next to other sideline events interfering with my concentration. Like the royal wedding of Philip to Elizabeth, that young girl I almost mowed down at the Royal Command Performance. Or someone discovering the Dead Sea Scrolls in Palestine. All of which happened that year, as did the very first Cannes Film Festival. Oh yes, and something called the 'Hollywood Ten' blacklist had just been issued, branding some of Tinseltown's rich and famous as Communists and drumming them out of the business.

None of which seemed as important as the piddling little picture with which I was about to get involved. A card-playing friend of mine, David Coplan, who was then the head of United Artists, had called me up to ask if I'd ever heard of an author named Richmal Crompton. Which, of course, I had. She was an extremely popular writer whose 'William' books, about a lovable rascal of a schoolboy, were inevitably best sellers. 'We've bought one of them,' said Dave. '*Just William's Luck*. Interested?' I was interested enough to leap at an invitation to his house in Seymour Street to discuss it over dinner. However, when I rang the bell, the last thing I was prepared for was to have the door opened by Chico Marx. Chico, the piano-playing wonder of the Marx Brothers, stared at me solemnly.

'Evening, m'lord,' he said. 'They can't afford a butler so I'm doing this for charity.' A grinning Dave was close on his heels, effecting the rest of the introductions. There was one other couple, William 'Buster' Collier Jr and wife. Buster, son of Broadway star, playwright and film character actor William Collier Sr, had been a popular leading man in silent films and had made an effective transition into sound before retiring to become an agent with the William Morris Agency.

Over dinner Dave filled me in about the prospective film. It was a small budget picture, but if it took off United Artists would make more of the 'William' stories. Buster Collier would be co-producing and it would be shot at Southall Studios. I could take the Richmal Crompton book home with me and they'd like a screenplay as soon as possible. All of which sounded fine, but where did Chico fit into all this? Throughout dinner I'd been wondering but had been afraid to ask. Could they possibly want me to write Chico Marx into *Just William's Luck*? The answer came with the coffee.

'Okay,' said Chico, 'we've had a great dinner, great cooking, great service and Val has agreed to write the great movie of the year. Now, wouldn't it be great if we got down to the really serious business of the evening?' At last I realised why he was there. Knowing Chico was an inveterate card-player, Dave had promised him an after-dinner game. Moments later I found out that he'd also promised I'd be the fourth player. 'I don't have much cash on me,' I hedged nervously as they took their brandies to the card table.

'No problem,' soothed Chico. 'UA can always take it out of your pay cheque.'

It was two in the morning before I finally got home, having just about broken even. Cash-wise I'd broken even, but life-wise, had I known, I was on my way to a jackpot.

It began during the second week of shooting *Just William's Luck*. We were on a night location at Englefield Green, near Runnymead. As so often on English film locations it was teeming with rain, so we were all huddled in our unit cars waiting for it to stop. There were three of us sheltering in my limousine. One was a 40-year-old character actress named Joan Hickson. How she would have laughed had I told her that in another 40 years she would become a television icon as Agatha Christie's indestructible Miss Marple. The other occupant was a stocky character actor with a pleasantly plug-ugly face and his name was Michael Balfour. He'd never worked for me before and was playing one of our crooks. He grinned at me between thunder claps, making conversation.

'You've seen our play, of course?'

'What play is that?'

'*Born Yesterday.*'

'I haven't had much time to see shows this year.'

'You ought to make time for this one,' he enthused. 'It's a knockout. So is the girl.'

'Yes, I read about her. I must try and get tickets.'

'Never mind try and get. I'll get. What night?'

'It'd have to be a Friday, the end of my shooting week.'

'Okay.' Michael Balfour was still grinning. 'But only *one* seat, in case I can talk her into letting you take the three of us out to dinner afterwards.'

'I'll make the booking tomorrow,' I said, going along with his joke. But he wasn't joking. He did get me one seat and he did talk his leading lady into letting him chaperone her on a blind date with his director! He wasn't joking about the show, either. It was a hilarious knockout. As for the girl playing the legendary Billie Dawn, that historic not-so-dumb dumb blonde, she was more than knockout. I thought she was incredibly talented, enchanting and someone I'd be willing to attempt a triple-loop for any day. Michael, very good in a supporting role as a hoodlum henchman, collected me after the show and took me down to meet the now-famous Yolande Donlan.

'It's Michael,' he called, tapping on her dressing-room door. And in we went. For a moment it was difficult to see her since the room was unexpectedly full of Laurence Olivier, Vivien Leigh, Jack Buchanan, Beatrice Lillie and the Duke of Bedford. Michael pulled me through the heady gathering. 'It's nearly always like this,' he whispered and pushed me towards his leading lady. 'Here's Val,' he said, cutting our introduction down to what was almost cable-ese.

'Hello, Val,' she smiled, shaking hands. 'I'm Yolande, and everyone calls me Yo.' Mentally I made a note to change my triple-loop to a quadruple-loop. Eventually, after the starry throng had left, she turned to me with a warm, disarming smile. 'Sorry about all that. Now – Michael's told me all about you. Where are we going to eat?'

Not just a pretty face, but a girl after my own heart. I told her I'd booked a table at the Four Hundred Club and hoped that was all right. 'Fine with me,' she said, grabbing her mink. 'I'm starving.' And away we went into the cold September night for my first chaperoned date with my future wife. I say 'first' because over the next few weeks we had several other dates but she always brought Michael, her dresser Grace, or some other conscripted bodyguard. It seemed I was still suspect material. Not that we didn't have fun. She had an infectious sense of humour and we seemed to find the same things funny. I learned she was over here with her mother and 18-month-old son, Christopher. So she was married? Oh, yes – to Philip Truex, actor son of the American comedian Ernest Truex, but it was going through a rather traumatic time at the moment, on top of which her husband wasn't at all happy about her going away to England for so long. I told her about my own marital situation and we commiserated with each other over Krug champagne and Dover sole. The chaperones, too.

One of her more frequent escorts, I found out, was producer-screenwriter-playwright Anatole 'Tolly' de Grunwald. No chaperone for him. Mind you, Tolly was in the top film echelon. He'd been a director of Alex Korda's Two Cities Films and had just formed his own production company. His screenplays included such acclaimed titles as *French Without Tears*, *Jeannie* and *The First of the Few*. To say nothing of the fact that he'd produced, as well as written, *The Way to the Stars* and was busy preparing *The Winslow Boy*. This was all rather formidable competition for someone making a small family comedy called *Just William's Luck* at the tiny Southall Studios and living in a minuscule mews flat over a garage in Devonshire Mews West. Not exactly a compelling image. Years later Yo told me it wasn't *that* image that had bothered her – it was my tan trilby hat, thin moustache, cigar and camel hair coat. 'You looked like someone I'd seen in gangster movies,' she laughed.

As shooting progressed, Michael Balfour would bring me updated Donlan progress reports. According to him her dressing room seemed to harbour an endless stream of British aristocracy and landed gentry with scores of invitations for weekends at stately homes and baronial castles, in which she almost froze to death. She even shivered at the Oliviers' Notley Abbey when Larry and Vivien took her down there for the weekend. And that, believe it or not, was to be the beginning of my salvation. How? Because the government had nationalised electricity. No, I'm not being frivolous. Here's how it happened.

Even two years after the war we were one of the few countries still caught up in rationing. On top of which there was now a fuel shortage and power supplies had been drastically cut. Most illuminated advertising signs were now restricted, including the front of theatres. Poor Yo, having spent most of her life working hard to become a star and get her name up in lights, there it was at last, in letters three-foot high and they weren't allowed to switch it on. Inside, audiences were suffering as well. Many times I saw people wrapped in furs and mufflers. On stage, in the first Act, Yo was dressed in a very glamorous chiffon negligée. Had the audience but known, she was wearing woollen longjohns underneath it. So you can imagine those baronial halls and their 60-feet long drawing rooms with no heat other than a fireplace at the far end. So how come Guest was blessed with a constantly heated flat in Devonshire Mews? Because the mews was directly behind the London Clinic, which had an uninterrupted power supply and luckily my little abode was connected to the same circuit.

It wasn't long before the news leaked out and suddenly I became the only person Yo knew in London who had constant central heating. Hey presto! Suddenly I was kilowatts ahead of the rest of the dating gang. From then on our friendship blossomed, chaperones were banished and we found all sorts of ways to keep warm. But don't think it was easy. The last American actress to capture London like this had been Tallulah Bankhead over 20 years earlier and, like Tallulah, Yolande was being courted and dated by the crème de la crème. So Guest had to grab his chances in between the big stuff.

One of her greatest admirers was the ubiquitous Noël Coward. Noel had been at her opening night and become, as he described it, 'her devoted fan'. He wrote her witty notes, invited her to his parties and generally treated her like one of the family. 'Yolande,' he said one night after seeing *Born Yesterday* again, 'I've made up my mind. You are going to be in a play with me.' It was a great compliment coming from 'The Master' and Yo was thrilled. The play he had in mind was a revival of his *Present Laughter*, which he had been thinking of doing for some time. However, *Born Yesterday* ran on and on and eventually Noël had to get going with his own production. But the unexpected Coward gesture had yet to come. On his opening night at the Haymarket Theatre, the curtain went up on a drawing room set with a grand piano. On the piano was a framed photograph. It was a photograph of Yolande. 'I said you'd be in a play with me,' he quipped afterwards, 'and I always keep my word.'

That year brought some sad news, too. My guru, chum and mentor, Marcel Varnel, was killed in a motor accident on his way home from Nettlefold Studios where he was producing *The First Gentleman*. He was driving alone when his car had swerved off the road, ending upside-down on a grassy bank. The cause of the crash was always a mystery. The weather was dry and clear, he was sober and medically fit, but I've long had a theory about what happened. Marcel had a horror of flies or any winged insect. Many times, driving with him, I'd witnessed his sheer terror at the sight or sound of something that had got into the car. We'd swerve dangerously until I'd either swatted it or shooed it out of the window. I'm sure something flew in that day and poor Marcel fought a losing battle. I still think of this talented, energetic little man with affection and gratitude for his contribution to my life.

On our last week of shooting Yolande paid her first visit to the set and there was great excitement, and publicity flashbulbs galore, when she met the cast. My biggest surprise was to find that the cast member most interested in meeting her was that distinguished veteran of the British theatre, A E Matthews. Matty, as he was fondly known throughout the profession, had been a popular star for decades, from his days as a matinée idol on Broadway and in the West End, playing opposite some of the great leading ladies of the day, until now, in his venerable eighties, when he was still one of the best light comedians in the business and at that very moment starring in his own hit play, *The Chiltern Hundreds*, at the Vaudeville Theatre. 'I've read about this Donlan,' he said to me with a mischievous twinkle. 'Always good to size up the opposition.'

The two of them bonded right away. They were both the same no-crap type of person and hit it off so well that Matty and his wife Pat became our good friends from then on. You'll also find Matty in many of my old films; in fact, he became the cornerstone of what was jokingly referred to as my rep company. This comprised a band of hand-picked, talented thespians who always tried to keep themselves free when I was preparing another film because they knew I'd try hard to write them into it somewhere. And quite a group it was, too. With the exception of Matty they were all aspiring performers in the early stages of their careers. Characters like Wilfrid Hyde White, Sid James, Leo McKern, Michael Goodliffe, John Le Mesurier, Reginald Beckwith, Jon Pertwee and Peter Butterworth – the list could go on. It would be nice to feel that in some small way all that early screen-time helped them to achieve their latterday acclaim.

There was another aspiring hopeful in the studio that day. A young composer fresh out of the Royal Canadian Air Force in which he'd had his own band. He was now striving to crash the civilian world and had brought some of his tapes for me to hear, with a view to writing some background music for the film. His name was Robert Farnon and I thought his tapes were great. Not only did they have vitality, they also had a sense of fun, which was exactly what *William* needed. I played them for our top brass who were not too impressed but allowed me to prevail. So not only did the talented Bob Farnon do his first film score for *Just William's Luck*, he also scored the sequal, *William Comes to Town*, as well as many other wonderful backgrounds for me over the years. And isn't it fun to know that his *William* theme has long since found its way into the world catalogues of classic light music under the title of 'Mexican Jumping Bean'.

Anyway, it was on that day, after our studio lunch, that Yo dropped her bombshell. *Born Yesterday* was closing in four weeks time. *Closing?* Panic! What now? She'd be gone. Back to New York with mother and Christopher and I'd never see her again. The whole thing was unthinkable. The last night of the show would be 29 November. Only 25 days to Christmas, so couldn't she just stay on for the holidays? She couldn't. 'I'm a working girl, Val. I have to go back and earn a living. But what I have promised myself is to steal a few days and see Paris before I leave.'

'Fantastic! We'll be wrapped up by then. May I come too?'

'If you have time...'

I warned her Paris was also on rations and still battling austerity. That didn't matter, she said. Her mother's side of the family were French, she'd spent her childhood writing postcards to her French grandmère in Paris and she couldn't be this close and not see France. What we didn't know was that on top of all its other troubles Gay Paree was in the middle of a garbage strike, as well as a power problem. Poor Yo: her first sight of the legendary City of Lights was an unlit Champs Elysée with the sidewalks piled high with sacks of rubbish and refuse bins.

That night I reserved a table at Scheherazade, one of the more romantic Parisian dining spots, long famous for its strolling string orchestra which serenaded the tables. 'I would wear something warm, M'sieur,' suggested our helpful concierge, Claude, at the Hôtel Vernet, my favourite French home-from-home at the top of Rue Vernet. 'The heating might not be what it should be. Les problèmes...' he explained.

And he was right. It was cool, it was romantic and gourmet-wise it rated at least four rosettes, but it was also mildly embarrassing because we seemed to be the only two diners in that elegant candlelit room. And as there was no one else for those strolling strings to serenade, they encircled our table for most of the evening requesting our requests and giving us their undivided all. The cello player even rested the spike of his instrument on the empty seat next to me. However, by coffee time they had taken their break and strolled away to the mens' room or the bar or wherever, and we both laughed at the sudden peace and candlelit cosiness of our table.

'Thank heavens,' said Yo. 'One more "Does Ma'm'selle have another request?"... I was getting ready for "Oui, allez vous ont!"'

'What if I had a request?'

'Such as?'

'Suppose one day you were single again and suppose one day I was too. And suppose I plucked up the courage to ask you....'

'Oh no, no, no, no,' she laughed quickly. 'Too many supposes for one evening. Just ask for l'addition, there's a good boy!'

Of course she was right. The village idiot had rushed in and asked the wrong question at the wrong time. But then, as you've probably gathered by now, he was well and truly smitten. And after all, it *was* Paris, to say nothing of all those violins.

So to the next problem. How do you show someone Paris in five days? Well, I did my best. The Opera House, the Louvre, up the Seine on the Bateau Mouche, les Tuileries and finally the lavishly spectacular Folies Bergères, where we and the rest of the audience sat in our overcoats and furs, sympathising with all those nude nymphs on stage. At least Yo, in London, was able to hide longjohns under her negligée to keep warm. Here they wore nothing to hide anything. And there was certainly no need for the Folies' sponge man that night.

Ah yes, the sponge man. You may well be puzzled. I only learned of this historic character because several years later I shot a sequence backstage at the Folies Bergères with Bebe Daniels and Ben Lyon. I was making a little epic called *The Lyons in Paris*, a sequel to *Life with the Lyons*, a comedy I'd made earlier based on their successful BBC series. Standing in the wings just before curtain-up, I was intrigued to see the topless showgirls stepping up to a serious young man clutching a sponge in one hand and a bucket of cold water in the other. Then, like some ancient ritual, he dunked the sponge in the bucket and dabbed it on each girl's nipples as she went on stage. House rules at the Folies, I learned later, demanded that whenever possible nipples should be erect. Further research into this ceremony revealed his name was Pierre and that not only was his job taken most seriously but, traditionally, it was usually handed down from father to son. In much the same way as the smuggling rights in Andorra. Whether Pierre ever performed this service for the star of the show, Josephine Baker, I never found out.

All too soon we were back in London and all too soon Yolande and family were packing to sail back to New York on the Queen Mary. And then what? Would I ever see her again? I was surprised how much that question haunted me. Until the day before she departed when, in the middle of a noisy thunderstorm, the answer appeared in the form of a Good Fairy. Actually he wasn't a fairy at all. He was a small, dark young pseudo-intellectual stage director named Peter Cotes. And it wasn't a wand he was waving but a playscript of Clifford Odets' Broadway hit, *Rocket to the Moon*. Odets was one of the brighter luminaries of the American theatre, author of many acclaimed works including *Awake and Sing*, *Night Music*, *Paradise Lost* and *Golden Boy*.

'Jack Hylton plans a London production of *Rocket* in the New Year,' declaimed young Cotes over the thunder. 'Probably the Duchess Theatre. I'll be directing it and we both think it would be a wonderful vehicle for you, Miss Donlan.'

'Well, thank you,' said Yolande. 'I never saw the show but I remember it had a wonderful leading female role. I'd like to read it.'

'It's a great role and great for you,' said Good Fairy Cotes. 'Read it on the Queen Mary, where better? Naturally, I'd appreciate a yes or no as soon as you've decided.' He weaved his way around the cabin trunks. 'Well, fingers crossed and bon voyage.' With that he was gone. Strangely enough, so was the thunder. As for me, I felt sure there had to be a rainbow out there as well.

'You'll come back in the New Year ?' I asked, hoping to clinch that rainbow.

'You never know,' smiled Mona Lisa Donlan.

CHAPTER
ELEVEN

That Christmas Eve I drove down to Virginia Water to spend the festivities with young David, Pat and my soon-to-be-ex in-laws. By now Pat and I had decided it was best for both of us to make the break legally and get on with the rest of our lives. All of which we agreed to do in the New Year without a lot of fuss and bother. How naïve can one be? Without fuss and bother? Neither of us could have imagined the unbelievable series of tragi-comic surprises the English divorce laws had in store for us.

As expected, it wasn't the merriest Christmas for any of us, but for the sake of young David we all made the effort and entered into the Yuletide gaiety. My inner emotions were a mixture of sadness and guilt. Sadness, because this was the end of a youthful dream and probably the last Christmas we would spend together. Guilt, because I felt that somehow I should have been adult enough to handle things differently and stop that dream from disintegrating.

'All right,' said Jimmy Granger when I'd let it all hang out at his New Year's Eve party, 'so you weren't grown up enough to handle it. Maybe she wasn't, either. It takes two to tango, you know.' He glanced over his shoulder and steered me to the drinks corner. 'Matter of fact,' he confided under his breath, 'you probably know, it's a bit dicey with me and Elspeth, right now.' I didn't know. In fact, I'd always regarded Stewart Granger and his highly respected actress wife, Elspeth March, as the perfect couple. 'We're obviously not very good at these things, are we?' shrugged Jimmy, refilling his glass. 'Well, we just have to bite the bullet, mate.' He raised his glass. 'To a New Year resolution: from now on we all grow up and handle the rest of our lives better.'

Not long after, around the time he was shooting *Adam and Evelyne*, Jimmy and Elspeth were divorced. And he obviously broke no teeth biting that bullet because almost immediately he upped and married his co-star who happened to be, surprise surprise, my little protégée, Jean Simmons.

And what did the new year hold for the resolved-to-grow-up Guest? Well, an item in my old desk diary, written for some reason in red ink, recorded my mad desire to buy the latest 'in' thing on four wheels. Some inspired person had produced a vehicle called a Land Rover which had caused a mild sensation when launched at the Amsterdam Motor Show and almost overnight became a status symbol for débutantes, Sloane Rangers, Hooray Henrys and the whole of the huntin' shootin' an' fishin' set, which, of course, included Buckingham Palace. Now if Guest had bought a status symbol – but he didn't. Not because he'd grown up. No way. He simply couldn't afford it.

I'm sure any psychiatrist could explain why this less-than-shattering event seemed worthy of recording in red, rather than some of 1948's more important milestones. For instance, why hadn't I noted that on New Year's Day the government upped and nationalised British Railways? Or about the historic birth of the National Health programme? Or even the first jet aircraft to fly the Atlantic to Labrador? The flight I did note, however, in thick black capitals, was that of a British Overseas Airways Constellation which touched down at London Airport and delivered a certain Miss Yolande Donlan to London's St Martin's Theatre for the Clifford Odets play *Rocket to the Moon*.

And once again she captivated me and all those formidable London theatre critics. YOLANDE DONLAN THE CONQUERING BLONDE headlined the *Evening Standard*. 'Mr Odets can write and Yolande Donlan can act,' wrote that doyen of West End critics, Beverly Baxter. 'Her playing is one of the best things we've seen for a long time.' And the *News Chronicle*: 'No play could possibly be unenjoyable which contained Yolande Donlan,' said their hard-to-please Alan Dent, 'that radiant, sulky, dumb, shrewd, spry, spritely and wholly delectable nymph – Mr Odets himself would find her innocent impudence quite irresistible.' Sadly, Mr Odets would not have found the almost overwhelming verdict on his play quite as irresistible. 'One of those disappointing rockets,' summed up the *Daily Graphic*, while the *Observer* observed, 'In spite of Miss Donlan's performance the play falls flat.'

Maybe they had found it hard to come to terms with a play called *Rocket to the Moon* which turned out to be all about emotional undercurrents in a dentist's reception room. Added to which, some critics even dared to suggest that Peter Cotes, its young, pseudo-intellectual director, had been rather more pseudo than intellectual. Anyway, one evening, at the end of the second week's run, Jack Hylton dropped by Yolande's dressing room. 'Business is okay,' he announced with a wry grin, 'but they're only coming in to see you. They think the play's lousy. How do you feel about it? Shall we keep it running?'

Poor Yo. What a decision to fling at your leading lady. She had a long, hard think and then said, 'No, if it's all right with you, Jack. I mean, I don't want people coming to see me in a play that isn't giving them a fun evening.' Two weeks later *Rocket to the Moon* left its St Martin's launch-pad and disappeared into the deep blue yonder. Which meant that any minute its star would do likewise and already I was beginning to feel deprived. I puzzled as to how a person I'd met by sheer chance, from the other side of the earth, had affected me this way and in such a relatively short while. It seemed that for the first time I had experienced an uncanny sense of bonding with someone and couldn't pinpoint the reason. How come I felt we had so much in common?

Or did we? True, we both laughed at the same things, both had a sense of the ridiculous, both liked good food. On the other hand, she liked to dance; in fact, in her Hollywood days she'd danced her way through some of MGM's greatest musicals with Gene Kelly and the rest of them, whereas I could barely one-two-three my way through the basic foxtrot. Furthermore, Yolande loved the ballet and opera, which for me were still unexplored territories. So it was obviously none of these things. Yet there was an indefinable something else and I was about to lose it again.

It was then I had one of my all too rare flashes of brilliance. What if I wrote a film vehicle for her and found some backing? Would she stay and do it? 'Such as, and when?' laughed the practical Miss D when I put it to her over dinner at Le Caprice. I was currently shooting the second 'William' picture at Southall Studios. The first had done well enough for Dave Coplan and United Artists to ask me to make another, *William Comes to Town*. But although there was only one week of filming left I knew I could never dream up anything concrete for Yo for at least another month. 'It's a nice idea, Val,' she smiled, squeezing my arm, 'but I have to get back to Christopher. If the play had run I was going to have Terry bring him over. Chris needs his mom.'

'So do I,' I grinned. 'And at least in the meantime Chris has his father.'

She was silent for a long moment. Finally: 'Not really. That's over. Terry says he rarely visits him so when I'm working here he doesn't have a mother or a father,' she said quietly.

It took another long moment for me to believe my ears. 'You mean, the marriage?' She nodded. 'Why didn't you tell me?'

She shrugged. 'I don't know. I suppose it's trying to figure out whether it was him or me or my obsessive career thing. You can't have it all.'

That's when I took a deep breath, plunged into the deep end and asked if she'd stay on until the end of shooting to join me on a brief Côte d'Azur holiday at Cap d'Antibes, Eden Roc and the fabulous Hôtel du Cap. 'Come and hear Grandmère's native tongue again,' I tempted. This caused a lot of pondering, right through les desserts, le café and even l'addition. Then her rather sad face creased into the well-known Donlan smile and I knew she'd decided it was an offer she couldn't refuse. Luck was a lady that night and even our lucky waiter got a larger tip.

Cap d'Antibes was as wonderful as always, perhaps even more so because I was showing it to Yolande for the first time. And it helped that André Sella, owner-proprietor of the legendary Hôtel du Cap, greeted us with smiles, recalling the fact that I'd met him way back with my old chum Frances Day. I had also managed to book one of his famous cabañas down on the rocks above their small private jetty. Here Yo and I lazed between swims amidst the ghosts of past literary icons such as Anatole France, F Scott Fitzgerald (who wrote *Tender is the Night* about this very place), Erich Maria Remarque, George Bernard Shaw and many other greats who used this haven for scribbling in the sun.

Which brings to mind another du Cap summer when I was holidaying in one of these cabañas, trying to finish writing a screenplay. Across from me, in the next patio, was an actor-director who has long since gone into filmdom's folklore as Hollywood's homme terrible. His name was Erich von Stroheim and when he wasn't directing he usually played stiff-as-a-ramrod, monocled Prussian Generals or similar heavies and had become known, fondly, as The-Man-You-Love-To-Hate. In later years he turned up as Gloria Swanson's butler in Billy Wilder's *Sunset Boulevard*. Anyway, that day at du Cap his ramrod back was hunched over a writing pad as he sat there hour after hour desperately trying to finish his autobiography. 'There's so much of it,' he kept grumbling. 'Why did I do so fucking much?' Poor Erich, I'm afraid I wasn't very sympathetic. At least he was writing about the life he'd lived, he wasn't having to dream up a new screenplay. Today, as I sit here trying to pen these words, my heart goes out to him, albeit belatedly. Yes, dear Erich, wherever you are – it's tough!

I had another interesting interruption that day. Two pleasant young American gentlemen paused at my cabaña and waited until I'd stopped tapping on my portable Olivetti, at which point the good-looking one smiled and said, 'Sorry to interrupt, but how do we go about getting a cabin like this?'

'Ah, you have to track down a chap called Marcel,' I explained. 'He handles all the bookings.'

'We've done that,' he shrugged. 'There's none free until next week and we're off in a few days. Is he the final word?'

All at once I saw a glorious excuse to stop typing for a few days. 'I'm afraid so,' I told him, 'but look, I have this one for the rest of the week. If you just want to relax and get some tan you're welcome to share it. My name's Val Guest.'

'Mine's Walter Annenburg,' he smiled again, shaking my hand.

And share it they did. Walter, it turned out when he gave me his card, was in journalism; in fact, his father was an important American publisher. At the end of the week my two new cabaña sharers bade me a grateful farewell, headed for the Haute Corniche, pointed their automobile towards Switzerland and drove out of my life. I never heard of Walter again until one day, decades later, when the front page of my newspaper announced that Walter Annenburg had become the new American ambassador to London. Today, my erstwhile cabaña guest has long since retired, had a theatre and museum named after him, become a public benefactor and one of the most distinguished and seriously rich people in California. How's that for a 'little did I think'?

One way and another du Cap seemed to have a penchant for the unexpected. Like the year French couturier Louis Reard descended on the Eden Roc pool with a battery of photographers and a model wearing his latest creation, the world's first skimpy two-piece bikini swimsuit. It had already caused a sensation at its Paris fashion show début a month before, when it was modelled by a stripper from the famous Crazy Horse Saloon and promptly banned in Biarritz and several other French resorts. Now here he was, immortalising his creation at one of the most famous pools in the world. The model had made less than a half-circuit before the horrified management ordered a pool attendant to cover her with a beach towel, smuggle her into the changing rooms and pretend it never happened. Remember, all this was in 1948, long before topless beaches. In fact it's hard to realise that it was not until the sixties that the first bikini was even accepted in America.

I suppose my happiest du Cap surprise came on the last day of my farewell week there with Yolande. We were reclining on our matelas, impressed by the fact that no less than the Duke and Duchess of Windsor had just bestowed on us a courteous, regal nod en route to their yacht, when a voice hailed us from the surrounding woods. 'Ma'm'selle Donlan, s'il vous plait.' We knew it wasn't the Duke because it had a French accent and it turned out to be the ever-smiling Chef des Cabañas, Marcel. 'Téléphone, Ma'm'selle.'

Puzzled as to who knew she was in the South of France, Yo followed him to the phone in his hut. The caller turned out to be Aubrey Blackburn, her cosy, fatherly London agent with the jackpot of all surprises. London entrepeneurs Linnit and Dunfee wanted her to star in a new musical due to open at the Strand Theatre in a couple of months' time. It was called *Cage Me a Peacock*, based on Noel Langley's book of the same name, and was an ancient Roman frolic about the rape of Lucrece. Langley himself had done the stage adaptation and especially asked for Yolande to be his Lucrece. Since he was a highly respected writer of many novels, to say nothing of screenplays for such classics as *The Prisoner of Zenda*, *Svengali* and *The Wizard of Oz*, it had to be worth looking into.

'Undercranked' is a film term for everyone moving at double speed. Which is exactly how it felt on our return to London. While I rushed back to the studio to finish editing *William Comes to Town*, Yolande read *Peacock*, liked it, signed her contract, launched into singing and dancing classes, arranged for Terry, her mother, to bring Chris back to London and decided that if we were still to be nesting under one roof, which happily we were, my small mews flat was far too tiny for Chris as well. Not only was it good practical thinking by this remarkable young lady but somehow, in between costume fittings, singing lessons, dance rehearsals and learning her lines, she also managed to find us a great two-bedroom maisonette in Montagu Square.

Terry, of course, was delighted to be coming back to London, but not so delighted that her daughter was sharing an appartment with a member of the opposite sex. 'Do be careful, dear,' she wrote in one of her many warning letters, 'it could harm your career. Look what it's done to Ingrid Bergman.' And she enclosed a sheaf of press cuttings to show how the Swedish star had been pressured to leave America on account of her liaison with Italian director Roberto Rossellini. 'You don't want that to happen to you,' added the well-meaning Terry, obviously swept up in their current wave of popular Puritanism and unaware of the slightly less censorious attitude in Europe.

However, it did make me doubly aware of the fact that at the moment ours was not exactly 'a consummation devoutly to be wished' and I vowed to do something about my side of it right away. Our friendly studio lawyer advised me that the 'uncomplicated and friendly' divorce Pat and I had discussed should be no problem if I provided her lawyers, unofficially, with proof of infidelity and the name of the co-respondent. It was shock number one to find that English divorce laws decreed there could be no such thing as an unnamed co-respondent – all names had to be named. Which seriously cut down the field, since who in their right mind would want to be named publicly as a co-respondent?

Then for some reason I recalled that in Fred Astaire's *The Gay Divorce*, actor Erik Rhodes had played a 'professional' co-respondent. Were there such things in London? If so, where did one find them? They certainly weren't listed in the telephone directory or even the Classified Sections. So one night, in desperation, I stopped by Al Burnett's popular night club in Cork Street, the Stork Room. Al, who had played a supporting role in an earlier film of mine and was the brother of my friend, impresario Bernard Delfont, looked aghast when I asked if he could arrange for me to pay one of his girls to help out. 'Are you joking?' he asked incredulously. 'Have one of my girls in court? What kind of a name would that give us?'

I was still getting nowhere fast. Until my second flash of light. Paris! The Hôtel Vernet! Give the address and dates to Pat's lawyers, then have them check the register for proof I had indeed stayed there with someone. And Claude, our friendly concierge, would certainly confirm it all. The lawyers thought this was a splendid idea and evidence of those visits would probably be enough to prove infidelity without having to name anyone.

Back in the real world life was racing on. Yolande's rehearsals were in full swing under the masterful direction of Charles Hickman, one of London's top stage producers who was later to become one of our closest friends. The second *William* epic was finished, delivered, press-shown and premièred. In June *Cage Me a Peacock* opened at the Strand with a fanfare of enthusiastic reviews and, as usual, Yolande seemed to scoop the cream. And soon it became the 'in' show with celebrity-studded stalls. After one of those shows a celebrity sent his visiting card down to Yolande's dressing room. It announced: Sir William Russell Flint. The name meant little to Yo, but left me slightly awed. Russell Flint was not only President of the Royal Academy of Arts, he was also an internationally renowned watercolourist whose paintings hung in museums and collections worldwide. Invited to her dressing room, Sir William told Yolande how much he had enjoyed her show and wondered if by any chance she would allow him to paint her as Lucrece for the Royal Academy?

After a moment of initial shock we realised this was another offer she couldn't refuse. She posed for him over eleven sittings at his Peel Street studio and when the painting was almost completed Sir William invited us to a small celebration cocktail party. Which was where he took me quietly by the arm and led me behind a screen. On the floor, leaning against the wall, was the unfinished portrait of Yolande in her Lucrece costume. Even unfinished I found it quite breathtaking and told him so. 'Thank you,' he said with a twinkle. 'I haven't shown it to Yolande yet in case she says, "My God, the guy can't paint!"' And if you think that can't be topped, you are wrong. Not only was the portrait hung at the exhibition of the Royal Academy of Arts but it was also voted painting of the year. When Yo's mother, Terry, saw it, she said, 'I think you should buy it. It shows you at the height of your good looks. From now on it's all downhill, you know.' So today it hangs proudly above our fireplace.

Would that the rest of my year had proceeded so well. My 'uncomplicated' divorce had developed another glitch. And his name was Claude, our friendly concierge at the Vernet. Faced with the lawyer's investigator and a photograph of me, Claude had immediately sprung to my defence, launching into a fierce cover-up on my behalf! 'Non, m'sieur, he was not here... Non, non, le registre est privé... Non,

non, non, I have not seen him, met him, or heard of him… Wrong hotel, m'sieur…' Dear Claude, loyal to the death – the death of my second flash of light.

Chris and Terry were now in London, Chris living with us and Terry in a small apartment Yolande had rented for her a few doors away in Montagu Square. Here she would stay until she decided to go home to California. I recall when she did there were still some months left on her rental lease so we put the flat back on the market. One day Terry announced that a young man and his wife had viewed the place that morning and wanted to move in as soon as possible. 'He says he's an actor,' she told us doubtfully. 'Do you think he's safe for the money?'

'What's his name?' asked Yolande.

Terry rummaged in her handbag and peered at a slip of paper. 'Peter Sellers,' she read and wondered why we laughed. At that time Peter was still a radio comedian but currently in a highly successful BBC series called *The Goon Show*. 'I think we can chance being Peter Sellers' landlady,' said Yo. 'He's such a comic genius I'd almost let it for free. What am I saying?'

It was around this time that I received a historic telephone call from Bebe Daniels. Historic for me, that is, since it triggered off a most important event. 'Val, dear,' said Bebe, 'would you do Ben and I a favour? There's this old vaudeville comedienne who's worked for us – Ada Adair. She's having a rough time. Her husband just died, on top of which she's about to be dispossessed. Be an angel, take a look at her, maybe give her some bit in your next.'

When Ada Adair came to Montagu Square for her interview she turned out to be perfect casting for an old vaudevillian, or perhaps a barmaid at the local pub. Plump, with a bubble-cut of peroxide hair, she had a mildly brash, music hall personality and chain-smoked. After regaling me with her past triumphs she confided that she'd now be grateful for even the smallest part as she was already two weeks behind with her rent.

Andy Warhol once said everyone has their 15 minutes of fame, to which we might add that everyone has their one moment of instant genius. I had mine sitting in front of Ada Adair that day. 'Ada,' I said quietly, weighing every word, 'could you play a co-respondent?'

All right, so you're ahead of me. When I explained the situation and offered to settle her rent arrears if she played the role, in name only, for one night at the Russell Hotel in Russell Square, she almost crushed my hand shaking it.

My lawyer said: 'When you get to the hotel be sure you make yourself memorable.' Dreading the night ahead, I checked the two of us into the Russell just before midnight and started making myself memorable by knocking over the receptionist's flower vase. Once in our twin-bedded room I rang Room Service to see what food was still obtainable and eventually a cheery little grey-haired sparrow of a floor waitress brought us some ham sandwiches, a pot of tea for Ada and coffee for me. Chatting her up as I signed the bill, making sure I stood in a good light so my face would be recognisable later, I learned her name was Millie, Millie Brown, and that she was 'on' most nights and had worked for the hotel 'almost since it was built!' I congratulated her and gave her a memorable tip. Twenty minutes later I called her again for a packet of Ada's cork-tipped Craven A cigarettes, making a big point of the cork-tipped bit. This, I thought, could be another piece of memorabilia. Millie's second tip certainly was.

Ada, who had disappeared into the bathroom with her overnight bag, now reappeared in a dressing gown carrying a large book of press cuttings which she handed to me with a smile. 'Thought you might like to glance through these – some of my reviews…' Whereupon she climbed into bed, lit a Craven A and eventually coughed herself to sleep. Realising it was going to be a rough night, I rang for a fresh pot of coffee, gave another memorable tip to the unsinkable Millie Brown, who was steadily becoming my star witness, and spent the rest of the night slumped in a chair with Ada's press cuttings book catching up on her career. Through Southsea, Huddersfield, Hull, Leeds, Scunthorpe and most points west, she'd played them all. By dawn's early light, while she was still asleep, I left a cheque and a thank-you note on Ada's bedside table, crept downstairs, paid the hotel bill and hurried out of my demi-monde into le monde-entière, wondering how any civilised country could devise a law that drove people to such lengths to get an amicable divorce.

Now, are you ready for the postscript? I wasn't. 'Thank you for the hotel receipt and name of co-respondent,' wrote Pat's lawyer to my lawyer. 'However, in regard to witness Millie Brown our enquiries have shown she passed away last week.'

CHAPTER
TWELVE

It is hard to believe it took another six months before the divorce courts decided there was enough evidence to grant Pat and I our friendly dissolution papers and on a wet July afternoon we stood under our umbrellas outside the Chancery Law Courts, shook hands, wished each other good luck and two wiser and hopefully more adult people moved off into the summer rain to get on with the rest of their lives.

Meanwhile, Yolande's *Cage Me a Peacock* had now transferred to the Cambridge Theatre where it was still nudging house records. And that's when an Angel came into our lives. An Angel called Danny, or to give him his full title, Major Daniel M Angel. And Danny was quite a character. Grandson of Morris Angel, the well-known theatrical costumier, he had spent his early days in the family business 'peddling clothes to film producers' as he put it. And he had hated it, although he was fascinated by the industry. So it was almost a relief to him when war was declared and the army posted him to India as a gunner in the Heavy AntiAircraft Regiment, in which he ended up a major. It was no relief, however, when he suddenly contracted polio, a disability he had fought with tenacious courage, getting around with the help of two canes almost as fast as many people did on two legs.

I had previously met Danny through his father-in-law, Vivian Van Damm, another fascinating character who had devised, founded and operated the near-historical Windmill Theatre. During the war I had often written comedy sketches, routines and musical numbers for him and his theatre had become the spawning ground for many new comedians, from Jimmy Edwards to Peter Sellers. After the war the Windmill's proud slogan was WE NEVER CLOSED – and they hadn't. Throughout the Blitz and the flying bombs Van Damm had run his non-stop shows day and night for troops on leave and anyone else who needed some laughs and beautiful girls as respite from the city's devastation.

For anyone too young to remember those bygone days of raised eyebrows, the Windmill was the only theatre in London's West End that was allowed to stage nude tableaux. The Lord Chamberlain, our stage censor, had made a special dispensation for Van Damm to use nudity but only in the form of artistic tableaux in which the girls had to remain motionless. The Lord Chamberlain's ruling: 'If You Move It's Rude.' And I can assure you that Van Damm – or 'VD' as he was affectionately or scathingly known, depending on your relationship with him – ran a very tight ship. He tolerated no nonsense in his theatre and to ward off any criticism of the nudity in his shows he used his own beautiful daughter, under the stage name of Betty Talbot, as his most delectable nude. Hollywood later made a film about the Windmill called *Tonight and Every Night*, starring Rita Hayworth, in which they all kept their clothes on, obviously because the reigning Hays Office had decided that even if you didn't move it was still rude.

Incidentally, I recall that on the opening night of every new Windmill show the Royal Box was always reserved for one of the most popular members of His Majesty's Government, the Hon George Lansbury. He and his family seemed to enjoy laughing at the new comics and seeing so much effervescent youth frolicking around the stage, to say nothing of all those tableaux. It is also mildly interesting to note that the Hon George Lansbury happened to be Angela Lansbury's grandfather.

VD became Danny's father-in-law when his lovely daughter, Betty Talbot, stepped out of her tableau one day and became Betty Angel, the wifely power behind Danny's throne. But when he came into our lives he was still working on getting his throne together and it would have been a brave man who predicted he would later become the important producer of such prestigious films as *Reach For the Sky*, *Carve Her Name with Pride* and many more. But when we met he had only made some documentary shorts, having peddled an idea to no less a personage than His Majesty King George VI for permission to film *All The King's Horses*, followed by *All The King's Men* and *All The King's Musick*.

This was the Danny Angel who called on us one day in Montagu Square peddling yet another idea, this one from Phil and Sid Hyams of Eros Films. They knew that already, during the run of *Peacock*, Sydney Box had persuaded Yolande to make a guest appearance in the Ralph Thomas film *Travellers' Joy* at their Lime Grove Studios and the Hyams had asked Danny to find out whether she would be interested in starring in her own film for them before she returned to America. If so, was there any particular subject that interested her?

The truthful answer to the last question was 'No', but I had long ago learned never to admit there is no 'subject' because if the worst came to the worst you just sat up all night and wrote one. Which is how Yolande Donlan's first tailor-made British film came into being. I just sat up several nights until I'd written the outline of a story for her, *Miss Pilgrim's Progress*, the tale of an American girl on an exchange visit to a little English village where she helps them save their sleepy, picture-postcard hamlet from the town planners. The next happy ending was that Yo liked it and so did the Hyams brothers. What's more, subject to script and availability, my old chum Michael Rennie agreed to co-star.

The next question was who would produce our epic? 'You,' said Danny. 'Not possible,' I told him 'I can't do that *and* write and direct. What's wrong with *you* producing it?' Danny's face was a picture of startlement. 'Me? Oh no, no,' he insisted firmly. 'I couldn't handle a full-length production!' But he did. And that was the launching of Daniel M Angel as a feature film producer. 'How soon can we start?' he asked excitedly, flushed with the scope of his new decision. 'Well, first I have to write a screenplay,' I told him, 'then we'll have to wait until Yolande is clear of *Peacock*.'

Poor Danny: here he was raring to go, wearing his brand-new feature-producer hat, and I'd just rained on his parade. I tried to explain that while it had been easy for Yo to 'guest' her way through the Ralph Thomas film with sequences all shot in Lime Grove Studios, *Pilgrim* would be a 90 per cent location job and, with Yo as Miss Pilgrim, she'd be in most of it. We'd be filming in some out-of-the-way country village and logistically, to say nothing of physically, it wasn't feasible to expect her to do a show every night, plus two matinées and all that travelling.

Danny nodded gloomily and with a frustrated sigh went home to commiserate with Betty. Twenty-four hours later he was back on our doorstep, grinning like Einstein must have done when he'd solved his relativity problem. 'What about the Windmill?' he beamed.

I looked at him blankly. 'What about it?'

'A film about it,' he enthused. 'While we're waiting for Yolande. So far the old man's been dead against filming it, turned down all kinds of offers, but he knows you and of course he knows me, so if you had the right story I think I could talk him into it.'

'You mean make it before *Pilgrim*?'

'Why not?'

It may sound crazy but that is what happened. Once more, to keep Danny's new career from marking time until Yo was ready for him, I sat up all night creating a musical-thriller called *Murder at the Windmill* and presented it the following morning. By noon Van Damm had given it his blessing and somehow I finished the screenplay in just over a week, taking another to compose the songs while Danny went ahead and raised the funds.

Within a month of burning that first midnight oil, with a cast of Jimmy Edwards, Garry Marsh, Jon Pertwee, Diana Decker, swing organist Robin Richmond and Sam Livesey to play 'Van Damm' – plus of course, the Windmill Girls, choreographed by the talented Jack Billings – we were off to the races! What's more we shot the whole one hour 40 minute musical at the theatre itself and Nettlefold Studios, in 17 days dead. Which is pretty much how we all felt at the end of it. But at least we'd blazed a trail for Rita Hayworth. Happily the picture turned out to be a popular success and they've even preserved a print in the National Film Archive as a piece of contemporary wartime history. As to its box-office, although it wasn't exactly up with *Gone With the Wind* and *Titanic*, it more than repaid Danny's moneymen who were now almost eager to pour some of it back into *Miss Pilgrim's Progress*.

By the time *Peacock* had closed and I'd completed a script for *Pilgrim* it was obvious there was no way we could start production that year, so it was to be 1950 before I made my first picture with Yolande. And, to be honest, I began it with a few secret qualms about directing someone with whom I was so close. Should we travel to location in separate cars? Would we be able to shut off the day's work coming home at night? And, as her director, would she be comparing me with Larry Olivier or Charles Hickman? All wasted worries. She turned out to be as professional in her work as she was responsible in her life and it became the first happy milestone in the six films we were destined to make together.

For our picture-postcard village we found a dreamy little place called Turville, nestling away near Aylesbury, where I surrounded her with my regular rep company and one newcomer, a good-looking young Canadian to play the US Consul. His name was Arthur Hill, it was his very first film and it turned out to be a milestone for him, too. Not only was he inducted into our rep but later it led to him playing opposite Yolande in another Garson Kanin play, *The Rat Race*, for the BBC. Which in turn led to Gar being impressed enough to whisk him off to play opposite Ruth Gordon in the Broadway production of the Thornton Wilder classic, *The Matchmaker*. From such little acorns big careers can grow and from then on Arthur's just grew and grew, collecting, among other tributes, a well-deserved Tony Award for his performance in *Who's Afraid of Virginia Woolf?* Our nice, quiet, talented 'new boy' had now made the biggest of Big Times.

On our last night of location shooting, under a full Turville moon and a sky full of winking stars, I walked my leading lady across the jasmine-scented village green towards our car and popped the $64,000 question. 'Yo-Yo, darling,' I whispered, 'I've had a great idea. To stop your mother sending us all those cuttings about Ingrid Bergman, why don't we just get married?'

In spite of the moon, the stars and the jasmine, my offer was gently but firmly turned down. Poor Yo, still coming out of her own marital trauma, she wasn't ready to even think about getting into any more knots for a while. And how long was 'for a while'? Well, I remember proposing to her regularly over the next four years. On a Sussex farm shooting *Mr Drake's Duck* with her and Doug Fairbanks; in the Spanish Pyrenees on location for *Penny Princess* with Dirk Bogarde; in her dressing room at the Vaudeville Theatre after the opening night of *Red-headed Blonde*, a play I'd written for her. I even proposed to her one Saturday in a New York taxicab racing to the airport to get us back to England in time for Monday morning shooting on *The Men of Sherwood Forest*, a film I was in the middle of making at Bramber Castle in Sussex! No one can say I didn't plight my troth persistently. And just as persistently my troths were lightheartedly rejected. Her down-to-earth reasoning being that with Chris and the two of us so cosy and content in our Montagu Square nest, why rock the boat?

'Anyway, I can't afford to get married,' she laughed one day. 'Tax-wise, with both of us working, we're better off single. Maybe one day, when the Church and the State get together...' I had to admit it was a sound point, but there comes a time when even the most ardent swain has to try and put his foot down. I'm sure even Romeo would have lost his cool if, after four years of balcony scenes, Juliet was still giving him a hard time. So one morning, four years and two dozen or so proposals later, I brought Yo her morning breakfast in bed, stretched out beside her, propped myself up on one elbow and said, slowly and distinctly: 'Earth calling Yolande Donlan – this is a global warning. Today is the last day of this astounding offer!'

By some miraculous chance it pressed the right button and almost before I'd realised it, Yo laughed, squeezed my hand and actually said 'Yes'. Of the many momentous utterances recorded in history, this one, for me, out-historied the lot of them. That same day I raced ahead organising a secret wedding at the nearby Marylebone Town Hall Registry Office. We wanted to avoid any publicity because, having lived together for so long, most people thought we were married already. Craftily, I slipped a five-pound note to the Registrar to keep our names off his Forthcoming Marriages board. Which he did. Then, even more craftily, he called the *Daily Express* to tell them what he'd done and they slipped him another one. The cat was now well and truly out of the bag. But more of that 'secret' wedding later.

Montagu Square was a cosy little community with its own railed gardens where Christopher used to play with the rest of the local children. We had a mixed bag of interesting neighbours ranging from high-powered government nobility, Lord Mancroft, to the equally distinguished Jeanne de Casalis, actress extraordinaire, ex-star of the Comedie des Champs Elysée and now a doyenne of the English theatre. Jeanne was an amusing character who always seemed to be throwing lunch parties for her royal friend Princess Alice, or her near-royal chums the Oliviers. As a matter of interest, when Larry and Vivien were illicitly courting, they had hidden in Jeanne's country house to do so.

But the best of all our neighbours lived at the far end of the square: Dr George Crosby and his retired actress wife, Vi. Over the years this warm, friendly couple were to become two of our best friends, George as our cosy family doctor and Vi as one of Yolande's closest girlfriends. Vi Crosby was a memorable lady. A fine cook, a great hostess and fun company, she would have made a wonderful mum, just like my own Vi in Winchester Road. Having no children of her own, she lavished all her love and encouragement on a very young nephew named Andrew and in doing so was largely responsible for launching him into musical history. If it were up to me there would be a Vi Crosby plaque on the wall of that Montagu Square house because but for her we might never have heard of the Andrew Lloyd Webber he grew up to be. Today we have a large coffee-table book in our house titled *Andrew Lloyd Webber, His Life and Works* and on the fly-leaf Andrew has written, 'To Val and Yo – the entire content of this book is questionable!' But one thing we know he didn't find questionable was the fact that even in the first chapter of the book there is a photograph of his beloved Aunty Vi.

Although Andrew came from a musical family, his father being no less a personage than William Lloyd Webber, director of the London College of Music, it must have been somewhat daunting for him to grow up in the shadow of such a musical pinnacle. Especially when Daddy writes church music and sacred songs while you seem to get turned on by Elvis or Bill Haley and His Comets. The trouble was that as young Andrew's collection of these records grew, so did his family's vague feeling of disappointment that he wasn't spending his pocket-money on the classics instead. But not Aunty Vi. Always happy to let him rock around the clock, she encouraged him to be his own person, have his own likes, do his own thing and grab whatever grabbed him. And it was Vi who introduced him to the theatre. When he was ten years old she took him to see his first stage musical, *My Fair Lady*, and —wham! – he was grabbed. Suddenly this wide-eyed child had an ambition and from then on I don't think there was a stage or film musical he didn't see, some more than once. In fact I think he saw *South Pacific* 12 times.

Andrew first came into our lives through the Crosbys, who by now were almost part of the family. He was then all of nine years old and one of the first things he said to Yolande, almost by way of introduction, was, 'Hullo, I'm going to write musicals.' The nine-year-old oracle had spoken. He was then a pupil at Westminster Underschool from whence he graduated to Westminster proper. As a 16-year-old student with a bright mind but not all that dedicated a scholar, he revelled in his moments of composing the odd musical score for the school pantomimes, one bearing the immortal title of *Cinderella Up the Beanstalk*. And then one day, to everyone's surprise, including perhaps his own, he won a scholarship to Magdalen College Oxford. Everyone was jubilant. Everyone except Andrew. To him, Oxford was just something that had come up to stop him writing musicals and he didn't want to go. Even Vi was unable to convince him and one day, tentatively, she conscripted Yo. 'Please, Yolande, will you talk to him? I'm sure he'll listen to you.'

What wouldn't I give for a tape of Yolande's fireside chat with Andrew. She had tried to explain to him how tough it was to earn a living just writing musicals, so it might be smart to have some other job to fall back on if the musical end didn't work out. And what better place than Oxford University to give him the groundwork for this? Whether it was Yo's homily or not, something somewhere must have rung a bell for in the autumn of 1965 Andrew did go to Oxford. Now, I know they say you can't un-ring a bell but something certainly un-rung this one because suddenly, just before Christmas, Andrew decided he'd been there, done that and promptly dropped out of Oxford for good.

So, after he'd made his first million writing musicals... No, no, I'm joking, it really wasn't that easy. For instance, I well remember the evening Andrew and his new writing partner, a cheery young lyricist named Tim Rice, dropped in to see us on their way back from Riverside recording studios. They'd brought us the demo LP record of their new brainchild. It was called *Jesus Christ Superstar*. Yo and I listened to the tracks and were carried away by their originality and innovation. Somehow they'd rustled up the finance to record it with the help of some singing friends and wondered where to go from here. Was there any hope of using it filmwise? 'I'm sure it could make a great and unusual film,' I enthused. 'In fact I'm going to take this LP to Elstree first thing tomorrow.'

Early next morning I played it for Elstree's head of production who, because I bear no grudges, can remain anonymous. 'Are you mad?' he asked. 'A musical about *religion*?' The head man at Pinewood told me, 'Oh, come on Val, can you imagine a swinging Christ at the local Odeon?' After trying Shepperton, MGM and even the Danzigers I'm afraid I gave up. Which, to tell it as it was, is how Yo and I lost our first million.

However, we couldn't complain about *Miss Pilgrim's Progress*, which had a successful London première and, true to form, Yolande collected most of the adjectives. Next morning I spread the critics' reviews over the bed. 'Don't you ever get *bad* notices?' I kidded. 'Of course,' she said with a straight face, 'and I hide them from you.'

It wasn't long before Danny Angel popped into our lives again. 'How soon can we make another one with Yo and Rennie?' he asked.

'You mean next year?'

'No, this year – while they're still hot.'

Every scribbler has faced that dreaded moment called writer's block, when the mind goes as blank as the paper and you're not even capable of writing a suicide note. Author John Steinbeck said he used to handle his by going around the house sharpening all the pencils to their finest points. It must have worked or he wouldn't have given us classics like *East of Eden*. However, I didn't think sharpening my four pencils would help the writer's block Danny Angel had left me with. Dream up and launch another film before the end of the year? In two words, no way.

Then suddenly a spark relit my pilot light and I started to think sideways. Sometimes the impossible becomes possible, especially if it gives a reason to stop the one you love from leaving the country again. Somehow the brain goes into overdrive and you're able to come up with a piece of lighthearted nonsense like *The Body Said No*, a comedy-thriller with music, set in a BBC TV studio. Which, miraculously, I did manage to write and shoot that same year. Whereby hangs a tale. In fact, two tales.

In one of our musical numbers we needed six dancing girls to back Yolande in a dance routine with Jackie Billings. We held an audition at the Prince Edward Theatre in Soho, which was attended by dancers from current West End musicals. It was one of the girls from the Cambridge Theatre's hit revue, *Sauce Tartare*, who seemed to stand out way above the others. Not because she was taller or her dancing any better, but her personality, smile and general attraction put her at the top of my pick list.

'OK, luv, you're in,' said George Fowler, my First Assistant, pencil poised. 'What's your name?'

'Audrey,' she smiled.

'Last name?'

'Hepburn. Audrey Hepburn.'

'And who do we talk to, luv?'

'Me,' answered a man's voice from the shadows. It was Cecil Landau, her escort and producer of *Sauce Tartare*. 'Audrey's one of my dancers,' he explained. 'How long will you need her?'

'Three days,' I told him, 'four at most. And don't worry, Cecil, I promise we'll get her off early enough for the show.'

'All right,' he nodded, 'but you'll have to give her a car.'

A car for one of the dancers? Mildly staggered, I explained this was impossible: next thing I'd have five other dancers wanting the same thing. 'Look,' he said firmly, 'filming all day and seven shows a week I'm not having her worry about public transport. Sorry, Val, no car no deal.' Which is why Audrey Hepburn never danced behind Yo in *The Body Said No*. Many years later, when Audrey was an international star and we met after some première or other, I recalled the story and it made her laugh.

'Funny, I often wondered why I never got that job,' she grinned. 'Had I known, I'd have made Cecil drive me!'

The second tale concerns the location shooting we did one night in Albion Mews, a picturesque residential hideaway near Marble Arch. As usual on these occasions the unit had been told to make as little noise and commotion as possible because, even though we had all the necessary permissions, one irate resident could wrap us up for the night. We had just finished the first long shot, a taxi pulling up and depositing Yolande, when a window opened noisily above our camera and a man's pyjama-clad top leaned out.

'What are you making?' he called down.

My ever-alert assistant hurried forward. 'We're just shooting a couple of scenes, Guv,' George smiled up at him. 'We'll be away before you know it.'

The golden rule of location shooting is to butter up the locals, charm them, soothe them, woo them, if necessary bribe them, but somehow or other keep the peace until you've finished.

'You film or TV?' probed the pyjamas and suddenly saw Yolande. 'Oh my!' he exclaimed and shut the window with a bang.

As we set up the next shot I was vaguely aware that somehow the man's face was familiar. And then it clicked. He was an actor named Geoffrey Sumner. I'm afraid the name won't ring a bell unless you were traipsing around during World War II. At that time Hitler had a renegade Englishman with an over-posh accent who did short-wave German propaganda broadcasts telling us to surrender, or else. In England he was derisively nicknamed 'Lord Haw-Haw' and Geoff Sumner had found fame doing a very funny take-off of Haw-Haw on radio, TV and the music halls.

We had just moved in for the close-shot of Yo paying the driver, when Sumner's front door swung open and there he stood in his dressing gown, clutching what looked like a script. 'Hullo,' he beamed, 'I'm Geoffrey Sumner.' And then to Yolande, 'Excuse me, Miss Donlan, I have a play I'd love you to read – it's perfect for you – written by a friend – in fact he wrote it for you – would you mind?' Whereupon he handed it to a suprised Yo who, with her usual charming smile, thanked him, handed it to me and went back to study her current script. I handed the play to George who handed it to his Second Assistant who put it in the back of my car. Where it remained for two weeks until I found it quite by chance while searching for something else. Which is just how close we came to missing a play that was to become the comedy hit of the London season and a new triumph for Yolande and Richard Attenborough, running well into its second year.

That evening, while Yo's mother Terry was preparing our dinner, I began reading the manuscript and even the first few pages had me laughing. 'What's so funny?' interrupted Yolande.

'This play – and I've only read a few pages.'

'Am I on yet?' questioned the practical Miss D.

'No.

'Then why are you laughing?' she asked with a straight face and insisted I read it aloud. Before long she, too, was laughing so much she sat on the floor doubled up as Terry popped in and out with her kitchen mitts to join the merriment. Was it just us, or was the play really that funny?

It was called *To Dorothy A Son*, was written by a virtual newcomer, Roger Macdougal, and there were only three characters in it: A husband, his pregnant wife Dorothy, who never appeared on stage, being a 'voice off' for the entire play, and his American ex-wife who drops in unexpectedly. With only two people on stage from beginning to end it was a challenging undertaking, but Yo liked it so much she decided to take the plunge, gave it to impresario Jack deLeon and offered to co-present it with him. To stage it they engaged Peter Ashmore, who had already distinguished himself directing the best in British theatre: Peggy Ashcroft, Wendy Hiller, Robert Morley, not to mention several of our of knights and dames. They also chose Richard Attenborough to hold the stage with her and Sheila Sim, Dickie's real-life wife, as the pregnant 'voice off'.

During rehearsals I remember a truly Marx Brothers routine regarding pre-London tour billing. 'Naturally,' said Attenborough's agent, 'his name will come first and on the left.'

'Not so,' replied Aubrey Blackburn, Yolande's agent. 'My client must have top billing.'

'Look,' arbitrated deLeon, 'I have a great idea. We put a flying stork on the billboards, left wing down, right wing up. So Dickie's name is down on the left wing and Yolande's up on the right wing. That way you both win your position.'

'Oh, come on!' laughed Yo when they put it to her. 'Let's share it. One week Dickie, one week me. Who cares?'

It has never ceased to amaze me how first or second billing troubles so many actors and actresses. Worry about the role, the director or even the money, but about first or second billing? Which reminds me, less than a year later I was to get an even funnier request. I'd written a film for Yolande and Douglas Fairbanks Jr called *Mrs Drake's Duck*.

'Douglas loves the script,' said producer Danny Angel, 'but wants us to change the title.'

'To what?'

'*Mr Drake's Duck*.'

We did. I wonder if Warren Beatty ever thought of changing his to *Clyde and Bonnie*?

To Dorothy A Son opened in Birmingham followed by an eight-week tour with the usual surgery, a nip and a tuck here, an implant there, good days, bad days and all those nightly inquests. The last pre-London date was Bournemouth, a lovely town where audiences were predominantly genteel retirees, known in theatre parlance as the 'grey and white' matinées. Yo and Dickie found them unresponsive. The big laughs had become titters and the titters had become deafening silences. Some of London's top managements hurried down to see the new play as did Laurence Olivier's entourage – his close friend, costume and set designer Roger Furse, with his personal manager Anthony Bushell. None of them seemed too impressed. 'My dear Yolande,' said Roger Furse afterwards, 'you go to London in this and next thing you'll be playing the cat in *Dick Whittington*.'

After the show that evening we gathered for a gloomy nightcap in the hotel bar. 'I don't agree with any of them,' I told Yo, Dickie and Sheila. 'It's a very funny, classy light comedy and you can't let Bournemouth be your last judgment. Half of them can't hear and the other half are too busy explaining what they missed.'

Dickie Attenborough shook his head. 'Well, I for one don't want to go in with it. Yo?'

Before she could answer I said, 'Okay, but make sure you all get seats for the opening night and watch someone else make a smash hit.' They looked slightly stunned at my outburst. Finally Dickie's face twisted into a wry smile. 'You bastard,' was all he said and I knew I'd won.

Not long after that, as Fate would have it, London's Savoy Theatre became available. After more decisions and more inquests they decided to move in, only to find there was still one more river to cross. Director Peter Ashmore, who was later to become one of out dearest friends, had retired from the fray with jaundice. So who would stage it in London? 'How about you?' threatened deLeon, daring me to say no. Which is how I ended up in the Savoy Theatre, on a cold November night, waiting for our first curtain to rise. Backstage, Dickie Attenborough stood in the wings ready for his first entrance. 'Never mind,' he sighed philosophically. 'It'll pay for the Christmas turkey even if we don't last till New Year.'

And up went that first night curtain on a halfway reluctant cast who could never have envisaged the reception they were about to get. Standing at the back of the stalls I, too, was holding my breath, until the first gale of laughter engulfed me, followed by another, and another. Suddenly I was laughing as well, but mine was a pent-up, almost maniacal laughter, realising my head was no longer on the chopping block and my predictions had been fulfilled.

As for Yolande, Dickie and Sheila, by the end of the first act they couldn't believe what had hit them. Gone with the wind were those grey-and-white memories of Bournemouth. It had worked in London! The audience howled and the critics raved. What's more, *To Dorothy A Son* became so much a part of the Savoy's history that even as I write these words they still have a cartoon of Yolande and Dickie Attenborough in their programmes.

And what of the rest of our friends during that funny, frenetic year? Well, Bea Lillie filled London's Café de Paris with a hilarious new cabaret act and dear Noël wrote, composed and directed his latest revue *Ace of Clubs*. Whereas Vivien winged her way to Hollywood to set them all on their ears again with

A Streetcar Named Desire while Larry O was impressing everyone in *Venus Observed* at the St James'. As for our old *Born Yesterday* chum Garson Kanin, as though to top them all, he not only revised the libretto of *Die Fledermaus* but went ahead and directed it at New York's Metropolitan Opera House!

Yes, that was a busy year, that was.

CHAPTER
THIRTEEN

My First Assistant, George Fowler, was quite a character. Small, verging on the chubby, he had a dimpled smile and was a warm, friendly personality who seemed to be able to handle everything and everyone. I had met him on the first *William* picture, at which time he was personal secretary to associate producer Buster Collier. 'He's dying to work on the floor,' Buster had told me then. 'He's a great organiser and I'll miss him like hell, but are you game to give him a try?' I was, and I did. Since when George had been on all my films and together we'd battled through the usual studio dramas, traumas, hold-ups and hiccups. Somehow he always seemed to be unflappable. Until the day Her Majesty Queen Elizabeth II bestowed a knighthood on Douglas Fairbanks Jr for 'furthering Anglo-American amity'.

We were a couple of weeks away from shooting *Mr Drake's Duck*, a lighthearted satirical comedy about Mr and Mrs Drake (Douglas and Yolande) honeymooning in their new farmhouse, and how her casual nod to someone at an auction unwittingly buys them two dozen ducks, one of which later lays an atomic egg and has the world's major powers fighting over it. Told like that at a story conference there would be a quick 'Thank you and goodbye', but it turned out to be a fun picture and, even today, is still a popular holiday re-run. If you happen to catch it sometime you'll see what I mean.

The Fairbanks 'knighthood' had received a barrage of press coverage and the reason I put it in quotes is because unless one is a British citizen it is an honorary title which does not bestow the right to use 'Sir' in front of one's name, although some do it unofficially. Non-Britons are dubbed Knights Grand Cross of the Most Honourable Order of the Bath, or Knights Commander of the same order, which allows them to put the letters KGB (not the Russian one!) or KCB after their names as many Americans have done, from Reagan, Bush, Schwartzkopf and Colin Powell to one of the more recent recipients, Bob Hope. As a matter of fact, Hope was actually born in Eltham but, as he explained later, left for America the moment he realised he could never be King.

So what was our George's problem when he came to me one morning, his usually unflappable face full of flap? 'Fairbanks,' he started without preamble. 'I mean, what do we call him, Guv? I mean, after all this? Is he Mr Fairbanks or Sir Douglas? I mean, I've got to warn the unit...' The sheer unexpectedness of the question made me laugh. Of all possible hazards at the start of a new production, this had to be the funniest. 'Your best bet,' I advised him, 'is to go and ask Fairbanks himself.' Doug Jr greeted George's question with the same merriment. 'Call me whatever you like,' he laughed. 'I answer to Douglas, Doug, or hey-you-in-the-blue-suit!'

Still concerned, George reported back to me with his next protocol puzzlement. The studio chair. What should they paint on the back of it? DOUGLAS FAIRBANKS JR or SIR DOUGLAS? Yolande happened in on the end of this bit and, playing it dead straight, announced, 'Listen, if he has "Sir Douglas" on his I want "Dame Donlan" on mine.' Which at least took care of the chairs.

We found Doug a joy to work with, professional to his well-manicured fingertips, always punctual, knew his lines and took the good-natured ribbing about his recent honour with charm and good humour. If we had any trouble at all it was trying to get him to Buckingham Palace on time. Buck House, as it was fondly known, seemed to be his second home these days thanks to his close relationship with the Royal Family, most of that closeness being with Princess Margaret and this time there was no need for a Palace fire escape.

From our farmhouse location in the village of Steyning, near Worthing, it was a good two-hour drive to Buck House so, on his Palace nights, I would try to arrange the day's shooting to speed him off early for his royal 'do', dinner or dance. On those mornings when his limousine brought him to location, it would sweep him up the long farmhouse drive with his bemedalled uniform jacket hanging in the car window. After a while I found this too hard to resist, so one morning I had the whole unit line both sides of the drive and as he swept by we all saluted that decorated jacket. Nobody laughed louder that Doug. Whereas Mrs Fairbanks would not have laughed. Mary Lee Fairbanks, formerly Mary Lee Hartford, the A & P heir, took the 'knighthood' business extremely seriously.

I well remember the night Yo and I were having drinks with some of the cast in our Worthing hotel bar. Present was the one and only AE 'Matty' Matthews, Jon Pertwee, Reginald Beckwith and the inimitable Wilfrid Hyde White when Mary Lee Fairbanks made her first entrance. With a gracious smile she crossed to our corner and announced, 'Hello, I'm Lady Fairbanks.' Without a moment's hesitation Willy Hyde White was on his feet offering a hand. 'Enchanted,' he smiled, 'and I'm Lord Hyde White.' To this day I don't know if she realised he was sending her up but we saw very little of Mary Lee after that.

As for Doug Jr, his popularity with the crew followed him back to the studio where, for a little surprise, the art department had built him a small portable 'den' which he could move from set to set. It contained a couch, an armchair and a small table on which, pretty soon, there was a telephone and a framed picture of Princess Margaret. One day, between takes, the voice of the studio switchboard girl reverberated over the stage tannoy. 'Telephone call for Sir Douglas Fairbanks,' it boomed. 'Would Sir Douglas please come to the telephone… Hurry, Doug, it's urgent!' Even Fairbanks fell about.

Incidentally, at a recent film festival an interviewer asked me, 'Of all the actors you've worked with, do you have a particular favourite?' He was surprised when I put Doug Jr in my top three, along with David Niven and Roger Moore. The reason being that all three of them made hard work fun. Had they asked me about actresses I might have surprised them even more. I've enjoyed working through a colourful assortment including Jean Simmons, Deborah Kerr, Bebe Daniels, Bette Davis, Margaret Lockwood, Claire Bloom, Joan Collins, Ursula Andress and Olivia Newton-John, to name but a few. So, my top three? Well, of course, working with Yolande was always my first joy and the next two — take a deep breath — were Ursula Andress and Bette Davis.

Apples and oranges? Not really, because they were both unusually professional, down-to-earth ladies. Ursula was nothing like the sexy, sultry screen siren she usually portrayed but had a zany humour, a delightful sense of the ridiculous and never took her 'most beautiful woman in the world' tag seriously. I recall a couple of moments on our Bond film, *Casino Royale*. We were on the casino set with 200 tuxedoed extras and Ursula in a close-fitting white evening gown. Just before a two-shot of her and David Niven I noticed she had dropped into a relaxed habit of hers, rounding her shoulders. 'Okay, let's shoot it,' I said, 'and Ursula – shoulders back, push those bosoms out.'

In front of the crowded set she turned to me with gloriously regal hauteur and said, 'You dare to talk like that to the most beautiful woman in the world?'

Collapse of crew, cast and crowd. On another occasion, after her contract had finished, I was down in the South of France using her double to shoot some location scenes when, on returning to the unit hotel one evening, there was a message to call her Berne home in Switzerland. When we got her on the line all she said was: 'Hello. Do you love me?'

Wondering what was coming I answered, 'Of course I do.'

'Then why aren't I down there shooting pro rata?' asked the down-to-earth lady.

Bette Davis? What can I say about Bette that hasn't already been said or written? Fun? Yes, once you got to know what she was all about and until then an exhilarating, never-a-dull-moment experience I wouldn't have missed for anything. As it was I could easily have missed it altogether if MGM's romantic heart-throb, Robert Taylor, hadn't been in Rome making a film, as well as a German actress named Ursula Thiess. Let me tell it as it was.

Shortly before we finished *Mr Drake's Duck* Danny Angel handed me a play called *Deadlock*, written by Leslie Sands, which he thought might make a good film. After reading it I agreed. It was a tense, tight melodrama about a woman who plans the perfect murder of her husband and ends up caught in her own trap. Danny, having had his first taste of using a Hollywood name, hoped this might be a good enough role to entice another one. He was right again and I knew just the person I'd like to write it for, a long time favourite of mine, Barbara Stanwyck. Stanwyck could play high melodrama like nobody else, she simply 'played against' it, played it down and made it all 100 per cent believable, witness her acclaimed perfomance with Fred MacMurray in Billy Wilder's now almost legendary *Double Indemnity*.

The very thought of working with one of my acting idols inspired a screenplay out of me in record time. And because, for some reason, no one seemed to like the title *Deadlock*, we changed it to *Another Man's Poison* and, thanks to the help of our new chum Doug Jr, we were able to bypass agents and dispatch it direct to the lady herself. Less than two weeks later we learned we'd hit the jackpot. Stanwyck liked the script and agreed to fly over and do it provided that before she started we let her make a surprise Christmas visit to Rome and her working husband Robert Taylor. Never was a contract agreed with such alacrity and an elated Danny went ahead booking his studio space for the new year. Which is when the gods stopped smiling on us.

A surprise Christmas it certainly was for Bob Taylor. 'Knock, knock, guess who's here?' And guess who answered the door. Correct. There and then Stanwyck decided she must go home immediately and start divorce proceedings. She telephoned us. 'There is no way I can come to England now. I have to get home right away.' In vain we tried to convince her it would be good to come over and work, take her mind off things for a while. But she didn't want to take her mind off anything. The following year she divorced Robert Taylor and he married his Fraülein. Which may have solved their problems but we still had ours. Here we were with a studio, unit, half the cast lined up and no star. This was obviously time for a shot of 'instant genius'. A Hollywood icon had just arrived in town, fresh from her triumph in Billy Wilder's *Sunset Boulevard*. Gloria Swanson had checked into the Savoy Hotel. Almost before she'd had time to unpack her eyelashes I was sitting in front of her. A tiny but striking lady, Swanson listened to me intently as I outlined the story. Then her large eyes seemed to blink in slow motion and I was almost expecting 'Ready for my close-up, Mr DeMille.'

'Macabre,' she murmured, 'but the subject that could really interest me is if someone would only make *The Strawberry Roan*. Have you read it?' I said I hadn't. 'It's about a woman who falls in love with her horse. Magical,' she purred. 'I'll send you a copy. Meantime, leave yours, I'll try to read it.'

Reporting back to Danny I was met by a glum face. 'You can forget Swanson,' he said. 'Distribution don't want to know. They say she'd empty theatres.' Back to square one. Luckily we were also back to Doug Jr who had become so involved with the project he now wanted to co-present it with Danny. 'Don't worry,' he told us, 'I'll take it back to the coast with me and see what we can come up with.'

And up he came with Bette Davis. She'd read the script, loved it and didn't want a word changed, he told us on the phone from Beverly Hills, and that went for husband Gary Merrill who was ready to play her screen husband. But there were three provisos. One: The deal would include transport for family and nurse. Two: She wanted her own director, Irving Rapper, with whom she had already made *Now Voyager* and *The Corn is Green*. Three: If possible she would like an Academy Award cameraman. All of which were reasonable and acceptable. The only slightly worrying thing was 'She didn't want a word changed.' Hopefully this was only meant as a compliment because it was obvious that a melodrama written for the subtle talents of Stanwyck would have to be toned down for the volatile talents of Miss Davis or we could end up with Grand Guignol.

I put this to Fairbanks, who understood but cautioned me to tread gently at all times. After all, he reminded me, the first lady of the American screen could at times be, how should he describe it, a trifle tricky. Then Danny Angel had a brilliant idea. Why not call my old friend Paul Henreid, who had starred with her in *Now Voyager* – he could give us a few do's and don'ts. 'Bette?' laughed Paul when I phoned him in California. 'She is a child.' Which was the last description I expected to hear. 'An insecure child,' he elaborated. 'Suspicious of new people. She's spent all those years getting up there and she figures any one of you could ruin it all. But get her confidence, Val, and she's a dream. Great fun. Please, give her my fondest.' Spoken like a true psychologist, but not a word about how to get the Queen of the Screen's confidence.

Our first meeting was at the Savoy, where Danny had arranged for her to stay until nearer production when Gary and the family would arrive. I found her a vibrant, instantly likeable, no-crap type of lady with smiling x-ray eyes searching for any hint of trouble. She also seemed to have a raucous sense of humour about everything except herself. Later, as we trod warily thought the minefield of my script refurbishments, she was unexpectedly co-operative. Until I told her about one of the British censor's objections. A line in which she told the police, 'My husband whipped me', about which the censor had written: 'We cannot allow the word WHIPPED, the connotation is sado-masochistic.'

For a brief moment Bette looked stunned. 'Is *what*?' she asked in that Davis voice.

'Look,' I said quickly, 'don't worry, it's an easy change...'

'I don't want it changed. It's a powerful line!'

'You could say "he hit me" or "he struck me"...'

'He *struck* me?' she spat. 'What am I, a boy scout for God's sake?'

'Okay, so we'll shoot it "he whipped me" for America and then "he hit me" for the UK.'

Her back straightened and her shoulders squared off. 'We will not,' said Miss Davis decisively. 'I have been engaged to make *one* picture.'

End of first script conference.

When Irving Rapper finally came to that scene he shot the two versions without any trouble, except for her comment on the British censor. 'I suppose we mustn't shock the poor man,' she shrugged. 'He was probably flogged at Eton.'

I don't know about the censor at that time, but a later incumbent, John Trevelyan, was never flogged as far as I know and, though a rather lean, gaunt-faced man whom many said looked perfect casting for the part, he was in person a friendly, mild-mannered and understanding soul aware of our problems as well as his own. I certainly wouldn't have wanted his job, having to tread the thin line between the public's acceptability and susceptibility. It is interesting to note that while the English found violence obscene and were open-minded about sex, the Americans appeared to be wide-open about violence and almost puritanical about anything remotely sexual. Which is why, in those days, you would so often hear the director say, 'Great, cut, print, now one for America.'

Any kind of nudity seemed to give them an attack of the vapours and even today they still paste stickers over pubics and airbrush bare backsides. I remember in the David Niven film, *Where the Spies Are*, much of which we shot in Beirut, I used a well-known Lebanese belly dancer whose bare navel sent the whole of the MGM hierarchy into a state of apoplexy. Within an hour of viewing our 'rushes' a top priority memo was delivered to the studio's optical department ordering them to digitally superimpose a rhinestone on every frame of that undulating navel.

I had another amusing skirmish with the American censor on a film called *The Full Treatment*, a psychological thriller set on the French Riviera. It included a scene in which a hot and depressed Diane Cilento, pacing the beach in the middle of the night trying to calm her fears, spontaneously slips out of her jeans and takes a nude swim in the Mediterranean. As was our custom, a copy of the script had already been sent to American censor, Eric Johnston, and back had come his swift reply: THE SCENE IN WHICH DENISE SWIMS IN THE NUDE IS COMPLETELY UNACCEPTABLE. SHE MUST OF COURSE BE FULLY CLOTHED. I couldn't resist cabling back: IS IT ALL RIGHT WITHOUT GLOVES AND HAT? And once again it was a case of 'Cut, print, now one for America.'

John Trevelyan's view of nudity was that if it was an intrinsic part of the scene and story he had no objections. If it was pulled in for the sake of sensation or voyeurism he was en garde with scissors at the ready. I remember how mad Laurence Olivier was when Trevelyan frowned at the nude Britannia in his film of John Osborne's *The Entertainer*, having already passed the nude tableaux in my film of *Expresso Bongo*. It did no good trying to explain that Larry O's Britannia appeared in a music hall act simply for a laugh, whereas our *Bongo* tableaux were the background to a legitimate Soho strip-club in which Laurence Harvey chats up Sylvia Syms, the show's leading lady.

I was once asked how one talks stars into baring all. The answer is, of course, one doesn't. They decide for themselves, having read the script, been satisfied there's a valid reason and whether they want to play the role or not. In my 60-odd years of filmmaking I probably had nudity or partial nudity in half-a-dozen pictures with not the slightest star problem. Correction, one slight moment, albeit an amusing one, with a worried Claire Bloom.

The picture, *80,000 Suspects*, with Claire, Yolande and Richard Johnson. The story, about a frightening smallpox epidemic in the city of Bath, had Claire playing a hospital nurse whose estranged husband, Richard Johnson, is a doctor in the same hospital. A crisis of such enormity demands all hospital staff fumigate their clothes and take decontamination showers before leaving the building. Due to nursing pressure, the decontamination times for doctors and nurses are changed and Richard, not knowing this, walks in on his showering wife. A moment which sparks off the rekindling of their romance. Claire had nothing against the scene as such and was quite happy to do the shower close-ups wearing a bra just below camera. But she was worried about the longer shots. Could she have a double? Of course she could. And could she help choose her double? Delighted. So one day, after shooting, four be-robed 'Claire' doubles were brought on to the set by the wardrobe mistress and we all bundled into a stage caravan. One by one they disrobed to show Claire their figures and after a brief, whispered consultation we chose one. But it was a strangely silent Claire who walked back across the stage with me. Suddenly she slipped an arm though mine.

'You know something?' she said quietly.

'What?'

'I have better boobs than that.'

'Meaning?'

'Hell, I'll do it!'

And she did. Needless to say we had no such problems with Bette Davis and the only things she bared were her royal fangs a couple times. One such occasion occurred in the studio projection theatre where Hairdressing, Make-Up and Camera had gathered to view her first hair and make-up tests. True to his promise Danny Angel had procured her an Academy Award cameraman in the person of the great Robert Krasker. Bobby Krasker had won it for his outstanding work on Carol Reed's *The Third Man*, in which his inventive shots of bomb-scarred post-war Vienna both above and below ground in the sewers had held filmgoers spellbound.

It was unfortunate that the night before these make-up tests Bette and husband Gary had been celebrating or commiserating a trifle too exuberantly. Next day Bobby Krasker had struggled valiantly with his gauzes and filters to compensate for the damage. The tests were now being screened, with Bette and Irving Rapper in the front row. After a few moments of silent viewing there were disapproving noises in the front. Then Bette's querulous voice pierced the darkness.

'And for *what* did this man get his Academy Award?'

From somewhere at the back of the theatre a voice answered, 'For shooting ruins.'

How can I describe the eternity of the next few nailbiting minutes? The breathless hush of the Bastille Day mob waiting for the first head to roll? The declaration of World War II? I can only tell you there were a lot of tongues being bitten and breaths being caught waiting for an explosion to top Hiroshima. But it never happened. Instead, la Davis rose silently, turned her back on the screen and made a truly regal exit from the darkened theatre.

Well, of course, there were profuse apologies from every department followed by flowers, candies, toys for the kids, soothing bottles for the parents and an assurance that the culprit had been severely reprimanded. After which Bette, like the old pro she was, seemed to take the incident in her stride. And although no one ever divulged the identity of the voice I think she had a shrewd idea it belonged to a junior technician with whom she'd had an earlier brush. Was she right? Well, just as Watergate's famed Woodward and Bernstein still won't disclose the name of their so-called 'Deep Throat', I feel the same about our so-called 'Smart Arse'. Not only because he has always regretted his youthful moment of folly, but also because he has since grown up and won his own Academy nomination.

There is a PS to this tale. The following year, when Yolande and I were on a Hollywood casting expedition for *Penny Princess*, Bette invited us to her large, typical early California-style family home. Typical, that is, except for all those Oscars scattered about, one even used as a doorstop. After lunch, as we all sat around the pool, she suddenly turned to me with an unexpected glint in her eye and said, apropos of nothing, 'I'm thinking of using another Academy Award cameraman for my next production. Arthur Edeson. Know him? '

'I don't think so.'

'And do you know what he got his Academy Award for?'

'I'm afraid not.'

'For shooting *Frankenstein*,' she answered and hooted with peals of raucous laughter. It was the first time I'd ever heard her laugh at herself.

All in all it had turned into a vintage year for me and somewhere along the line I'd also written a musical for Vera-Ellen, Cesar Romero and David Niven, *Happy-Go-Lovely*, which American director Bruce Humberstone was at that very moment shooting on location at the Edinburgh Festival, bagpipes and all. It was also the year we were invaded by some of 'The Hollywood Ten'. Headlined as such, they had all been blacklisted by their own industry after being branded as Communists. Since we no longer had Nazis to hate it had been decided to hate the Communists even more and America had taken it to extremes. In Washington an overbearing, over-righteous, over-patriotic zealot named Senator McCarthy had been running a Communist witch-hunt, pulling in some of Hollywood's most talented actors, writers and directors and labelling them as dangerous un-American threats to democracy. Half of these had now emigrated to Britain where they hoped they could still earn a living by working under assumed names.

Amongst them were some heavyweight talents. Like Dalton Trumbo, with top screenwriting credits as long as your arm with titles such as Ginger Rogers' *Kitty Foyle*, Spencer Tracy's *A Guy Named Joe* and Katharine Hepburn's *A Bill of Divorcement*. He even served a ten-month jail sentence for refusing to testify before the House Un-American Activities Committee about his alleged membership of the Communist Party. Why do I find it droll that while in jail he actually managed to smuggle out scripts for underground sales using a pseudonym? Perhaps the biggest lunacy of all was in 1956 when his story for *The Brave One* collected an Academy Award for someone called 'Robert Rich'.

Writer-producer-director Carl Foreman was another of our London immigrants. Carl had already given us great film archive material in *Home of the Brave*, *Young Man with a Horn* and *Cyrano de Bergerac*. Now listed as 'un-American' he wasn't even allowed to receive either of his two Oscars, one for the screenplay of the epic *High Noon*, the other as co-writer of *Bridge on the River Kwai*. Then there was director Joseph Losey. When Joe settled here and made his first English film, *Sleeping Tiger* with Dirk Bogarde, on the credits he had to use producer Victor Hanbury's name as director. Incidentally, film buffs might care to notice on those same credits the screenplay was credited to 'Derek Frey' – who happened to be Carl Foreman. All of which, in this day and age, seems slightly ludicrous to say the least. Especially since poor Carl had to wait until he was dead before the Academy finally granted him both Oscars posthumously.

Not so our old prankster friend Hitchcock. His film *Rebecca* had already won 'Best Picture' in 1940 and although he'd been nominated for 'Best Director', he hadn't won it. But now he'd just made a new thriller, *Strangers on a Train*, which was receiving such raves everyone was convinced it would bring him his first Academy Award. In view of this I couldn't resist writing a suggested acceptance speech, which I cabled him for a laugh. It went: 'My thanks to all of you for this great honour. I would also like to add that but for the constant help of my agent, my manager and my family I could have won this years ago.' Knowing Hitch, he might well have used it had he won. Five years later, when he did win it for *Psycho*, he'd probably lost my notes anyway, which perhaps was just as well.

CHAPTER
FOURTEEN

Some people remember 1952 as the sad year we lost our much-loved King George VI, or the happy year Egypt's corrupt and degenerate King Farouk was deposed and fled the country before they could string him up like Mussolini. Other Senior Citizens may even recall that nostalgic July day when London's last tram clattered through the capital's bus-filled streets. And who could forget that gem of film folklore, Stanley Donen's *Singin' in the Rain* with the incomparable Gene Kelly.

The rest of us old-timers may well recollect different events to pinpoint this particular anno domini. As for me, I always think of it as the year Yo and I tried to help a young singer named Frank Sinatra restart his flagging career. 'The year you did *what?*' I can hear your snorts of disbelief, so I had better start from the top.

The Rank Organisation had asked me to find another film vehicle for Yolande so I'd written a lighthearted fantasy called *Penny Princess* for her and a yet-to-be-cast co-star. It was the story of a young New York shop assistant who, through the death of a distant relative, suddenly finds she's inherited a small European principality in the Pyrenees and is now their Head of State. On arrival she discovers the entire economy of her new kingdom is based on a potent, home-made produce called Schneeze, a mixture of Schnapps and cheese, which they smuggle across the borders into France, Spain and Switzerland. I'd based the story on the little principality of Andorra where smuggling rights, as I've mentioned before, were actually handed down in the family. However, on my short location recce I realised the governing Andorran Council weren't at all happy about the idea, so I renamed our principality 'Lampidorra' and arranged to shoot it elsewhere. More of which later.

So here we were, looking for a light romantic comedy co-star to play Fortnum & Mason's food department buyer sent to suss out the saleability of Schneeze. Cary Grant? Bob Cummings? Michael Wilding? I even sent a script to Montgomery Clift, hoping maybe he'd like to change gear for a moment. His brief but pleasant reply had ended, '...thanks for the script, thanks for the thought, Europe would have been fun but dates alone make it impossible. Regards, Monty Clift.'

Okay, next please. Cary Grant was his usual charming, amusing self, bought us a lunch at 20th Century, offered to loan us one of his automobiles for the rest of our stay, wished us good fortune with our venture and got on with his busy life. Bob Cummings happened to have married an ex-dancer who way back had been in the same Earl Carroll show as Yolande and would have loved to join us in the Pyrenees but was so involved in planning *The Bob Cummings Show* for TV we might have to wait for the millennium. As for Michael Wilding, his agent said no one had even had time to read it yet.

One evening in the Polo Lounge of the Beverly Hills Hotel we were having a little ponder about things when in walked another of Yo's old buddies from her Carroll days. His name was Howard Snyder and for many years he'd been one of Bob Hope's top gag writers. Right now, he told us over drinks, he'd written some patter for Frank Sinatra who was about to try out a new nightclub act at the Ambassador Hotel's Coconut Grove.

'Frankie's had a rough ride lately trying to restart his career and he's thrilled to get the date.'

'Are you serious?'

Howard shrugged. 'That's how it goes – you're in, you're out – you're a phase, you're a phizzle, you're old hat and the bobby-sox are screaming somewhere else.' Apparently Sinatra's career had really hit one of those lows. It seemed his voice had suddenly haemorrhaged, his agents MCA had dropped him and he'd even lost a recording contract. 'At the moment he needs all the help he can get,' added Howard. Then suddenly, 'Listen, want to be a couple of friendly faces at the ringside opening night? I have a table and he'll need friendly faces around that floor.'

Which is how Yolande and I came to be at the Coconut Grove the night Frank Sinatra launched his comeback act and it was a surprisingly small audience, although he had quite an act. Not only vocally but for Howard's patter material with which Sinatra sent himself up. 'It's difficult to please everybody,' Frank told the audience with a grin. 'When you're up in the bright lights and get a longing to revisit your old home-town, you go back and the inhabitants stare at you and say, "What are you doing back here, slumming?" And when the lights aren't quite as bright, you go back and they say, "You're only here because nobody else wants you." There are times when you can't win.' The whole act had such charm and humour he completely capti-vated that sparse Coconut Grove audience which, hopefully, might bring in other worthwhile bookings. Then, out of the blue during an orchestra break, Howard said 'This actor part you're looking for. Would Frank be any good?' Seeing the look of blank surprise on our faces he added, 'I don't know the character, but it would do Frank a power of good to get away right now and I think he might go for it.'

It took a while for the off-beat idea to sink in but the more we thought about it the more we felt it might work. After the show Howard told Sinatra, who said it was a great idea and we could call him 'collect' from London anytime! Two days later we were winging our way back to Pinewood Studios and our executive producer, Earl St John. 'I think we can get Frank Sinatra,' I told him.

He looked at me, puzzled. 'Frank Sinatra? What can we do with Frank Sinatra? He's finished. Won't sell a ticket, Val. Why aren't we thinking of Dirk?' Dirk was Dirk Bogarde, one of their contract play-ers. Why weren't we thinking of Dirk? He was one of the best and most sensitive actors, winning all sorts of critical honours for dramas like *Boys in Brown*, *The Blue Lamp*, *So Long at the Fair*, but in those days one didn't immediately think of him as a light comedian. 'So you can lighten him up,' said Earl. 'Get him a good tailor, give him some square shoulders. Why don't you test him?'

It escaped me what square shoulders had to do with lightening somebody up but we tested Dirk with the shoulders he already had and, of course, he was great. In later years I was amused to read his account of all this in one of his autobiographies. 'Poor Val,' he wrote, 'he wanted Cary Grant and got me.' Dear Dirk, it wasn't poor Val at all. Dirk was not only a joy to work with but he and Yo made an endearing, fun couple. But what about poor Frank Sinatra sitting by his phone waiting for our collect call? You need-n't feel sorry for him either because not long afterwards he managed to talk his way into a supporting role in *From Here to Eternity* and promptly won an Oscar for it. What's more, as Frank confessed later, he did it for 'the almost insulting fee' of $8,000. Just think of the deal Earl St John might have struck.

Penny Princess was quite a milestone for us, being the first film to be made with our own company.

During the run of *To Dorothy A Son* Yolande, Tony Beckwith and myself had decided to form Conquest Productions and, like it or not, from there on I would be wearing three hats as writer, director and producer. As producer one of the first contracts I signed was with a much-in-demand costume designer named Beatrice Dawson. It had been Tony Beckwith's idea. 'If you want someone really fabulous for Yo's clothes try and get Bumble Dawson,' he said. Seeing the blank look on my face, he added, 'Bumble Dawson – her real name is Beatrice but everyone calls her Bumble. She's mostly theatre, Vivien Leigh won't do a play without her and Larry uses her too. She does all the big ones,' he laughed. 'See if she can do Yo.'

After such a build-up what else could a new producer do but contact her? Luckily the busy Bumble was between 'big ones', who had also included Marlene Dietrich. Thus another memorable character came into our lives, not only as a costume designer for so many of my future films but as a dear friend and one of Yolande's closest buddies. In her late fifties, with a chubbily round face, Bumble always wore extra-large spectacles which sometimes gave the impression of a friendly owl. I'm sure Roget's Thesaurus would give us many adjectives to fit this delightful lady but let's just say she was worldly, sophisticated, amusing, at home with king or commoner and somehow seemed to know someone somewhere no matter what out-of-the-way country we happened to be in. Except, of course, 'Lampidorra'.

For our tiny, fictional principality we chose the small, picturesque sheep-rearing village of Montseny, high up in the Spanish Pyrenees. It had no electricity so we sent our generators ahead to supply it. As for the plumbing, the word 'basic' would be a wild exaggeration and our always inventive property department produced buckets punctured with holes for everyday showers. Our one lifeline to the outside world was in the tiny hosteria, an ancient wall telephone which looked like Graham Bell's 1876 research model with a side-handle to wind in the hope of waking an operator on the other end.

Otherwise, we were a happy crew of filmmakers bringing daily amazement to the wide-eyed villagers and struggling with the usual foreign location gremlins. For a start, our cameras had been held at the border by Spanish Customs so our first week's filming was nada. Then Rank made an unsuccessful attempt to use some of their frozen Barcelona pesetas and the unit's first weekly pay envelopes were also nada. Which is when Yolande decided everyone needed cheering up, marched our English unit to the nearest fonda bar and showed them how to click their fingers and heels and dance flamencos with the locals. It was also when I put on my new producer hat and told the director, 'Somehow we have to pick up shooting-time this week.' And wearing my director hat I told the writer, 'What sort of clot are you to dream up this kind of location?'

My production manager brought me the next eye-opener. 'The village insurance,' he said. 'We're going to be over budget.'

'I thought they'd already agreed the figure.'

'That was for people. This is for sheep.'

'What have sheep got to do with it?'

'In Montseny they're worth more than people.'

Knowing how Yolande and I felt about our dog Figaro, I conceded they could have a point. That evening the whole unit turned out to cheer the camera trucks which at long last were clattering into the village square. Next morning it was all systems go and we were off on our first independent production. The sheer relief of no longer just sitting around seemed to spur everyone on to superhuman efforts and we even picked up the week we'd lost. Our only minor problem was organising the crowd scenes we needed. The entire village population plus half our unit would have raised barely 50 people and I needed at least a hundred for my night scenes of Lampidorrans smuggling their contraband Schneeze up the mountains and over the borders. It was obvious we would need people from surrounding villages but the only way to contact them was to send someone up there by mule cart.

Then the redoubtable George Fowler came up with a brilliant idea. Get word to the villages that the night before we needed extras, Montseny's padre would ring his church bells as a signal that there was work for anyone who showed up in the village square at 7.30 the following morning. The padre agreed to help out and George's scheme worked wonderfully. Until the evening the local fonda owner was married and after the ceremony, what else, they rang the wedding bells. At 7.30 next morning there were nearly a hundred extras in our village square who all had to be paid off. The Production Office scurried about trying to scare up enough pesetas as we kept little extra cash in the village because Montseny's solitary policeman had advised us not to. 'Peligroso!' he had warned. 'Bandidos en montanos!'

Which was sound advice because any mountain bandit would find a visiting film company irresistible bait. So every Friday our accountant would drive down to Barcelona, pick up the week's cash and drive back, closely followed by a heavily armed posse of Spanish policea. Giving us one more unexpected budget heading: POLICE PROTECTION.

However, I still have the happiest memories of *Penny Princess*, made even happier by a fun cast led by Dirk and Yolande with the rest of my merry rep company who were fast becoming a family: AE Matthews, Peter Butterworth, Reggie Beckwith, Desmond Walter-Ellis, Kynaston Reeves, Edwin Styles, Laurence Naismith, all of them on their way to further glories.

But perhaps my most abiding memory of Montseny is the night we shot the smuggling scenes. Under a brilliant full moon I was shooting a wide-angle shot of the mountainside covered with climbing villagers, sacks of contraband Schneeze slung across their shoulders and Schneeze-laden mule carts navigating the twisting mountain roads. It was a most impressive scene, until four pairs of headlights suddenly swept across and ruined it. Two Guardia Civil cars and two Policea vans screeched to a halt behind us, disgorging a wave of uniforms, half of which fanned out over the mountainside, the rest of them racing after the carts. Within minutes the Policea had corraled our mountaineers and the mule carts were surrounded by Guadia Civil. The reason? News had spread about our night smuggling scenes and under cover of the arc lamps and general production activity we'd been infiltrated by real smugglers who were doing their own thing as part of our crowd. Someone had tipped off the Policea and here they were putting término to my night's filming. We shot it again the following night, under Guardia Civil supervision which gave us another unwanted budget heading: SMUGGLING COCK-UP.

Returning to the soothing chaos of Pinewood Studios we found we'd missed the opening of Noël's new play *Quadrille* at the Phoenix with Alfred Lunt and Joyce Carey which had been a great success, even without the help of Yolande's photograph on the piano. However, we came back just in time to be caught in London's unprecedented four-day 'killer fog', so named because it actually caused the death of over 4,000 people with its deadly mixture of oxide and sulphur fumes from coal smoke. It would be another two years before the government passed the Clean Air Act which banned the burning of any more untreated coal.

But for happier memories I recall Yolande deciding on an early present for my upcoming 41st birthday. To celebrate it, she would take me to Covent Garden to see her idol and friend, the Royal Ballet's prima ballerina assoluta, Margot Fonteyn. It was then we learned the sad news, not only had Margot injured a foot, she was also battling a prolonged bout of diphtheria, which had played havoc with her performance schedules. But now, defying doctors' advice, she was determined to return in one of her favourite ballet pieces, *Apparitions*. What courage, what stamina, what a lady!

Yolande and Margot had become friends after they met by chance at a small cocktail party given by our good friends Leslie and Evelyn Kark. The Karks owned and operated the prestigious Lucy Clayton Model Agency and that evening the world's greatest ballerina had weaved her way across the room to say how much she had laughed and enjoyed Yo's performance in *To Dorothy A Son* and how she'd seen all her shows starting with *Born Yesterday*. Yo was stunned and delighted, the more so because she had long been one of Margot's devoted admirers and told her so. After which the two had become fast friends. They had a lot in common as well, both having started their careers in their early teens, worked hard and become the sole support of their families. Margot was a truly delightful person and, just like Yolande, had a contagious sense of humour.

I still laugh at the wonderful story she told against herself and the legendary Perle Mesta. This formidable lady was the US ambassador to Luxembourg and gloried in being known as 'The Hostess with the Mostest'. In fact, Irving Berlin's Ethel Merman musical *Call Me Madam* was written about the redoubtable Perle. Her parties and balls were consistently graced by the greatest talent currently available, with whose work she always claimed to be au fait. It was at one of these celebrity-studded evenings that Margot was a star guest. One by one each new arrival was announced by a liveried major-domo and one by one they stepped forward to be greeted by the smiling ambassadress. 'Miss Margot Fonteyn!' boomed the major-domo. Margot walked forward, Perle Mesta grasped her hand warmly and gushed, 'Miss Fonteyn, it's an honour and a privilege to have you with us. I just can't wait to hear you sing.' Before Margot even had time to smile the major-domo was booming the next arrival. 'Miss Maria Callas...!' Margot told us that sadly she was unable to hear whether the Hostess with the Mostest had said she just couldn't wait to see Callas dance.

It would have taken a Nostradamus to predict that on a cold February night, exactly ten years later, Yolande and I would be sitting in Covent Garden's Royal Opera House for the opening of Margot's *Giselle* in which she would be dancing for the first time with a brand new partner, a young Russian defector who had escaped through the Iron Curtain to freedom in the West. His name was Rudolf Nureyev. And what a night that was. If it isn't in *The Guinness Book of Records* it should be. Has anyone else ever taken 23 curtain calls? Well, that night Margot and Rudi did just that and it went into the annals of ballet history.

But back to fog-bound London. As Ira Gershwin wrote: 'A foggy day in London Town, it had me low and it had me down.' We'd come to the end of another non-stop year which was about to be topped by a hard-to-forget New Year's Eve Fancy Dress party at the home of theatredom's favourite cartoonist, Arthur Ferrier. Not that one would forget any of Arthur's New Year's Eve parties because, apart from the one at the Albert Hall, they were among the best year-enders in town. Pre-party weeks would find London's theatrical costumiers bombarded with requests for toreadors, Orientals, Hawaiian or clown outfits for the evening. But this particular one has stayed indelible because of what happened ahead of the party, rather than at it.

First, let me tell you a little about Arthur Ferrier. Every new London stage production worth its salt would hope to see a Ferrier cartoon of the show in the following Sunday's *News of the World*. He not only drew a great likeness of the great but added his own amusing comments about them. Later, his drawings would become collectors' items and some of the originals of Yolande's shows are hanging on our walls to this day. His New Year guest lists resembled pages from 'Who's Who in Show Business' and, unlike Perle Mesta, he not only knew what they all did but had sketched them doing it. It was considered something of an accolade to be on one of these lists and, since Arthur and his fun wife Freda were two of our longtime buddies, we were on them. In fact, over the years I'd turned up there disguised as everyone from Fu Manchu to Groucho Marx. Security at these affairs was always tight and there were guards at the entrance denying admittance to anyone without a printed invitation.

This year, a week before New Year's Eve, we still hadn't received the invitation Freda had said was in the mail. So I telephoned her. 'Oh no!' she cried. 'You too? That bloody office boy, he's forgotten to post half the invitations! Just come, anyway. Arthur will warn them at the door.'

'You know what?' said the ever-practical Yolande when I relayed the message. 'I believe they've invited too many people and this is their diplomatic way of losing some of them. I think we should help out and stay home.' Which we did. But around six o'clock on New Year's Eve a nagging thought began to trouble me.

'Look, Yo,' I said tentatively, 'if I hadn't already called Freda I wouldn't worry, but now they're expecting us, don't you think it might look rude if we don't show up?'

Yo stared at me open-mouthed. '*Now* you tell me! At this hour! How can we show up? We don't even have any costumes to wear!'

'Couldn't we dream up something or other, from somewhere or other...?'

Yo took a deep breath before hurrying upstairs to Christopher's room, returning with an armful of props, two of which she thrust on me. 'Here's a headband with feathers and a tomahawk – you're an Indian,' she told me. 'And pin the Navajo rug on you.' For herself she'd found a cowboy hat, a holster, an ammunition belt and a couple of spurs. It wasn't long before a cute-looking cowgirl and a war-painted Indian brave set off for the Ferrier abode. My feathered headband kept hitting the car roof so I took it off. My Navajo rug wasn't too comfortable either because of the safety pin under my crotch. Eventually we arrived, a little late, but happy to have made it. The car valet took our vehicle while I explained to the security guard that Mr Ferrier was expecting us so would he nip in and confirm it.

'Put your feathers on!' hissed Yolande as we waited. I did as she bade and raised my tomahawk to complete the picture, at which moment the door opened to reveal Arthur in his dinner jacket. But that wasn't all it revealed. Behind him was a room full of people in faultless evening attire.

'Oh, my God,' said Arthur, trying not to smile at the be-feathered Indian with a tomahawk standing on his doorstep. 'You didn't get the invitation. It said this year we weren't going to... Never mind, come on in as you are...'

'Oh no, no way!' said Yolande quickly. 'We'll go home and change.' And home we went, not without some prickly comments en route. 'You couldn't check it wasn't Costume tonight?'

'Yo, be fair – why would I check when it's always been Costume? Just try and think how we'll laugh about this in years to come.'

'Well, I'm not laughing now.'

'It won't take us long to change.'

'Change? I'm not going back there.'

But we did go back and strangely enough no one seemed to have noticed our first visit. Except for Michael Wilding, who later in the evening tapped me on the shoulder and said, 'Happy New Year, Val. Weren't you here earlier as an Indian?'

It so happened that come the new year another Indian would become a talking point but this was an Asian Indian from Nepal and, unlike my one-night-stand on the Ferrier doorstep, his one-night-stand went into the history books. His name was Tenzing Norgay and he was the Indian Sherpa who in the merry month of May, with New Zealander Edmund Hillary, stood on the summit of Mount Everest, the first two people ever to do so.

'Now there's a script in that,' said Earl St John over lunch one day at Pinewood after the story broke.

With a straight face I asked, 'For Dirk to play Tenzing or Hillary?'

'Neither,' said Earl, his face just as straight, and then with a smile, 'Nor Sinatra. Someone like Gregory Peck.'

'Are you serious?'

Earl shrugged. 'Show me a script.'

I can't imagine Gregory Peck ever wondering why the Rank Organisation never asked him to climb Everest for them, but the simple reason was that no one ever wrote them a screenplay to send him. I certainly didn't. Instead, I decided to do my bit towards making it a year of historic 'firsts', took a sabbatical from dreaming up screenplays and launched into trying to write my first play for the theatre. Having read some of the playscripts managements had sent in for Yolande's consideration I thought, with inexcusable conceit, that I could write one at least as good as some of them, so why not try and keep it in the family? At worst it would be an exciting new challenge. Yolande was unaware of my foolhardy decision until one day she dropped by the office, saw me tapping away on my faithful Olivetti and asked, 'What are you working on?'

'A play.'

'Whose play?'

'Mine.'

For a moment she looked at me as though I'd announced I was writing a sequal to *Hamlet*.

'Why a play?' she asked in a voice she might have used at a counselling session for Cretins Anonymous. 'That's not your scene, don't waste your time, get on with your film scripts where you know what you're doing.'

Nevertheless, over the next few weeks I continued to work on it surreptitiously. I called it *Red-headed Blonde* and it was about a Hollywood blonde bomshell who had rocketed to fame after singing and dancing on screen with Gene Kelly in a couple of hit musicals. And how a London theatre impresario, loosely based on Jack Hylton, announced his coup of the year by bringing her to London to star in his new West End musical, only to find that in real life the blonde bombshell was not only a redhead but could neither sing nor dance, having been doubled in the Kelly films for both accomplishments. So now they have the chaos of attempting to give the poor girl singing and dancing lessons trying to ready her for opening night while attempting to hide it all from the press. I thought it might be a fun vehicle for Yolande and as soon as I had a finished playscript I sent it to Jack de Leon with whom we'd done *To Dorothy A Son*. A couple of days later Jack called me.

'I like it it,' he said. 'When is Yo free to do it?'

'Yo doesn't even know about it yet.'

'Doesn't even know about it?' echoed de Leon.

'No. You see, Jack, I want this play to come to her from a management and not from me.'

Which left someone else thinking I was cretinous. But he did as requested and one morning I carried our usual breakfast tray up to the bedroom and put it on the bed together with the morning mail, amongst which was a large envelope from the de Leon office. Yo looked at it curiously, turned it over. 'Now what's he found?' she said, opening it with the butter knife. And out popped my play. Glancing briefly at the title without registering the playwright, she thumbed idly through the pages, chuckled a couple of times and turned back to check the fly-leaf. Which is when the penny dropped. After a moment spent digesting the awful truth, she laughed loudly. 'You stinker!' was all she said before she went ahead and read it.

Which is how, with perfect timing, my first play came to open at London's Vaudeville Theatre on April Fools' Day. What's more I was lucky enough to get Yolande and Naunton Wayne heading a sparkling cast of light comedians including Lionel Murton, Jerry Desmonde, Anthony Oliver and an ambitious young choreographer named Lionel Blair in his first acting role. We also managed to get our old friend, director Charles Hickman, to give it his usual sophisticated touch and, although by no stretch of the imagination could it be called a 'historic first', it was an evening of fun and even more fun the night Gene Kelly himself came to see it.

'I was told your play mentioned me at least a dozen times, so I came to see if I could sue,' he joked afterwards, adding, 'That's why I brought my lawyer,' indicating the person coming into Yo's dressing room behind him. His 'lawyer' turned out to be none other than MGM's icon of screen musicals, Arthur Freed. The prodigious Freed had not only produced such film landmarks as *Broadway Melody*, *Meet Me in St Louis*, *An American in Paris* and *On the Town* but had also written songs for them, classic standards like 'I Cried for You', 'Our Love Affair', 'Singin' in the Rain' and too many others to mention.

Yo was surprised and delighted to see them. Even more so because the last time they met she had been Arthur Freed's youngest contract dancer at MGM, dancing around and about Gene Kelly and Lucille Ball in *Dubarry was a Lady*, or with Mickey Rooney and Judy Garland in Busby Berkeley's *Girl Crazy* and other Freed musicals. It was during the latter production that Yolande had gone to Arthur's office one day to drop her bombshell. Would he please let her out of her contract? She'd like to leave because she had the chance of a role in a new stage show opening in Chicago and she wanted to go on the stage. It was the most mind-boggling request Arthur Freed had ever heard. At which point I can do no better than to quote Yo's account of that incident from *Shake the Stars Down*, her own hilarious autobiography.

"'Leave?' he repeated faintly. "Do you realise Miss… er…" I filled in the 'er' for him. "…that people all over the world are clamouring for your opportunity of being here in Hollywood under contract at MGM?" The mere idea of someone asking permission to leave his Shangri-La seemed to numb him for a moment and he took a deep gulp from his glass.'

Eventually he came to terms with the unthinkable, shook her hand, wished her good luck and, as Yolande wrote, even helped her to the door in case she wasn't capable of finding it herself. 'And if you ever want to come back,' he had told her gallantly, 'the job's still here.' And now, all these years later, they were meeting backstage in London's Vaudeville Theatre. After the initial hugs and congratulations Freed turned to her other visitors. 'This is the only girl I ever made a star by firing her,' he laughed.

In the world of writing there have been many historic firsts. I think we could safely call the 1886 appearance of Conan Doyle's Sherlock Holmes historic. Also Agatha Christie's Hercule Poirot or Georges Simenon's Maigret. Well, this year was about to see the birth of another and this one was born almost by accident. The instigator was a scribbler like myself who had once tried to be an actor before turning to journalism. During World War II he had distinguished himself and become a commander in the RNVR. He now lived partly in Jamaica where one of his friends and neighbours was Noël Coward. He was also about to get married to his longtime girlfriend but admitted he wasn't too elated with the idea, feeling they were both happy enough staying single. However, as his loved one was pregnant by him for the second time he was now behaving like an officer and a gentleman. And to soothe his pre-marital nerves he decided to bury himself in his typewriter and launch into one of his dreams, to see if he was capable of producing a novel. 'I'm toying with the idea of writing a book,' he told Noël one day. 'Any advice?'

'Yes, dear boy,' said our Noël. 'Stop toying and start typing.' And type he did. In eight weeks, just two months before the marriage, he had finished his first novel. It was called *Casino Royale* and in it he had created a Secret Service agent named James Bond. That author's name, of course, was Ian Lancaster Fleming. But how did Guest fit into all this? Simply that *Casino Royale* would eventually take up a year of my life which was more hysterical than historical, in fact one might even call it maniacal. For a short trailer let's press the fast forward button.

It is now 12 years later and I'm making *Where the Spies Are* with David Niven and Françoise Dorléac. We had been night shooting in Covent Garden at the Royal Opera House and I returned home to hear our telephone ringing insistently. Thinking it was Yolande, who was away on the Côte d'Azur taking a well-earned break, I raced to the nearest instrument to find it was my agent, John Mather, London head of the William Morris Agency.

'Charles Feldman is in town,' he said without preamble. 'He's planning a new Bond film, *Casino Royale*. Would you be interested in doing it back-to-back with John Huston?' Well, I'd been asked to do some strange things in my career, but back-to-back with John Huston? 'He wants to make it a send-up of all the Bond pictures,' Mather enlarged, 'with different directors doing different segments.'

'How many directors?'

'I don't know. So far he's only signed Huston but he wants to meet you for dinner tomorrow night.'

Charles K Feldman was certainly a name to conjure with. President of Famous Artists, one of the leading Hollywood talent agencies, he had represented top producers, directors and actors. Until one day he decided to become a producer himself, going on to make such wide-ranging quality productions as *The Glass Menagerie*, *A Streetcar Named Desire* and *The Seven Year Itch*. What could be nicer than working for someone like him?

Had you asked me that same question after the first month's shooting the answer would have been,

'Anything!' Not that Charlie Feldman wasn't instantly likeable and full of warmth and charm but he was also a master of indecision, so on alternate days you either wanted to hug him or throttle him. 'I'm sure we'll have fun working together,' he smiled the day we shook hands on the deal. 'It's going to be a great picture. Sort of a psychedelic send-up, with half a dozen big names playing James Bond and lots of guest star appearances – which of course includes you,' he quipped with a playful punch to the chin.

At that moment there was no script, only the barest story outline since each director was supposed to work on his own segment of the screenplay. However, having the Charlie Feldman clout, he already had tentative agreements with Peter Sellers, Ursula Andress, David Niven, Woody Allen and Orson Welles. Not bad for starters. With that lot we had to have fun. But we also had twice the normal production headaches. Such as trying to cope with a producer who changed his mind every night and usually called you in the middle of it.

He also seemed to live every day off the top of his head. 'We can get Bardot next Wednesday,' he phoned me one dawn. 'Write her into whatever set you're on.' Then came the Jean-Paul Belmondo night. 'He'll be in town Saturday week. He's Ursula's current lover, so work him into one of her scenes.' And little hiccups like trying to contain the feud between Orson Welles and Peter Sellers, vain attempts to stop Orson referring to him as 'that fucking amateur', or at least lower his voice a couple of decibels when Pete was in earshot.

All this was merely the tip of the *Casino Royale* iceberg, more of which later. For now, let's rewind back to Ian Fleming, flushed with the accomplishment of completing his first novel and meeting his own iceberg of publishers' rejection slips. It seemed no one wanted to know about a new Secret Service agent named James Bond, until brother Peter came to the rescue. It was Peter Fleming, a successful author in his own right, who persuaded his publisher, Jonathan Cape, to read Ian's MS. And although they didn't think too much of it, almost as a favour to brother Peter, they went ahead and published it.

'I saw Bond as a suave, debonair Englishman with a sophisticated twinkle,' Ian once said. 'Like David Niven.' So it wasn't surprising that an early copy of *Casino* dropped into David's lap while he was filming *The Moon is Blue* with William Holden. 'I thought it was a fun read,' David told me later. 'So I sent it off to Dick and suggested we might do it for one of our television shows.' Dick was fellow actor Dick Powell and between them they were co-presidents of the very successful American TV series *Four Star Theater*. 'He read it,' grinned David, 'and said I was out of my tiny mind.' It seems hard to believe, but it would be another ten years before Harry Saltzman and Cubby Broccoli thought of making the first Bond picture, *Dr No*.

However, it was now coming to the end of my 'year of firsts'. Tensing and Hillary had done it, Fleming had done it and, in my small way, I had done it. Yet there was still one more person whose 'first' had a glancing future connection with both Ian and me. His name was Hugh Heffner and in December that year he achieved his very first issue of *Playboy* magazine. Years later, when we were shooting *Casino Royale*, Heffner came to visit us on the set having been amused to learn that in our frenetic screenplay, Bond's chief protagonist had his secret underground HQ in the cellar beneath the Playboy Club. Charlie Feldman considered that a piece of psychedelic writing.

Anyway, come the year of firsts' Christmas Eve I was walking down Wardour Street and bumped into Ben Lyon coming out of Hammer House. 'Well, well' he laughed, 'speak of the devil! Just been talking about you with Jimmy Carreras. Bebe and I have signed with Hammer to make a film of our BBC series *Life with the Lyons*. Would you like to do it for us?'

Which was the blissfully haphazard way I began my long association with the redoubtable James Carreras and his merry band of enthusiasts who somehow managed to make successful films, destined years later to become international cult viewing, with no other studio than an old country house in the village of Bray, where to get far enough back in the living room for a full shot the camera operator had to wedge his bottom into the fireplace. Could Cecil B DeMille have done that?

CHAPTER FIFTEEN

Bebe Daniels was an unforgettable character. Golden favourite of the silent screen, she had blazed an incandescent trail all the way from Hal Roach's two-reeler comedies to superstardom opposite everyone from Harold Lloyd to Rudolph Valentino, with a couple of Cecil B DeMille epics along the way. Together with Pola Negri and Gloria Swanson, she was the most popular Paramount star of that era. And when so many of them failed the dreaded sound barrier test, Bebe crashed through it victoriously with a record-breaking musical called *Rio Rita* and became the all-talking-all-singing idol of a new generation.

At one point she actually sat down for a moment wondering if it wasn't time to consider slowing up. 'I really did,' she confessed when I asked her one day between London Palladium rehearsals. 'After all, I'd had a busy life, from the age of four when I toddled about the stage in my father's touring company. I mean, it seemed I'd done most things and there comes a time,' she laughed, 'when old circus ponies should be turned out to grass.'

It was husband Ben Lyon who scoffed her out of that. 'You couldn't retire if you wanted to,' he told her. 'What are you going to do, take up needlepoint?' So, back into the ring she went, made the classic Busby Berkeley extravaganza, *42nd Street*, and was up there in lights all over again. Now here she was, topping the bill with Ben at the London Palladium, which is where I first met them while still involved with George Black and Val Parnell, writing numbers and comedy material for their various shows.

Ben Lyon was a character of a different kind. Good-looking leading man of many Hollywood silents (who fell in love with and married one of his leading ladies who happened to be, you guessed it, Bebe), he first hit box-office headlines with the early Howard Hughes talkie *Hell's Angels* starring opposite newcomer Jean Harlow. What you probably didn't know was that he not only flew his own plane in that film but was actually responsible for some of the picture's award-winning aerial photography. It seems ironic that in spite of his many achievements the one thing that could lock him into filmdom's folklore forever is the fact that in 1946, when he became a temporary executive talent director at Fox, he gave a year's contract to a young would-be starlet called Norma Jean Mortenson, paid her $125 a week and renamed her Marilyn Monroe.

It says a lot about this remarkably unsung gentleman that when World War II broke out he chose to come to Britain, join the Royal Air Force as a combat pilot and eventually fly himself up to a senior rank. Even the Queen thought this was quite a gesture and made one of her own by honouring him with an OBE.

By the time we met, Ben's commanding officer was the indestructible Bebe herself. This incredible woman not only acted as their business manager but also devised and co-wrote their radio programmes. When you recall that among these was the BBC's long-running *Hi Gang!*, as well as their number one family series, *Life with the Lyons* (which also featured their own teenagers, Barbara and Richard), you'll realise what a dynamo of a lady Mrs Lyon had become in her second childhood. What's more, the public adored both of them because, unlike many others, they had stayed on when they didn't have to and helped us to laugh through the wartime horrors of our Blitz.

I have always held fond memories of the three films I made with them. Hard-working pros to their fingertips, they had none of those delusions of grandeur nurtured by some of our Hollywood imports. I recall a location incident while filming *The Lyons in Paris* one night in that famous City of Lights when the only lights that were missing were ours. I was rehearsing a scene on the Champs Elysée with the Arc de Triomphe as background when my long-suffering lighting cameraman, Jimmy Harvey, came up to me shaking his head gloomily. 'Can't do it, Val. They haven't given me enough lights to cover that much background. Could you cut it down a bit?'

'Wait a minute! Hold it!' Ben's voice came out of the darkness as he stepped up to the camera. 'Look, this may sound crazy, but I take it we have permission to park our vehicles here. Right? Okay, so why not put them in strategic positions, like they were extra lamps, and when Val says "Action" switch all headlights to full beam until you've shot it?' Crazy or not, that's exactly what we did and managed to shoot my one-and-a-half-minute scene successfully before a motorised detachment of Gendarmerie screamed up the Champs Elysée, came to a siren-screeching halt in front of our camera and let forth a stream of French threats about blinding oncoming traffic.

Whereupon, like the Good Fairy in a Christmas pantomime appearing out of the star trap, there was Bebe. 'Hullo,' she said, giving the Law her most infectious grin. 'Je suis Bebe Daniels... Permettez-mois?' And almost before they could react she was in the middle of those angry uniforms, linking arms and calling our stills man to take pictures. As the camera flashed she joked and kidded with them, promising they would all get prints next day at their commissariat. Every flash seemed to lessen our worries about spending a night in the Bastille and pretty soon not only did she have them laughing with her but asking if she and Ben would sign their incident books.

That was Bebe Daniels and Ben Lyon, two rare examples of the three social Rs — Reliable, Resourceful and Real people. Yolande and I spent many enjoyable times at both their London and country homes, sometimes joining their Sunday canasta parties at which you could find yourself partnering anyone from the Spanish ambassador to MGM's starriest diva, Jeanette Macdonald.

It was shortly after the Parisian interlude that another 'real' person came into our lives. A popular star of radio, variety and cabaret, his name was Frankie Howerd. Here was another of that rare breed of performers beloved and admired by both public and fellow professionals alike. Another pro's pro like the Beatrice Lillies, Noël Cowards and Jack Bennys of the entertainment world. With two feet firmly on the ground and a bemused view of the vagaries of life, Frankie had an incredible mind behind all his buffoonery. He could hold a conversation with anybody about practically anything, for which the intellectuals adored him too. I remember at one of Frankie's parties the distinguished theatre critic Kenneth Tynan said to me, 'He's wasting his time as a comedian, he should be running the country.' Which is probably why, when it came time for the yearly *Evening Standard* Drama Awards, it was always Frankie Howerd they wanted to MC it. Dear Frankie, he became one of our closest friends and we still miss him greatly.

My first meeting with this unique character was backstage in his dressing room at the London Palladium where he was topping the bill of a long-running variety show. Thus far he had starred in every medium except films and both Yolande and I thought it was time he took a crack at that too. 'Films?' His large brown eyes surveyed me querulously before giving me one of his deep rumbling laughs. 'Oho, that's a dangerous game. Get your name up there outside a cinema and if they don't go in it's all your fault! Thank you but no thank you!' he chuckled. 'I'm safe where I am.'

I had just met the first actor in my entire career who didn't want to make a film. However, after promising to write a vehicle especially for him, he finally capitulated but with three even more unexpected stipulations. One: I had to write a comedy-thriller so that if the comedy part of it wasn't any good the thriller might be. Two: under no circumstances would his name be first above the title, and Three: he'd like to be in it with his favourite comedy character actress, Margaret Rutherford, who had already co-starred in several hit films. 'And *she* has to have top billing,' insisted Frankie.

So, back home I went with the once-in-a-lifetime assignment to write a comedy-thriller for two artistes, one of whom would only sign a contract provided he didn't get star billing and the other who was only offered a contract if she agreed to accept that billing. Even in films you'd think a situation couldn't get much wilder than that. Wait.

I sat down and wrote a lightweight comedy-thriller called *The Runaway Bus*, about a British European Airways bus driver, Frankie, who gets lost in a fog with a coachload of passengers, some of whom are up to no good. I persuaded Margaret Rutherford to be in it and agree to top billing and somehow was able to get the whole project off the ground so that just over a month later we were actually shooting at London Airport.

Next day, sitting in the projection theatre viewing the 'rushes', it was obvious Frankie Howerd's screen persona had surpassed even my optimism. Every raised eyebrow, querulous inflection and bristling body-language had the unit and cast laughing out loud, even though they'd seen him shoot the same scenes only the day before. I returned to the set blissfully unaware that I was about to be confronted with the wildest twist of all. It was heralded by a tug at my sleeve. The tugger was Margaret Rutherford.

'He is a very funny man,' Maggie said solemnly.

'He certainly is,' I agreed happily, 'and you two will be a knockout twosome.'

'Be that as it may,' answered my co-star, 'but I certainly am not taking top billing over him. He is the star of this picture and his name has to come first.'

'But, Maggie...'

'No argument,' she held up her hand. 'He has first billing. I'm calling my agent now.'

Which is the unlikely way Francis Howerd got his first star billing in a movie, launching him high into the box-office firmament. We had another launching on that production. A child singer from the BBC whose screen credits thus far included being the youngest daughter in Rank's popular film series about the Huggett family. And now, at the ripe old age of 20, she desperately wanted to put all that 'child' stuff behind her and be taken seriously as a grown-up actress. So I up-aged her to being our love-interest, the air stewardess in charge of the bus. Her name was Petula Clark and it was to be the first film she had made without Daddy Clark being on the set to watch over her. That alone was a historic step for our Pet and the first of many steps, if not leaps, through an impressive career on stage and screen, to say nothing of becoming a top-ten recording artiste with her own record label. Later still she was destined to win critical acclaim as the star of Andrew Lloyd Webber's *Sunset Boulevard* on the London stage. Dear Pet, she grew up magnificently.

My film encyclopedias tell me that 1954 was a busy year. For my part the most memorable production was Hammer's *Break in the Circle* because it was during this shoot that Yolande finally decided to make an honest man out of me by becoming Mrs Guest. I have already recounted how the Marylebone Town Hall registrar blew the gaffe on our 'secret' marriage, but there was an amusing prelude to this involving one of that picture's stars, Hungarian actress Eva Bartok. A few weeks before our wedding Yolande had joined me on location in Cornwall where we were shooting some sequences in the little village of Polperro. Eva and our other star, American actor Forrest Tucker, were staying at the same hotel as us, a small tavern on the bay, run by a rather toffee-nosed couple who seemed to be glad of our business but suspicious of our profession.

At that time Eva was having an undercover fling with Germany's current heart-throb film star, Curt Jürgens. It was during our second week of shooting that she informed me Curt had just completed his film in Munich and would I mind if he came over and joined her in Polperro. No problem, I told her, so he flew in and moved in. To her double room.

It only took two nights before Madam Toffee-nose corralled me into her office. 'I cannot allow this sort of thing, Mr Guest,' she trembled. 'I am told that gentleman is not Mr Bartok so we can't have them sharing the same room. This is not that kind of hotel, Mr Guest. He must move out immediately.' I nodded as understandingly as I could, calmed her down, told her I would explain to Miss Bartok and wondered what sort of convulsions the hotel would have if they knew there was another unwed couple sharing a room on the same floor. Anyway, next morning we moved Eva and Curt into a hotel that was a little less inquisitive.

The tag to this story came a couple of months later when the news of our marriage had appeared in the English press. It came in the form of a letter we received from that same Polperro hotel. 'Dear Mr and Mrs Guest,' it read. 'Now we know your guilty secret may we wish you both Good Luck and a lifetime of Happiness and Prosperity.' A charming gesture, if only to let us know we had their absolution. I often wondered if they sent a letter to Eva and Curt when they, too, got married later that year. Although, sadly, their marriage barely lasted long enough for a letter to reach them.

1954 was also a landmark year for young Michael Carreras. Until then Michael, son of James Carreras, executive boss of Hammer Films, had never produced a feature film, only a few musical shorts. 'And now you're going to show me how to film a full-length one,' he joked when we were setting up *The Men of Sherwood Forest*, Hammer's first feature film to be shot in colour. I was to make several more films with the energetic and enthusiastic young Mike, who was a quick learner and soon turned into one of the most organised producers for whom I had ever worked. Somehow he managed to deep-think his productions so that everyone felt secure knowing that come hell or high water what had to be done would be done and what had to be there would be there, even if he had to think sideways to get it there.

I first became aware of this talent on *Break in the Circle*, after we had moved our location from peaceful Polperro to hair-raising Hamburg where Yolande and I were fated to spend a working honeymoon. One evening I was out shooting on the famous, or infamous, Reeperbahn, that neon nightmare of nightclubs, bars, strip-joints and brothels. After a hard day's night coping with sightseers, drunks, bouncers and broads, we eventually called it a 'wrap' and I couldn't wait to go back to the luxurious comfort of our Vier Jahreszeiten hotel and get on with my honeymoon. Not so the rest of them. Led by the tireless Michael Carreras, they scuttled off to explore Hamburg's nightlife for themselves. But even while exploring, Mike's agile production mind was still thinking sideways and before he eventually went to bed that night he summoned the Third Assistant and instructed him that at 5.30 the following morning he was to make the rounds of the Reeperbahn clubs, bars and brothels, winkle out any members of the unit he might find there and make sure they were on set on time for the 7.30 call. Quite seriously, I cannot recall any producer with whom I've ever worked who was capable of thinking as sideways as that.

I finished the picture and our honeymoon in marginally more sedate Britain, or as Bob Hope used to call it 'Good old Jolly', where Yo and I took time off to catch up on some of the shows we'd missed. I remember *An Evening with Beatrice Lillie* at the Globe. Also the Phoenix, where Larry Olivier and Vivien were appearing in *The Sleeping Prince*, a new play by Terence Rattigan. We were doubly interested in seeing this because Terry, who was a good friend of Yolande's, had said he originally wrote the piece with her and Olivier in mind. We also knew that Vivien wasn't at all happy playing the role and was only doing it because Larry O had talked her into it. Later, of course, he filmed it as the ill-fated *The Prince and the Showgirl*, of which Vivien wanted no part. So he brought over Marilyn Monroe to be his co-star.

I call it ill-fated because somehow it all went wrong and, according to chums who were on it, became an unhappy production on which everyone seemed to hate someone else. Everyone, that is, except dear old Bumble Dawson whom Olivier had engaged to design Marilyn's wardrobe. Bumble, as always, loved everyone and everyone loved Bumble. 'Poor Larry,' she told us later. 'And poor Marilyn. If ever there was a non-meeting of minds...'

'Poor nothing!' snapped one of the sorely tried assistants. 'She was a pain in the arse. Mostly late and seldom knew her lines.'

'Yes, she *was* a little tiresome,' understated kind, gentle Richard Wattis who played Mr Northbrook in it. 'And yes, a trifle unpredictable.'

Perhaps the ultimate summing up of screen goddess MM came from Tony Curtis years later when I was shooting *The Persuaders!* with him and Roger Moore in the South of France. One of the French crew couldn't wait to know how he'd enjoyed making *Some Like it Hot* and his love scenes with la sexy Monroe. 'It was like kissing Hitler,' said Tony. End of conversation.

Somehow Bumble managed to handle her. 'Desperately insecure, of course,' she told us over dinner one night, 'but so far I've managed.' She beamed through her owl-like spectacles. 'The only demand she makes of me is that all her costumes are, as she puts it, "cupped under the ass".'

Still, even Bumble admitted the lady could be unpredictable. Like the night of the Royal Command Film Performance when Marilyn drove in from the Englefield Green house she and husband Arthur Miller had rented, to Bumble's Eccleston Square flat to be fitted into the dress Bumble had designed for the royal occasion. She arrived wrapped in a voluminous sable coat. 'Okay, fit me,' smiled Marilyn, dropped her sable and stood there naked as she was born.

Bumble gasped. 'Have you driven all the way from Englefield Green like that?'

'Uh-uh,' nodded Monroe as though it was a silly question 'I figured I'd be wearing your dress home anyway so why bother with all the other stuff.'

'But what if you were in an accident, or stopped by the police...?'

'Never thought of that,' laughed the goddess. 'You think I'd have gotten a ticket?'

However, she had at least brought a bra which she'd stuffed into her evening handbag. And speaking of bras, not long after Monroe returned to Hollywood, one of her bras showed up in Bumble's closet. Grinning like a Cheshire cat Bumble brought it around to our flat one evening and waved it at Yolande. 'She's the same size as you,' she chuckled, 'so you might as well have it.' No one recalls what happened to that bra after Yolande dropped it into her lingerie drawer to be lost to posterity but years later, recalling the incident, Yo shook her head and sighed. 'Can you imagine how unaware we were then? Just think what a Marilyn Monroe bra might fetch at Sotheby's today!'

It will just have to join all the other 'what ifs'. Such as what if I hadn't said no to *Dr No*, the Bond film that unlocked all those millions, or no to a studio car for the young Audrey Hepburn? In fact, I almost said no to the picture which, surprisingly, has been screened at more worldwide film festivals than almost any other I've made. *The Quatermass Xperiment.*

Quatermass had been a BBC science fiction serial that kept everyone riveted to their TV sets for six suspenseful weeks, although I must admit I was one of the few people in Britain who didn't see any of it. Firstly, because I had never been a science fiction buff and secondly because I just didn't have time to watch it. So when producer Anthony Hinds called me to say Hammer had just bought the screen rights and how did I feel about making it into a film, he must have been mildly surprised at my lack of enthusiasm. The main reason, apart from knowing so little about the property, was that Yolande and I were about to take off the following day for a well-earned holiday in Tangier. So far it had been a pretty hectic year for both of us. We'd not only shot *They Can't Hang Me*, based on a thriller by *Daily Express* film critic Leonard Mosley and starring Yolande, Terence Morgan and André Morell, but I'd made *The Men of Sherwood Forest*, *The Lyons in Paris* and *Break in the Circle* for Hammer already.

I told Tony we were booked on the early morning British European Airways flight out of Northolt. 'Fine,' he said. 'I'll bring them to the airport. You can read them on holiday.' 'Them' turned out to be a parcel of six TV scripts, which really isn't the first thing you'd choose for hand luggage on a crowded plane. However, I nursed them safely to our Tangier en pension, plonked them on the floor at my side of the bed and promptly forgot all about them.

Tangier had long been one of our favourite getaways. A fascinating mixture of biblical and modern, it was then one of the few international ports administered by French, German and Spanish authorities taking turns to run it for a year at a time. Its inhabitants were an intriguing pot-pourri of VIPs, villains, spies and a lot of other interesting characters who called it their home. Characters like American author and composer Paul Bowles and Woolworth heiress Barbara Hutton, who actually had a palace in the Casbah with a constant stream of guests from Charles Chaplin, Garbo and Cecil Beaton to Aristotle Onassis and Maria Callas – you name them, they were all there. And, of course, what would Tangier's social whirl have been without that witty pillar of Tangerine society, the Honourable David Herbert, son of the 15th Earl of Pembroke. David, besides keeping the locals amused by appearing at all their charity musicals in full drag, was a great cook, delightful company and also happened to be, hey-ho, the Queen's cousin.

It was a week before Yolande noticed the still-unopened parcel of scripts at the side of the bed.

'What about all that?'

'Haven't read them yet.'

'Aren't you even curious?'

'Well, they're science fiction and that's not really my scene.'

'Since when have you been ethereal?' asked my practical Yolande.

So, next morning I lugged the six scripts down to Robert's Sun Beach Café to laze by the surf and read them. Robert was a cheerful, smiling Brazilian who ran this small, unpretentious patch of plage which seemed to have become the favourite spot for many of the more colourful visitors. A perfect place to relax, swim, and expect the unexpected which, as often as not, was what you got.

For instance, not more than a dozen yards to my left was another Sun Beach denizen similarly immersed in a pile of manuscript to which he periodically added some scribbles. His name happened to be Tennessee Williams and the manuscript he was scratching at happened to be a little something he was dreaming up called *Cat on a Hot Tin Roof*. At the same time, from inside the Sun Beach Café behind us, like background music helping our muses along, came the tinkling sound of Robert's upright piano. At the piano, in beach-robe and sunglasses, a pencil clenched between his teeth, was Phil Green, one of

Britain's most popular composer-conductors, trying to finish his soon-to-be famous background theme for a new film called *John and Julie*. All of which was the kind of goings-on one simply took for granted at Robert's Sun Beach Café in Tangier.

Then there was the gentleman to my right. For several days he'd been reclining on one of Robert's matelas, a pleasant fellow with a mid-European accent, a ready smile and a daily nod of greeting. 'What you read?' he asked one morning, stabbing a finger at my pile of scripts. When I explained they were something I might be filming it seemed to amuse him. 'Movies! You do the movies,' he chuckled. 'Perhaps I sell you my story. Yes?' I smiled my 'thanks, but no thanks' smile which promptly added another 'what if' to my life because that afternoon four French Sûreté vans squealed to a halt behind the café, disgorging a dozen heavily armed policemen who quickly surrounded the man on the matelas, pointed 12 guns at him, slapped on handcuffs and whisked him off without further ado or argument. It was only later they told me my friendly beach neighbour had been 'Der Teufel', one of the most wanted terrorists in Europe. So, what if I *had* bought the exclusive world rights to his story? Ah well, you can't win 'em all.

My next Sun Beach surprise was reading *Quatermass*. I found Nigel Kneale's visionary tale of what a manned space ship unwittingly brought back to Earth both absorbing and suspenseful. Whereupon, to prove to Yolande I wasn't ethereal after all, I called Tony Hinds in London to say if he still wanted me I'd love to do it.

It is hard to believe that *The Quatermass Xperiment* was eventually made for the tiny budget of £42,000, due mainly to the painstaking diligence of Tony Hinds who turned out to be one of the most charmingly money-careful producers I'd met thus far. He had, in fact, only been given £40,000 to spend on the picture but when actor Jack Warner ran into a few pro rata days the figure had rocketed to a reckless £42,000. Needless to say none of us was able to retire on what was then jokingly called our salary. Had I known then that in years to come our film would become what is lightly known as 'cult viewing', I might have plucked up the courage to ask the charming Tony for a mite more wages, perhaps stretching his budget to an exorbitant £43,000. And I wouldn't have got it.

There's an amusing postscript to that story. For old times' sake I sent Tony Hinds a copy of it and back came this reply. 'Dear Val, How kind of you to send me that extract from your memoirs. My pre-*Quatermass* memory was slightly different. Over lunch at Kettners (I think it was) I told you I had three films to make – a Robin Hood, a POW story and a science fiction and asked you which one you would like to direct. No hesitation – you said: "All three"! And you did.' See what I mean about the man being a charmer?

It wasn't easy condensing six weeks' television into a screenplay for a 90-minute feature film and of necessity a lot of the TV scenes and dialogue had to go. To this day I don't think Nigel Kneale has forgiven me for that. Sorry, Nigel, but c'est le cinéma and you should see what they did to Leo Tolstoy when they filmed *War and Peace*. Nigel, or 'Tom' as he liked to be called, was also unhappy about the choice of Hollywood's Brian Donlevy to play his Quatermass. He had written him as a dedicated English professor and here was some insensitive, money-minded American distributor insisting on a recognisable marquee name.

For my part I couldn't have been happier. It fitted into my idea of shooting the picture in a cinéma vérité, almost documentary style, sometimes using hand-held cameras to give it a newsreel quality, thereby bringing a space-orientated subject right down to earth. And who could be more down-to-earth than the Oscar-nominated Brian Donlevy? Brian had been-there-done-that and, he told us proudly, ours would be his 57th motion picture. What's more he was a delight to work with, being sure enough of his trade to realise, unlike so many other 'names', that he didn't have to be difficult to hide his insecurity.

In fact, the only trouble I had with Donlevy was trying to keep his toupée on, or as he used to call it, his 'rug'. In our second picture together, *Quatermass 2* (which America chose to retitle *Enemy from Space*), we had several sequences involving the elements. At one time on location, high on a windy hill, we were adding to the wind trying to simulate a hurricane with aeroplane propellers at full blast. Twice Brian's 'rugs' had taken off into the dust-filled yonder and we were now down to the last one Hairdressing had with them on location. 'Whatever you do,' I instructed Brian, 'keep facing the propellers and we'll be okay.'

He did just what he was told and we got one of the best shots of the day. 'Great. Cut. Print. We got it!' Whereupon a jubilant Brian turned to grin at me and away went his last 'rug'. I will never forget the scene that followed as the whole unit tried to get it back to earth. Prop men, electricians, assistants, hairdressers trying to swat it by throwing scripts, towels, gloves, clapperboards and anything they could get their hands on as Brian Donlevy's toupée swirled above us like some demented bat. All to no avail and I had to spend the rest of the day shooting scenes with his hat on tight.

He was also a great coffee drinker, constantly carrying a mug of it in and out of his caravan. Which made him a kindred spirit because I, too, liked my coffee and there was usually a thermos of it by my chair. Kindred, that is, until halfway through our location shooting when my Third Assistant discovered Brian's mugs were always laced with brandy. Not that it affected his work; he was never late and knew all his lines, although it did seem to explain why by mid-afternoon he was sometimes a little hazy about the storyline.

'Where are we? Give me a breakdown so far,' he'd often ask me before a scene.

'The rocket's landed, the astronaut's disappeared and you're going home to get some rest.'

'You got it,' he'd nod. 'Let's go.'

He was never one who needed a motivation for things but just liked to check whether he should be happier, angrier or more professorial. Motivation was left for the so-called Method actors, who sometimes have to go into a corner and pretend to be a frog or something before they can 'feel' the scene. Not that there aren't some very good Method actors but they can sometimes use up precious shooting time. I once spent a whole morning trying to get a Method actor to re-voice one of his own location lines in the dubbing theatre. His trouble was that having Methodised the line when he first said it, he couldn't find the same rhythm again.

And speaking of motivation, it recalls that historic day at MGM when the great Spencer Tracy stood watching a Method actor worrying about his motivation for coming into a room. Spence finally weighed it up for him.

'You come in the fuckin' door because it's the only way to get into the fuckin' room.'

Collapse of Method actor and the whole of Stage 3 at Culver City.

CHAPTER
SIXTEEN

I suppose at some time or another every diarist, memoirist and autobiographist has paused, stared at a blank page and asked, 'What am I doing? Does anyone really care about all this guff?' Perhaps even Samuel Pepys layed down his quill one day, sighing, 'Tis a waste of time, Samuel, t'will never be read.' And what about Tolstoy? It took him three volumes to write Childhood, Boyhood and Youth, but why did he never sit down and write Manhood?

'It doesn't matter if nobody else reads it,' said my down-to-earth Yolande. 'At least you owe it to the family to leave a record.' I can just imagine the family one day blowing the dust off this pile of MSS and chuckling, 'Oh, look, here's something the old fart wrote.'

I must say, it seems impossible and also a little scary to realise that what 'the old fart' has written so far seems to have covered a lifetime, when in fact it's only just over half of one. As Erich von Stroheim had grumbled back in Cap d'Antibes, 'Why did I do so fucking much?' Anyway, from now on, if anyone's still there, I'll try to undercrank it.

Somehow over the next two years I managed to make six more films. Today, the mere thought of it exhausts me. There was *It's a Wonderful World*, *The Weapon*, *Quatermass 2*, *The Abominable Snowman*, *The Camp on Blood Island*, *Carry On Admiral* and *Up the Creek*.

The Camp on Blood Island was an interesting and controversial film. I was told that this story, about an infamous Japanese prisoner-of-war camp, evolved from a handful of notes scribbled on yellowing scraps of newsprint, lavatory paper and crumpled envelops smuggled out of that very camp by an inmate who later, believe it or not, became the front of house manager of London's Lyric Theatre.

It was all tough shooting on the realistic prison camp that Hammer's art department created at their Bray Studios' lot. The most unexpected deep-breath moment came, however, the day the Crowd Artists' Association informed us they couldn't supply the 20 extras we needed to be Japanese soldiers and prison guards as they had no more that half-a-dozen Japanese on their books. Which is when everyone prayed for a flash of light. Luckily one came from our production department. 'Why not scour all the Japanese restaurants in town,' they suggested. 'Get their waiters to join the CAA and become extras.' Which is what we did and what they did and the *Camp on Blood Island* casting was complete.

Incidentally, from then on, whenever Yolande and I went to a Japanese restaurant our friends were constantly amazed when all the waiters called me Val.

Carry On Admiral started life as a successful stage farce about the navy called *The Middle Watch*. 'Not a good film title,' said Renown Films producer George Minter when he asked me to adapt and direct it. 'See what you can come up with.' I came up with *Carry On Admiral*. 'Sold,' said George and off we went on location with Peggy Cummins, Brian Reece, AE Matthews and a castful of top farceurs. But George Minter either forgot or didn't feel it worthwhile to register the title. Less than a year later along came a couple of charming pickpockets, or title-whippers, named Peter Rogers and Gerald Thomas and started their own historic Carry On series.

Up the Creek, of course, was the screenplay I wrote to try and launch Peter Sellers in his first starring film. I use the word 'try' because I had one hell of a time convincing Hammer's Jimmy Carreras that it was worth it. 'He may be great,' shrugged Jimmy, 'but his name won't sell a ticket. Needs somebody known up there.'

The somebody I managed to get him was David Tomlinson, a popular young light comedian who had starred in many plays and films and would later go on to Hollywood for *Mary Poppins* and *Bedknobs and Broomsticks*. *Up the Creek*, my second naval comedy, was about a 'mothballed' cruiser, its crew led by a wily bo'sun who, amongst other fiddles, raised poultry aboard, selling navy provisions and eggs to the local inhabitants. Peter was to play the wily bo'sun who tries frantically to keep the whole clandestine operation from the newly posted Commanding Officer, David Tomlinson. At last everyone was happy. Everyone, that is, but Sellers himself. All at once he was scared stiff. He was used to playing a stream of hilarious characters in short radio and TV sketches but wasn't at all sure he could pull it off, playing one character for the length of a feature film.

'I mean, what is he?' asked a worried Pete. 'Cockney's too corny. Scotch? Irish? Welsh?'

'What's your most comfortable?'

'Maybe Irish – but what kind of Irish? He has to be special Irish.'

Suddenly I had an idea. 'Come on and I'll show him to you!' I bundled him into my car and drove him to a block of tenement flats called Peabody Buildings off Shaftesbury Avenue, behind the old Shaftesbury Theatre. They had a Residents Only car park which I'd tried to drive into one day and had been stopped by the most unusual Irish car park attendant I'd ever encountered. What made him memorable to me, apart from his warm Irish brogue, was that he was so profusely apologetic for turning me away he was almost unctuous about it. 'Lend an ear to this,' I alerted Peter as we approached the parking lot. 'You're about to meet the Emerald Isle's Uriah Heep.' True to form the same attendant was there to stop us, practically wringing his hands in despair at having to do such an awful thing. Peter listened intently, trying hard not to break up, but finally exploded. 'Great! Great!' he laughed at the astonished man. 'And begorrah we'll be seeing you get tickets for the première!'

I am sure none of Her Majesty's cruisers ever had such an unctuous bo'sun as ours but it rocketed the Peter Sellers name into the 'known up there' film bracket from then on. It is interesting to note how accents play such a role in helping actors flesh out a character. I recall when we were about to make *Expresso Bongo* with Laurence Harvey, Yolande and our young Soho discovery, Cliff Richard, as pop star Bongo Herbert. Harvey was playing Johnny Jackson, his hard-selling agent, and was undecided on the kind of accent he would give the character. 'Any ideas?' he asked me.

'I'd say he was part Soho, part Jewish, and part middle class,' I told him.

'Thanks a lot,' grinned Larry.

It was then I realised the accent I had described was practically that of the talented Wolf Mankowitz who had not only written the original stage version of *Bongo* but several bestselling books as well, including *Cheaper by the Dozen*, *My Old Man's a Dustman* and *A Kid for Two Farthings*. Wolf was a rotund, grandiose, self-contained anarchist with a biting wit and, according to Yo and the other girls, an underlying sex-appeal. This larger than life character, who was also a Cambridge MA and worked on the screenplay with me, would himself have been good casting for young Bongo's agent. So Larry arranged a couple of lunches with the unsuspecting Wolf to pay attention to the way he spoke. 'I think I have it,' said Larry by the time we started shooting, 'but you'll have to watch I don't lose it along the way!' And one day he did. I stopped shooting immediately so that he could call Wolf from the set and chat to him on the phone. After a few minutes Larry hung up. 'Okay,' he joked. 'Better roll before I forget it!'

As for dear Wolf, I used his sparkling literary talents several times after that and we became fast friends, but I don't think he ever realised that when Laurence Harvey won critical kudos for his performance as Johnny Jackson in *Bongo* he won them partly for sounding like Wolf Mankowitz.

We had no such accent problems on *Yesterday's Enemy*, a Japanese war drama set in the Burmese jungle. I had adapted it for Hammer from an exciting television play of the same name and my only worry was how to shoot a complex, realistic jungle war film when your budget won't allow even a quick trip to the nearest jungle. The answer is you get a brilliant art director like Hammer's Bernard Robinson who not only fills an entire stage at Shepperton with Burmese jungle but builds different sections of it on revolves so that without having to move the unit it can be turned around to look like entirely different locations. It was truly Academy Award art direction and garnished with Arthur Grant's incredible photography we even fooled Burma war supremo, Lord Louis Mountbatten. Our première at the Empire in Leicester Square was in aid of the Burma Star Association, of which he was president, and I had the honour of sitting next to him during the screening.

'I know that place...' said Mountbatten at one point, stabbing his finger at the screen jungle. 'Know it well... Can't put a name to it... Where the hell was it?'

Not having the courage to tell him it was the large stage at Shepperton, I lied diplomatically. 'I'm afraid that was second unit stuff, sir, so I really wouldn't know.'

That was the season when London's West End was alive with the sound of music. We had George Chakiris and Chita Rivera in *West Side Story* at Her Majesty's and a delightfully grown-up Julie Andrews and Rex Harrison in *My Fair Lady* at Drury Lane. And guess what was at the Saville Theatre on Shaftesbury Avenue, a new musical with Paul Scofield and Millicent Martin called *Expresso Bongo*. At the time I was only vaguely aware of this show until Yolande went to see it with a friend and came back telling me what a great film it would make. Then, deciding my reaction to this piece of news wasn't positive enough, she whisked me off to the Saville to judge for myself.

It would be easy to say I came, I saw and was immediately conquered, but I wasn't. As a show it was bright and entertaining but I felt a little unsure as to how a story about a streetwise agent launching a new pop star would be accepted by filmgoers. In fact, left to my own devices, I would never have become involved in what would later turn out to be one of my favourite and most popular films. But when Yolande gets a bee in her bonnet she is not satisfied until she has the whole hive working for her. So, surreptitiously she called our friends and neighbours, Peter and Mary Noble, and hatched a plot to bring me and the prodigious Wolf Mankowitz together accidentally on purpose. To achieve this Peter and Mary invited all of us over to one of their frequent showbiz parties. And, just as my clever little beekeeper had figured, it worked. In no time at all Wolf and I were huddled together working around the clock on our first film script and, with Yolande cooking for us in her ever-open canteen, pretty soon it was completed. Now all I had to do was find the money to make it.

My first port of call was Nat Cohen. Nat's baptism into the feature film business had been when Danny Angel asked him if he'd like to put some money into *Mr Drake's Duck*. He did and must have been pleased with the results because he continued to stick around Wardour Street until he became the all-powerful, Lord-High-Panjandrum of Anglo Amalgamated Pictures. Nat listened attentively as I outlined the project, then his smile faded and he shook his head.

'Who cares about rock'n'roll?'

'They care about Elvis Presley.'

Nat shrugged. 'When you get Presley, talk to me.'

In a way I could see his point. There were several good English pop stars floating around – Tommy Steele, Marty Wilde, Adam Faith, Billy Fury – but by no stretch of the imagination could they be said to have international pulling power. In fact, during my search to find the right one to play the young Bongo I had covered most of them. Tommy Steele was probably the best known but somehow he didn't have the vulnerability needed for the role of a slightly bewildered teenager rocketed to unexpected stardom. Marty Wilde was a possible choice but then again I felt he was just too tall to command the necessary sympathy. After my search had been reported in the London press I received a telephone call from one Tom Littlewood, who owned the small 2 i's Bar on Soho's Old Compton Street.

'Got a kid working here, might be worth a look-see,' he told me. I had my look-see that evening when, down in the tiny cellar of the 2 i's, I watched a small good-looking bundle of vitality with dark eyes, an angelic face, a good voice and a gyrating body that showed he was an Elvis fan. Tom said his name was Cliff Richard and the four lively lads backing him called themselves the Drifters. And that, to tell it as it was, is how Sir Cliff landed his first starring role in *Expresso Bongo*. At which time, being still under age, he brought his mother along to sign the contract for a heady £2,000 plus his one request: 'Can my mates be in it too?' And in it they were, but since there was an American group already named the Drifters, Cliff's mates were launched as the Shadows, under which name they went on to achieve their own share of fame.

Meanwhile, Larry Harvey had read the script, couldn't wait to play Johnny Jackson with Yolande playing Dixie, a waning headliner who tries to hook herself on to the new pop star's tour. Together with Sylvia Syms as Johnny's strip-show girlfriend we seemed to have everything going for us. Everything except the backing. On top of which the time was creeping up when not only would we lose Harvey to his next Hollywood assignment, I might also lose Yolande who had previously committed to do a new play for *Mousetrap* impresario Peter Saunders. Titled *Suddenly It's Spring*, to co-star Yolande with my old workmate Margaret Lockwood, it was due to start rehearsals in August and here we were in June already.

Suddenly, wham-bam, it started to come together. Alex Korda's ex-associate, Steven Pallos, the first to see *Bongo's* potential, had talked John and Roy Boulting into giving us a British Lion distribution contract. Armed with this, my cast list, a copy of the script and crossed fingers I went to see the independent producer's Fairy Godfather, John Terry of the National Film Finance Corporation, to ask for a loan. It was two more days before he called to tell me I could uncross my fingers, the Board had agreed to put up the cash. All I had to put up were my last two pictures as collateral. C'est le movies.

Then, before you could say 'Pierre Balmain', Yolande had whisked dear Bumble Dawson off to Paris to arrange for the great Pierre to design her clothes for the picture. And since the great Balenciaga was only a few rues away, why not suss out his end-of-season collection for the play? Two haute couturiers for two haute productions for the price of one round trip? How's that for instant genius? Meanwhile, back at HQ, young Cliff had settled down to learn his first leading part and Larry Harvey was practising his Johnny Jackson Mankowitz.

Which is probably as good a time as any to recall one of life's more improbable coincidences. Living as we do in California's Palm Springs, fondly labelled 'Tinseltown Two', we have always had a gaggle of celebrity neighbours. Sadly we no longer have Alice Faye and Phil Harris, Ruby Keeler, Ginny Simms, Charles 'Buddy' Rogers, Francis Lederer, Loretta Young and Frank Sinatra. But we do have Caroll Baker, Bob Hope, Kirk Douglas and one who could almost be described as part of the landscape since we see his works here in the parks and even the streets. I'm referring to that internationally known sculptor, John Kennedy. And what a fascinating story his life has been.

To begin with, he wasn't always a sculptor. When Yolande and I first knew him, back in London's swinging fifties and sixties, he was famous for two other things. For dreaming up and opening the town's trendiest night spot, the Ad Lib Club in Charles Street and – wait for it – being the almost fabled manager of pop star Tommy Steele and heaven knows how many other teenage idols. And the coincidental tag to this story? When Wolf Mankowitz sat down to write *Expresso Bongo*, guess who he chose as his model for agent Johnny Jackson? Who else but our friend and now neighbour, Johnny Kennedy. Who, it's only fair to add, sounds nothing like Larry Harvey playing Wolf Mankowitz!

I have many fond and funny memories of shooting *Bongo*. Such as that endearing comedienne Hermione 'Tottie' Baddeley on night location in Soho playing one of the area's happy hookers and getting propositioned by a passing car during an actual 'take'. Being the ultimate professional, Tottie shouted an exorbitant price to the driver while still playing her scene. Then there was the delegation of local street ladies who came to me protesting that our arc lamps and tannoys were ruining their trade. Which reminds me of the top window in Old Compton Street that seemed like the ideal spot from which to take a high shot of Soho at night. It turned out to be the bedsit pad of a hustler named Mabel who demanded £50 for the use of her room for one hour. 'That's what you're costing me in business,' she insisted. We gave her the fifty, even though the shot took less than half-an-hour. When we finished shooting that night I heard my First Assistant laughing, 'Okay fellers, it's a wrap and if anyone fancies half-an-hour with Mabel, it's paid for.'

Perhaps one of my most delightful recollections was working with Kenneth MacMillan whom I had engaged as our choreographer. That was before he became an artistic icon as director of Covent Garden's Royal Ballet, creating all-time classics for the greatest dancers of our day. But right now, down at Shepperton Studios poor Ken was struggling to get our six topless strip-club dancers to dance and sing to playback at the same time. 'It's the simplest routine,' he despaired to me in the canteen one day. 'They may have looks, legs and tits but they have no co-ordination!' Eventually, they not only sang and danced at the same time but did it stylishly, thanks to Ken's persistence and application. Years later, after Sir Kenneth MacMillan had received his knighthood and world acclaim, we would tease him that, who knows, he might never have achieved any of this but for his early groundwork with our *Bongo* strippers.

All in all that was a conspicuous year for Yo and I, ending as it did with an unexpected Donlan-Guest double-feature when, during a cold and rainy November, Yolande's play with Maggie Lockwood opened at the Duke of York's quickly followed by our Haymarket première of *Expresso Bongo* at the Carlton. Happily, not only were our joint notices heartening but so were the umbrellas that lined up at both theatres. A few weeks later, after the trade papers had listed our Carlton box-office figures, I saw Nat Cohen at an Arthur Ferrier party. As soon as he spotted me he left his blonde to push his way across the crowded room with a grin on his face and hand outstretched. 'Shake hands with the schmuck who turned down *Bongo*,' was all he said before pushing his way back to the blonde.

The year's end was not without its moment of sadness for me because 'Nipper' Lupino Lane died at the ridiculously early age of 67. You may well ask what's so ridiculous about the age of 67. It's simply that when you reach my number of years you feel that anyone who falls off his perch before you has done it too soon. My philosophy has always been that age is only important when you die and, as some fireside philosopher once asked, 'How old would you be if you didn't know how old you were?'

Strangely enough, of all the countries in which I've lived and worked, I found America the most age-fixated place of all. It seems to turn up, in brackets, with almost every other item they print, like a human sell-by date. Pick up any paper and there it is: 'Fanny Phanackapan (25), Arkansas' champion apple-dunker' or 'Joe Jehosophat (82), the world's loudest hog-caller'.

Lucille Ball was another anti-ager. 'The secret of staying young,' Lucy opined one day, 'is to live honestly, eat slowly and lie about your age.' 'But if you didn't lie?' someone laughed. 'Come on Lucy, you're among friends, how old are you?' 'Ten years younger than you think,' answered everyone's favourite redhead.

And while we're on that subject, a New York columnist called me recently for a telephone interview, at the end of which he asked, 'Incidentally, what is your correct age?'

'Why, does it have any bearing on the story?'

'No no, but the *World Film Encyclopedia* says one thing and *Motion Picture Almanac* says another. We'd just like to get our records straight.'

'Well, here's a clue,' I said helpfully. 'When Beethoven was my age he'd been dead 50 years.' And I hung up. As a matter of fact, because age has meant so little to me, I'm often momentarily stumped to give an exact answer. But with the help of my fingers, my calculator and my unmathematical mind I've decided the simplest way to remember is that if I'm writing this in the nineties and I'm only in my eighties, the century is ten years older than I am.

While Yolande and Maggie Lockwood still kept audiences laughing at the Duke of York's, Jimmy Carreras had asked me to make them laugh in the movie theatres with a sequel to *Up the Creek*. But this time there was no Peter Sellers because Pete had already rocketed to busy stardom, so I wrote it for our other favourite funny man, Frankie Howerd. Following this, also for the Carrerases but this time with son Michael, I filmed *Hell is a City*, a murder mystery involving the Manchester Police with the redoubtable Stanley Baker. This film has always been one of my own top four.

And yet the production I had most most fun on as we launched optimistically into the sixties was a psychological thriller called *The Full Treatment* (which American distributors, with their usual restraint, retitled *Stop Me Before I Kill*). Apart from shooting most of it on the French Riviera, which is always a joy, I was working with two living legends of the French cinema, Françoise Rosay and Claude Dauphin. Both wonderful professionals, wonderful people and wonderful performers. My Australian leading lady, Diane Cilento, was also no slouch as a performer. A product of New York's Academy of Dramatic Arts and London's RADA, she would shortly be Oscar-nominated for her performance with Albert Finney in *Tom Jones*. But back then, on the beautiful Côte d'Azur, Di was mildly apprehensive about her one nude scene in our film. As the tormented heroine of the story, pacing a deserted Theule beach one hot night, trying to ease her tension she slips off jeans and top for a therapeutic swim in the Mediterranean.

'You will make sure it's deserted,' she probed hesitantly.

'Of course,' I reassured her. 'There'll be no one around but the unit, and you needn't worry about them, they've seen it all before and unless you have three of anything they'll be too busy filling in their time-sheets and Football Pools.'

'Thanks,' she nodded and with a beautifully straight face added, 'You needn't worry either. I promise I don't have three of anything.'

This was the sequence on which we shot the usual cover for the American censor. Even our own John Trevelyan gave me some pre-shooting advice. 'We don't mind the topless bit,' he warned, 'but we won't allow pubics.'

Above: *Up the Creek* in Weymouth, with David Tomlinson, Peter Sellers and assistant director John Peverall in 1957.

Left: With leading lady Sylvia Syms, on the Shepperton set of *Expresso Bongo* in 1959.

Above: *Hell is a City* was shot on location in Manchester and the Yorkshire Moors in 1959. Stanley Baker played the no-nonsense Inspector Martineau.

Right: Meeting Harold Lloyd, and Harold Lloyd Jr, during production of *The Full Treatment* in 1960.

Below: Edward Judd and Janet Munro, who played the troubled young lovers in *The Day the Earth Caught Fire* (1961), between takes on location in Battersea.

Below: Val Guest and Yolande Donlan holding the British Film Academy Award for *The Day the Earth Caught Fire*. Left to right (standing): Tony Sforzini (make up), Bill Lenny (editor), Pamela Carlton (continuity), Bernard Williams (second assistant director), Geoffrey Tozer (art director), Maureen Comfort (production accountant), Barry Davis (assistant accountant), Wally Byatt (camera focus). Seated: Frank Sherwin Green (associate producer), VG, YD and Moray Grant (camera operator).

Below: On the set of *80,000 Suspects* (1963) with Richard Johnson, former
Daily Express editor Arthur Christiansen and Claire Bloom.

Right: Filming *Where the Spies Are* in Beirut in 1964. Left to right: David Niven, his wife Jhordis, and Françoise Dorléac.

Opposite: Trying to make sense of *Casino Royale* in 1966, with a captive Daliah Lavi and an enthusiastic Woody Allen.

Below: Face-to-face with Ursula Andress, 'the world's most beautiful woman', at Casino Royale.

Bottom: Hugh Heffner visited the set of *Casino Royale*, and was amused to learn that James Bond's chief protagonist lurked in the cellar beneath the Playboy Club.

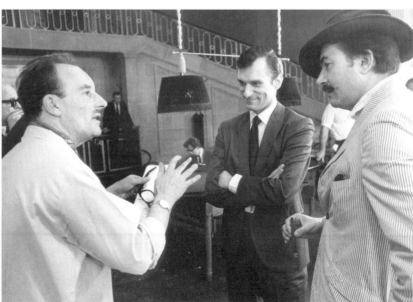

Above: Shooting the ill-fated *Toomorrow* in 1969, with nervous-looking newcomer 'Livvy' Newton-John.

Left: On location in Johannesburg with Peter Fonda and Maud Adams for *The Diamond Mercenaries* (1975).

Above: Trevor Howard and Diane Keen in *The Shillingbury Blowers* (1979). Trevor promised there'd be 'no tots on any shooting day.'

Right: Val and Yolande, with Palm Springs neighbour Loretta Young.

'What do you have against pubics'?' I laughed.

'Nothing at all,' answered John, ' but we don't like them flashed gratuitously.'

'The trouble with you censors,' I joked, 'is that you all have dirty minds.'

'We are paid to have dirty minds,' explained John Trevelyan.

Then there was Di Cilento's steady beau-on-the-woo, a handsome, likeable chunk of charm made even more interesting by what we had heard of his background. Whereas Diane was the daughter of eminent attorney Sir Ralph Cilento and Lady Cilento, noted gynaecologist, the boyfriend's father had been a truck driver and his mother a char lady, having an uphill struggle to raise a strong-minded, ambitious son who had left school at 15 to join the Royal Navy, left that to become a bricklayer, dropped bricks to become a lifeguard before becoming a coffin-polisher. How's that for a conversation-stopper? 'Hands up anyone who's met a coffin-polisher.'

But that wasn't the end of his fascinating CV. A body-building enthusiast, he drifted into modeling swim-shorts which in turn led to, wait for it, representing Scotland in the Mr Universe contest. Sadly he didn't win it, but he did win a job in the chorus of *South Pacific* at Drury Lane, just a hop-skip-and-a-jump into acting. But although he was now gainfully employed in what are euphemistically called 'supporting roles', his career seemed to be going nowhere in particular. What fun to have had the loan of Madame Zaza's crystal ball and been able to tell him that in less than two years time he would not only be married to Diane Cilento but also on the way to becoming a world superstar. Not as Mr Universe but as Ian Fleming's first 007, alias James Bond, alias, of course, our old friend Sean Connery.

Back in London the Donlan-Lockwood play had come to a successful close which, as far as Christopher and I were concerned, couldn't have occurred at a more opportune moment as we had finally made the momentous decision to leave our longtime Montagu Square flat. We were making a historic move into a historic house we had bought in St John's Wood called Peartree Cottage. I use the word historic advisedly as the star names that made it so were no less than that of its first tenants back in 1784, when it was a royal hunting lodge at which His Majesty King George IV conducted his clandestine love affair with the notorious Mrs Fitzherbert.

The house also had a stable for horse and carriage with a room in the rear for the coachman. Although this had long since been turned into a garage, the coachman's room was still there and we found it almost as fascinating to learn that the Aga Khan, spiritual leader of millions of Moslems, had also stayed in that very room while courting Joan, mother-to-be of the young Prince Aly, who would later grow up and marry Rita Hayworth. As you can gather, our new home had plenty of interesting vibes, not forgetting those of celebrated author F Tennyson Jesse, from whom we had bought it. And now it needed all of Yolande's time to help us move, refurbish and settle in.

Our love affair with Peartree was anything but clandestine and we were to live and love in it for many happy years to come. That is, after we got the painters out. Having arranged for a couple of our studio lads to do the job they had taken more time than Michelangelo did on the Sistine Chapel and eventually we had to move in to move them out. Even as they carted their gear through the front gate, our own very first 'historic' visitor squeezed his way in. It was Yo's chum and family friend, 'Uncle' Harold Lloyd.

The term 'legendary' is used all too loosely in the film industry, but if anyone really deserved the adjective it was Harold Lloyd, alongside the other two members of filmdom's great comedy triumvirate, Charles Chaplin and Buster Keaton. Back in the twenties Harold had become the funniest man on the American silent screen as well as Hollywood's highest paid actor whose drawing power had surpassed even Chaplin and Keaton. He had come into Yolande's life when her father, character actor James Donlan, appeared in several of Harold's pictures and the Donlans and Lloyds became fast friends.

In London for a short visit, Harold had dropped by to say hullo and, in passing, ask what we thought of an idea he was mulling over, to piece together some comedy routines from his old movies and release them as *Harold Lloyd's World of Comedy*. Not only did we think it a fabulous idea but even more exciting for me was when he asked if I would like to help choose some of the clips, to include snippets from time-honoured classics like *Safety Last* and *Professor Beware* (with Daddy Donlan), plus a library-full of other gems he'd made with his old sidekick Hal Roach. *Harold Lloyd's World of Comedy* turned into such a huge success they raced into a sequel, *The Funny Side of Life*, which also delighted the box-office. I wish I could claim some iota of credit for any of this but the funny finger of Fate had other plans for me and before I could see one reel of Harold's dream I had a dream of my own come true.

Every writer, every director has had some pet project they've struggled over the years to get made. I had one I'd been bashing against Wardour Street walls to no avail for the best part of seven years. It was a story I'd dreamed up called *The Day the Earth Caught Fire*, my vision of a future when mankind had done so many things to the atmosphere, then topped everything by inadvertently testing two atomic bombs at opposite ends of the globe at the same moment. All of which had altered the earth's orbit by one millionth of a degree and set us spinning slowly but surely towards the sun with disastrous climatic changes. Whereupon the government puts a security clamp on the whole incident which is eventually ferreted out by a relentless Fleet Street reporter. Since I had wanted to use the *Daily Express* as the newspaper that uncovered the story I sent a synopsis to their science editor, Chapman Pincher, asking for his comments. And he gave them. 'Good story, but a lot of balls,' he said cheerfully.

Mind you, at that time I had no idea how near I was to predicting global warming. I had even less idea that the finished picture was to win me a British Film Academy Award which would be presented to me by HRH the Duke of Edinburgh, or that Eleanor Roosevelt would ask for her own personal copy and that President Kennedy would screen another print in Washington for a meeting of foreign correspondents. I mean, come on, for someone still in the throes of struggling to get it set up this would all have sounded like demented pipe-dreams from the opium den. Which merely proves the worth of that sterling British Army advice in World War I: 'Come what may, we press on regardless.'

The one who had done just that and pressed on regardless was the indefatigable Steven Pallos. Once again he seemed to have achieved the impossible by getting no less than Sir Michael Balcon and co-producer Maxwell Setton on our side to the extent that the three of them were willing to form a new company, Pax Films, just to co-present the picture with British Lion. My first reaction was to jump three feet in the air, yell 'Whoops!' and do the Twist, the world's current dance craze. My second reaction was mild panic. I still had a couple of weeks' filming left on *The Full Treatment*. At the same time it was imperative to come up with a finished screenplay of *The Day the Earth Caught Fire* before anyone changed their mind. As usual, it was the Donlan brain that went into overdrive. 'Why not get some help? Like Mankowitz. You did a great job together on *Bongo*, why not another one?'

Within the hour I had tracked Wolf to the Wedgwood china shop he ran with his sister in Piccadilly. 'Trouble is, I'm in the middle of a book...' he began.

'Never mind the book, publishers wait. This is a film and they won't wait.'

My illogical logic either impressed or confused him because he signed the swiftest contract he'd ever signed and worked the longest hours he'd ever worked, with Yolande soothing us, coaxing us and feeding us until we had completed our second lucky screenplay together. In fact the first one, *Bongo*, was still doing so well I was able to put it up as collateral for the National Film Finance loan they were giving me towards making the new one.

In retrospect, *The Day the Earth Caught Fire* was possibly the toughest film assignment I'd ever set myself. For instance, one line in the screenplay reads: 'They cross a debris-strewn Fleet Street, derelict and almost deserted...' How easy it had been to write. Now try to shoot it. Would the City police even co-operate? Miraculously they did, thanks mainly to the efforts of one of Fleet Street's almost mythical characters, Arthur Christiansen. Having been Editor-in-Chief of Lord Beaverbrook's *Daily Express* for almost 25 years he had recently retired and I'd been lucky enough to sign him as technical adviser for my newspaper sequences. 'Chris' Christiansen, of course, knew everyone who mattered, from Police Commissioners upwards and downwards. In fact it was he who talked the eminent Beaverbrook himself into allowing us to shoot in the *Express* offices as well as using that newspaper as the one in my story. But it was me who actually talked 'Chris' into immortality by playing himself in the actual film.

Strange how sometimes one's mind retains minor memories while rejecting others. I still recall the day in Fleet Street when, coming out from a recce of the *Daily Express* building, I ran into one of the industry's busiest production managers, John Palmer. John had worked with me in the past and I well knew his prodigious capabilities. Half jokingly I said, 'Oh, boy, could I use you on this one. Have I got problems!'

'Want to trade?' he smiled and proceeded to tell me how he'd just returned from a location recce in Jordan with David Lean. 'In the desert. For *Lawrence of Arabia*. On top of which,' he laughed, 'we have Marlon Brando playing Lawrence. And you think you have problems?' Eventually Brando decided that instead of Lawrence he would rather play Fletcher Christian in a remake of *Mutiny on the Bounty*, so at least John Palmer had one less problem. Why do I remember this incident? Because, by sheer coincidence, almost a year later – on 16 May 1961 to be exact – David started shooting his *Lawrence* (with Peter O'Toole instead of Brando) on exactly the same day I began filming *The Day the Earth Caught Fire* in Battersea Park.

Of course, as John had predicted, we both had problems. But while they had to battle with sandstorms, we had to juggle with fog, our own man-made fog. It was for a sequence in which climatic changes bring a mysterious fog swirling up the almost waterless Thames engulfing South London and Battersea Park where lines of people are queueing for their water rations. Armed with all the neccessary permits, our machines were happily belching out clouds of lovely grey fog when a gentle breeze began wafting it across the Thames to the Chelsea Embankment. Within minutes a squad of police cars had raced to our location, ordering us, permits or no permits, to shut down production immediately. It seemed our fog had not only drifted across the Embankment but was swirling over the Royal Chelsea Flower Show which Her Majesty the Queen was at that moment trying to declare open in rapidly worsening visibility.

Hey-ho and lackaday. Somehow we managed to finish shooting while our brilliant PM and assistants double-talked the police about how long it took fog machines to shut themselves off, as well as using various other delaying tactics so that when we finally wrapped up we had managed to shoot all we needed without anyone being arrested, sent to the Tower or beheaded.

Emptying Fleet Street was a different nightmare. For the benefit of any future filmmakers or curious filmgoers it might be of interest to know I had to plan it like a battle campaign. The police agreed to close down one of the busiest streets in the City provided I shot early Sunday morning when they would place NO PARKING signs along all the pavements from the Law Courts to Ludgate Circus, so at least it would be empty of parked cars. All our scenes would have to be rehearsed during the normal traffic flow and every 15 minutes, on a radio signal and whistle, they would stop traffic at both ends for exactly two minutes, during which time I would have to get my shot before another whistle let it flow for another 15 minutes.

But that was only half the operation. At the start of each two-minute session a couple of motor-cycle cops accelerated up both sides of the street kicking down the NO PARKING signs so they were out of sight of the cameras. They were closely followed by our open-backed property truck, filled with rubble and dust which two energetic prop men shovelled into the now empty street as they sped after the motorcyclists. The moment they were out of sight behind the Law Courts I'd shout 'Action!', whereupon my actors, Leo McKern and Edward Judd, would saunter out of the *Daily Express* building to play their scene as they crossed a debris-strewn, deserted Fleet Street. In two minutes flat another whistle heralded the roar of London traffic taking over again. So, if you ever catch one of the re-runs you can now watch those scenes with added curiosity.

Anyway, the gods must have been smiling on us because somehow or other the picture I'd wanted to make for so long was finished in just under eight weeks of shooting and had its world première four months later at the Marble Arch Odeon. What's more those gods continued to smile right into the new year when Yo and I were on location in Peacehaven filming *Jigsaw*, an off-beat murder tale involving the Brighton Police.

Back at the hotel one night there was a message for me from London. Would I please call Theo Cowan. Theo was an old Gainsborough friend who had looked after star publicity there and, in passing, had long had an unrequited crush on Maggie Lockwood. He was now PR for the Society of Film and Television Arts. 'British Film Academy Awards,' he said briskly when I called him. 'You've been nominated. Best screenplay. *The Day the Earth Caught Fire*. Thought you'd like to know. Dorchester, April fifth. See you there. Love to Yo.' After I'd caught my breath I realised it was less than three weeks away and we would still be in the middle of shooting. My diary showed 5 April was a Thursday, which meant a late night at the Dorchester followed by a dawn rising to get back to work. To be honest, I really didn't think there was much chance of winning anything when the list of other screenplay nominees included *The Guns of Navarone*, *A Taste of Honey* and *Whistle Down the Wind* for starters. Still, at least it was exciting being nominated.

That year the award ceremony was to be held in the Dorchester Hotel Grand Ballroom with a reception at 6.30 and dinner at 8.00 followed by the awards presentation by guest of honour, Prince Philip. On the big night I arrived home from shooting wondering if I had the energy or will to struggle into a dinner jacket and go. 'Look,' said Yolande firmly, 'you've been nominated. You have to be there, win or lose. But they don't need me. So, if it's all right with you, Christopher and I are going to have an early night.'

Which is how I found myself dining at a table for eight people with an empty chair on one side of me and a charming young documentary director on the other. His name, he told me, was John Schlesinger and he too was in a state of suspended animation because his *Terminus*, a 45-minute film about Waterloo station, had been nominated for Best Documentary. A clairvoyant would have told him to relax because his documentary would not only win tonight's award but also First Prize at the Venice Film Festival and then launch him into full-length features. 'Just listen to old Nostra, John, because a few years from tonight you'll have directed a film called *Darling* which will not only win the New York Critics Award but get you an Oscar nomination for best director and best picture.' I wasn't clairvoyant, however, so we both just sat there tensely, wishing they'd get on with the ceremony. Suddenly a bustling Theo Cowan was at my side tapping the empty chair.

'Where's Yo?'

'She has an early call, Theo, so she's made it an early night.'

'Has she now?' he grunted and bustled off as they readied things for His Royal Highness. In the meantime I found myself fascinated by the neatly turned out lady sitting across from me. Attractive, in her late fifties, with a highly alive face, it was Sheilah Graham who happened to be, along with Hedda Hopper and Louella Parsons, one of the most powerful columnists in Hollywood. But that wasn't what fascinated me. It was her life story, which someone had once described as a supercharged soap opera. Starting life as a little cockney girl named Lily Sheil and brought up in a London orphanage, she went on to become a showgirl and model before descending on Hollywood to make her mark as a respected writer. She then topped all that by becoming famous, or infamous, for her turbulent four-year love affair with F Scott Fitzgerald. It sounded just like a screenplay. In fact it did make a screenplay and film, from her own book *Beloved Infidel*, which she wrote about those four torrid years. But somehow Gregory Peck and Deborah Kerr, good as they were, didn't make them torrid enough for me.

Anyway, I found it mildly amusing that here I was, waiting to hear about a writing award while chatting it up with the mistress of one of the great writers of the 20th century. And it was while we were chatting that my eyes suddenly popped and my mouth dropped open. Miss Graham looked at me with a mite of concern.

'Are you all right?'

'Oh yes, yes, sorry, but I've just seen my wife.'

In any other scenario the line might have had a dozen interpretations, but that night the correct one was that I'd just seen Yolande, in full evening attire, threading her way through the tables towards us. What's more she had young Christopher at her side, dressed for the occasion in his own little tuxedo.

'Theo called me,' she explained breathlessly as they found another chair for Chris. 'Said we'd better get here fast because he thinks you've won.'

'Good old Theo,' I laughed, 'and good old you! That must have been the quickest quick-change you ever made.'

'Quicker than the quickest,' grinned Yo. 'It's so exciting I don't even know if I have matching shoes.'

As I've already told you, we had indeed won and it was an unforgettable moment walking up to the dais where a smiling Duke of Edinburgh was waiting to hand me my British Academy Award.

'Congratulations,' said the Duke as he shook my hand. 'And what are you up to now?'

'I'm making a murder mystery with the Brighton Police, sir.'

'How bloody boring,' said Prince Philip and turned to check the next recipient.

Coincidentally, the following April almost to the day, David Lean's *Lawrence of Arabia* would collect not one but seven American Film Academy Awards. However, as David was over in Los Angeles he wasn't able to bore the Prince with what he was up to now. And while we're on the subject of *Lawrence*, it was to become one of Yo's all-time favourites which she saw four times. It's also interesting to note that Noël Coward felt the same way. 'Absolutely splendid,' the Master pronounced. 'As for Peter O'Toole, if Lawrence had looked like him there would have been more than 12 Turks queueing up in the buggering scene.'

What a shame they weren't able to use this quote.

CHAPTER
SEVENTEEN

1963 kicked off with the one of the coldest Januaries on record. Normally one would simply grumble and put on extra woollies but this time, alas, it wasn't that easy for poor Yolande. Let me tell you the whole shivering story.

We had just begun shooting *80,000 Suspects* with her, Richard Johnson and Claire Bloom in the beautiful old city of Bath. The first night's location was with 200 extras making merry with New Year's Eve revels outside Bath's historic Pump Room and Roman Baths, all of which our art director had festooned with decorations and lit trees. Everything was fine except that earlier that evening Mother Nature had decided she wanted to help the art department by dropping the year's first light carpet of snow. It certainly looked good but what if it didn't continue? What if tomorrow night all that beautiful white carpet had become brown slush so that nothing you filmed then would match anything you were about to film now?

Decisions, decisions. Send the 200 extras home and try again tomorrow? Or take a chance and shoot? I braved the latter but telephoned Pinewood Studios to have four truckloads of fake snow standing by to be raced down to us should we need to lay our own carpet on the morrow. As it happened, Mother Nature played ball and we never needed those trucks, but with every fall of snow it got colder. So cold that for our street tracking shots with Claire and Richard we had to light up every brazier and oil stove we could find, lining the sidewalks with them just below camera level to keep the actors thawed out. Which was mere child's play compared to what was in store for Yolande in those ancient Roman Baths.

Considered among the finest Roman remains in the country, they were built in AD 75 and consist of an Olympic-sized bath, open to the skies, surrounded by sculpture-faced columns and still fed by Britain's most famous hot-spring water. Our big question was how hot is hot-spring water on the coldest night of the year? Because that was when we were scheduled to shoot a scene in which a merrily tipsy and romantically mixed-up Yolande, in her Christian Dior party gown and a moment of bravado, jumps into the water and swims to the middle, taunting Richard Johnson to come in and get her. And while I knew the spa water was purported to heal all kind of things I was pretty sure it didn't include pneumonia. Obviously the schedule would have to be rearranged but, even as the production office looked into alternatives, the news trickled through to Yo who promptly stamped her little foot.

'No way,' declared my undauntable wife. 'Let's shoot and get it over. Okay, so it's minus something or other, tomorrow it could be more minus.' A typical example of Yolande's Positive Thinking. So once again I decided to plan the sequence like a battle. With three cameras placed in strategic positions around the Baths we meticulously rehearsed the whole sequence on dry land so that once in the water Yo could stay in until the whole sequence was shot and then climb out surrounded by more towels, robes and heaters than any Roman Emperor ever had. Came the night, we shot it diligently, she played it delightfully as did Richard Johnson, all of which helped towards making *Suspects* the picture Rank chose to represent them at that year's Edinburgh Film Festival.

To unwind, and to get Yolande's circulation back to full throttle, we decided to spend Easter in Paris, followed by a quick sortie to Cannes and Monte Carlo which we used as a recce to find some locations needed for my next production, *The Beauty Jungle*, a lighthearted exposé of the machinations of the Beauty Queen circuit. It might be amusing to note that shortly after a columnist broke the story I received a warning letter from Eric Morley, the impresario who ran, organised and presented the yearly Miss England contest. In effect, it advised me that: (1) Miss England, Miss World and Miss Universe were all registered titles and woe betide anyone who used them without authority, and (2) he would like to see a copy of the final screenplay before shooting commenced.

Poor Eric Morley, I don't know what he thought I was about to expose but my immediate reply was that: (1) my contests were called Miss English Rose and Miss Globe, titles which were now our copyright and woe betide anyone who used them without authority. However: (2) while no scripts were being handed out to anyone I would be delighted to see he was given two seats for the première, one for him and one for his lawyer. I never heard whether he saw the film or not but I still can't wait for someone to use the title Miss English Rose or Miss Globe.

The star role in *The Beauty Jungle* (*Contest Girl* in the US) was that of a local girl spotted by a press photographer at a Butlin's holiday camp beauty contest and persuaded to let him promote her into the big time and Miss Globe. What's more, I'd spotted the girl I thought would be ideal for the part, a comparatively unknown young repertory actress I'd first seen in a film called *Crooks Anonymous*. Her name was Julie Christie and I sent a full synopsis of the story to her Earl's Court address, saying I was considering her for the leading role and how did she feel about it?

A week later the synopsis came back with a note scribbled on it. 'Reply follows JC.' A few days later that too arrived. 'I'm so sorry I didn't phone before I left for Birmingham but my phone was out of order and I just didn't have time to go out to a public phone box, with all the last minute things to do... Hope you got the script back promptly – just about managed to stick the envelope down myself!' Poor Julie, rehearsing at the Birmingham Repertory Theatre, trying to learn her lines and brace herself for an opening night, all she needed was reading the synopsis of a film she might or might not be in. Her letter went on: 'It certainly is the most marvellous part. Very difficult, too. I *think* I could play it – at least I understand it.' *Think?* Dear, uncertain Julie, less than two years later this virtually unknown young actress would win not only the prestigious New York Film Critics Award but the Academy Award too for her performance in *Darling*, a far more difficult leading role than mine. 'I would love to talk about it,' she ended. 'Anyway I hope I will see you soon.'

So I arranged a quick trip to talk to her over dinner one evening after the show. Not being up on Birmingham eateries, I thought it easier for us to go back to my hotel dining room which at that hour would still be just about open. It wasn't her most glamorous night out, but at least we were able to chat over some rather tired-looking lobster salads. It seemed the thing that daunted her most was the screen test. I tried to soothe her daunt.

'Just relax, Julie. It's not to see if you can act. I've seen that. It's only to show Earl St John how you'll look in those Miss Globe outfits and your bikini.'

'I don't have a bikini,' laughed Julie.

'Then I'll bring you one from Cannes,' I promised, 'a white one. I'm there any minute to finalise locations. What size?'

A couple of weeks later I was flying back from Cannes with my PM, Bob Lynn, when he looked up from one of the London papers the steward had given us. 'Weren't you thinking of Julie Christie?'

'I still am, why?'

'Great minds think alike,' he grinned, folding over the showbiz column for me. And there it was, top item. The clever John Schlesinger had now landed his second full-length film, *Billy Liar*. Hooray for John! And who had he signed up to play opposite Tom Courtenay in her first leading role? Double hooray for Julie! And that's how it happened – or didn't happen, according to the film you were on. After which a might-have-been-famous white bikini disappeared into some drawer to get lost forever along with Marilyn Monroe's bra.

I then went ahead and tested at least half-a-dozen names, near-names, no-names and Janette Scott. Jan's name was certainly known. She'd made many films from child actress to ingenue leads and I thought it an excellent test, but somehow Earl wasn't happy. 'She's good,' he shrugged, 'but wrong type, too girl-next-doorish, has no – what d'you call it? – woomph.'

A couple of days later we gave Jan a full Beauty Queen make-up, a striking blonde wig, a phoney name and did another test which I slipped in amongst some of our next day's rushes. Earl perked up when he saw it. 'Now that's just the type of girl you need, why don't you use her?' Since an executive producer's word is almost a law unto itself I said I'd take his advice. And that's how ex-girl-next-door Janette Scott got the part and was able to add another credit to her collection.

We shot the finals of our Miss Globe contest at London's Talk of the Town, with a guest star jury comprising Norman Hartnell, the Queen's dressmaker, Linda Christian, the Duchess of Bedford, and current pop favourite Joe Brown. The press had a ball with Norman's name – HART-NELL TO DESIGN ROYAL BIKINIS? asked the *Evening News*' Show Page headline and even Norman laughed. But just three weeks later we were to be stunned by another headline: PRESI-DENT KENNEDY ASSASSINATED.

Altogether that year had been a mixed bag of headlines. We had the Christine Keeler-John Profumo call-girl scandal in which somehow our chum Doug Fairbanks Jr's name had become involved. One of the other girls, Mandy Rice-Davies, had named him as being present at one of those infamous nude swimming parties on Viscount Astor's Cliveden estate. When challenged by a defence lawyer that Mr Fairbanks denied this, she delivered the classic reply, 'Well, he would, wouldn't he?' After which this line was used in some form or other by almost every comedian in the land.

August had brought us Britain's Great Train Robbery when some villains hijacked a fortune in banknotes from a Cheddington mail train. I well remember returning from a Monte Carlo location the following day and finding the papers full of it. I also found a message about it on my Ansafone. It was from Peter Sellers and said, 'I know it's tough to find money for films but this time you've gone too far.'

And so, on into another year. It isn't often a new year starts with an occasion that is difficult to top, but for this one my clever Yolande managed to arrange it. Using her not inconsiderable influence she managed to jump-start a cold January by getting us two tickets for *Tosca* at the Royal Opera House Covent Garden with Maria Callas and Tito Gobbi to warm us up. There must be a single adjective to describe an evening that was unforgettable, spell-binding and magical, but for the life of me I can't think of it. The Opera House has always said it can judge a hit or miss by the First Interval buzz in their famous Circle Crush Bar. Well, that evening the buzz was an electric one.

For the benefit of those unlucky enough never to have been in the Crush Bar it is a spacious, lofty room, richly carpeted, warmly lit by little pink-shaded lamps and scattered with small tables and chairs plus two bars flowing with champagne and smoked salmon. That evening, amidst the buzzing splendour of dinner jackets and haute coutures we spotted our old *Bongo* buddy, Ken MacMillan, for a change just a member of the audience like ourselves. 'It certainly is a night to remember,' he agreed and then, with a wicked smile, 'But I'll let you into a little secret – neither of them can sing and dance at the same time.'

Which brings me to the moment when it's all too easy to write 'Little did I know' or 'Who'd have thought', phrases that drive me up the wall in anyone else's book. Instead let's just say that one year later, almost to the week, I would be sitting in this same Crush Bar with David Niven and his French co-star Françoise Dorléac. But this time there was no crowd other than ours and the only thing flowing was the location caterer's tea trolley as we completed the last day's shooting on a picture called *Where the Spies Are*. Having just returned from several arduous weeks of filming in Lebanon, the Opera House seemed like a haven of peace. The management had given us permission to use their hallowed precincts provided we shot on a Sunday and left the place as hallowed as we found it. All of which was a lot easier to comply with than some of the rules we'd been given for leaping around the Middle East!

It had all started when I read a best-selling thriller by James Leasor called *Passport to Oblivion*, a lighthearted tale of an English country GP, Dr Jason Love, who holidays in Lebanon and lands knee-deep in some international spy capers. So I bought the film rights, corraled Wolf Mankowitz again, beavered our way through a screenplay and submitted it to MGM. 'We like it,' said Maurice Silverstein, vice-president of MGM foreign productions, 'but the title's no good. You can't call it *Passport to Oblivion*. Most people will think Oblivion is a sleeping pill.'

A week later Culver City came up with one from their Unused Titles drawer – *Where the Spies Are*. In retrospect I'm surprised no one ever questioned *Gone With the Wind* because most people would think it was a flatulence pill. However, there we were all set up with *Where the Spies Are* starring David Niven and Françoise Dorléac, supported by my wonderful rep company. Now all we had to do was shoot it.

Jimmy Leasor had set his original story in Tehran but a friend of ours in the Foreign Office had warned us confidentially we'd be ill-advised to consider making a film there. 'The whole of Iran is still somewhat volatile,' he explained in Foreign Office speak. 'Just the sight of someone running across a street could spark a revolution. You get my point?'

I did and immediately rewrote all our Middle East locations into the Lebanon and Beirut. I can almost hear your ribald laughter. Beirut? He was out of his mind! Well, not completely because at that time it was still a popular city for package tours and cruise ships. It would be several years before intriguing Beirut erupted into its civil war between Muslims and Christians and, even later, got itself bombed and battered in the conflict with Israel. Luckily we were there while they still had a sparkling nightlife and a splendiferous casino. What's more, who should be starring at that casino but Shirley Bassey and she'd fallen head over heels for the city. 'Love it, adore it!' enthused our Shirl-girl. 'Can't wait to buy a holiday pad here!'

Happily we were able to talk her out of that immediate decision, although it was easy to see the appeal of the place with its fascinating mixture of biblical and modern. However, getting a film unit over there was to be even more fascinating. Apart from the usual innoculation and visa problems I received a summons from the Lebanese ambassador to visit him at his embassy in Kensington Palace Gardens. He was charm itself as he informed me how delighted everyone was that we would be the first international picture to be filmed in his country and how he wished to give us all possible help. In view of this he had asked me there for some unofficial tips on how my unit should fill in their visa requests. 'Firstly,' he told me with a smile, 'there will, of course, be no Jews on your unit. Where the visa form says 'Religion' they will write Protestant, Catholic, Quaker, whatever. Do you understand what I'm saying, Mr Guest?'

Only too clearly. Furthermore, he suggested with even greater charm, if by some unhappy chance anyone had a passport with an Israeli stamp in it they might be advised to get a temporary document for this visit without that cancellation. Thanks to His Excellency I was learning a few tricks of the diplomatic trade and less than a month later Middle East Airways were able to transport two planeloads of Catholics, Quakers, C of E and even, I'm told, a couple of Mormons safely into Beirut airport. There we were met by the indefatigable Frank Green, my AP, who had flown ahead to organise the Arab side and now whisked us through the ancient streets to our new home and HQ, that Beirut landmark called the Phoenecia hotel.

To celebrate our first night in residence on biblical soil a few of us met up in the famous underwater bar. Known as such because it was below ground and had one plate-glass wall through which one could see the bottom of the hotel swimming pool. It looked like an aquarium except that instead of watching colourful denizens of the deep one had a parade of flailing legs, diving torsos and underwater swimmers who sometimes pressed their faces against the glass trying to see who was in the bar. On this particular night they would have seen Yolande, on location holidaying with us, taking a well-earned rest from the theatre, together with the irreplaceable Bumble Dawson, who by luck had been available to join us and costume la Dorléac. They might also have seen the delectable Françoise herself, that talented young French actress who so unfairly appeared to live in the shadow of her more famous sister, Catherine Deneuve.

Not that it seemed to worry Françoise, who at that moment was more concerned about her sister's state of mind. Catherine, she told us, had recently split with live-in boyfriend, French director Roger Vadim. Vadim, who had previously discovered, married and divorced Brigitte Bardot, had now moved on again, leaving Catherine to care for their two-year-old love child and fight off an understandable attack of 'the glums'. 'She's between work,' said Françoise one day. 'I'm sure it would help if she could join us here.'

Which is how Catherine Deneuve came to be in Beirut at the same time as top British portrait photographer David Bailey. David had been commissioned to take some special publicity shots of Françoise amongst the ruins of Baalbeck and Byblos, but although the beauty of Baalbeck's Temple of Jupiter took his breath away it was nothing to what his first sighting of Catherine Deneuve did to him. I think there was once a book called *Love Among the Ruins* but, be that as it may, suddenly we were faced with the usual plot in an unusual setting when Boy unexpectedly meets Girl, Girl unexpectedly likes Boy and eventually, even more unexpectedly, Boy pitches his woo and marries Girl. To this day I don't know whether or not we did Catherine Deneuve Bailey a favour by inviting her to Beirut because her 'Love Among the Ruins', sadly, was destined to end up in more ruins.

Perhaps the most unexpected hazard we encountered in Beirut was on our Byblos location. It came in the form of a not unattractive young ma'm'selle from the *Paris Soir* newspaper who was anxious to interview M'sieur Niven. I explained that David was still in Nice finishing the Peter Ustinov film, *Lady L*, in which he was currently co-starring with Sophia Loren, but that he would be with us before the end of the week.

'Ah,' nodded Ma'm'selle, 'it is about his work with Miss Loren I wish to ask him.'

'Might be easier for *Paris Soir* to talk to them while they're both still in Nice,' I suggested.

She shook her head vigorously. 'No, no, is my exclusif about David Niven.' Then, seeing my frown, she laughed. 'No, no, no, is not scandal, but I have curiosité how he charmed Arabs into a visa after he and Sophia have already filmed in Israel.'

It took a moment for the full meaning of her words to sink in and start my three-alarm firebells ringing. I wasn't aware David had done a previous location shoot in Israel and, I was willing to bet, neither were the Lebanese. All it needed was for her story to hit the news stands and at best we'd all be expelled and escorted on to the next MEA planes for London. Suddenly this smiling Miss *Paris Soir* had become a walking time-bomb and I could almost feel the 5000 BC remains of ancient Byblos rumbling under my feet.

That evening, over a drink with her in the underwater bar, I tried to explain the disaster her story could wreak on our production and would she please hold it until after we'd left the country. Sorry, no way, said the smiling time-bomb, because others might get the story and 'boum!' would go her *exclusif*. It could also mean that 'boum!' would go *Where the Spies Are*. By the end of that week no one was more anxious than I to meet the last incoming plane from Nice with David Niven aboard, even to the extent of passing up a delicious couscous dinner with Yolande, Bumble and Shirley. As the plane taxied to a halt I was already out there on the tarmac waiting to greet the surprised David at the foot of the aircraft steps.

'Hello, chum,' he grinned cheerfully. 'Nice to see you, how's it all going?'

On our drive back to the Phoenecia I broke it to him gently. 'So please, David, somehow or other try and talk her out of it,' I begged. 'Maybe give her another story, chat her up, charm her, take her to dinner, do anything you can to persuade her not to print until we've left the country.'

For a moment he turned to look at me in silence, then the Niven twinkle appeared. 'I gather what you're trying to tell me is that whatever it takes to accomplish the assignment I just have to lie back and think of Val Guest Productions.'

'Spoken like an officer and a gentleman,' I said, and we both laughed while I crossed my fingers on both hands.

What else can I say except that we were able to finish our locations smack on schedule without even the smallest paragraph appearing in *Paris Soir*. And although I was grateful for the fine co-operation of the Lebanese army, air force and police, none of us, including MGM, should ever forget the sterling undercover work of one David Niven, Ian Fleming's original conception of 007. I never asked him when, where or how his mission was accomplished because, my dear chap, that simply isn't the sort of thing one asks an ex-officer and a gentleman. However, I will say that over the years, if David and I happened to be anywhere when someone mentioned trouble in the Middle East, our eyes would meet and there would be a twinkle in his, followed by a slow wink.

We flew back to dear old Jolly the day before Xmas Eve only to find the electorate had taken advantage of our absence and changed governments. It seemed that Labour was now in charge and our new Prime Minister was Harold Wilson who, in his early Downing Street euphoria and before anyone could say 'British Empire', had magnanimously handed over the last of it, the tiny Mediterranean island of Malta which, after 140 years of British colonial rule, had now been given its independence. Hardly a world-shaking event but it certainly shook a few of the British. Not because they'd lost another colony but because suddenly they'd gained another tax haven.

As a newly independent republic, Malta had a Nationalist Prime Minster, George Borg Olivier, who was to go down in history as the man who gave his blessing to an income tax agreement whereby Sterling residents only paid sixpence in the pound. That alone would have made him historic, and you can imagine the sudden property boom caused by ex-patriates who settled there and became known fondly as 'The Sixpennies'. In fact, several of our own friends and acquaintances had already domiciled themselves on this 95-square-mile piece of paradise where both the skies and the natives were always sunny.

There was the glamorous star of English silent films, Estelle Brody, together with husband, top showbiz agent Bob Fenn. There was that celebrated painter of royal portraits, Vasco Lazzolo, whose Lija home was as spacious as his parties, to say nothing of best-selling author Nicholas Monserrat who had moved all his books and typewriters to Malta's even smaller island of Gozo. Anyway, it wasn't long before my gregarious Yolande, deciding it would be fun if we too had a holiday pad on the island, promptly flew there and bought us a sunny penthouse with a breathtaking view of Balluta Bay. I'm afraid ours wasn't for tax reasons, but simply to give us a fun pad we could fly off to between plays and films.

And what fun it was. Not only the inhabitants but Malta itself seemed to be an island where they were always entertaining. I well remember our first Maltese New Year's Eve party at a resplendent house in the native M'dina to which everyone who was anyone had been invited, including their 'historic' Prime Minister George Borg Olivier. A few minutes before midnight I hurried to the men's room to spend a quick end-of-year penny and found myself standing next to Borg Olivier himself doing the same thing. Even as we stood there the cathedral bells began chiming midnight. Whereupon a smiling Borg Olivier turned to me, lifted one arm over the small partition between us, said 'Happy New Year' and shook my free hand. Just another 'historic' moment in my incident-packed life. I mean, how many people have shaken hands with a Prime Minister in the middle of a pee?

Let's move from the historical to the hysterical and my saga with one of the great mind-changers of the century, the likeable, hateable, exhilarating, exasperating yet sometimes almost lovable Charles K Feldman. This Hollywood producer extraordinaire had bought the screen rights of *Casino Royale*, the only Bond book Cubby Broccoli and Harry Saltzman didn't own. After which, undecided at which of our three major studios he would make it, he built sets in all of them, Pinewood, Shepperton and Elstree's MGM. At the end of a day's shooting one could often hear the unit plea: 'What studio are we at tomorrow?'

Be that as it may, at least he decided to contract me for the picture. Shortly after which I received a beautifully engraved card from Columbia Pictures inviting me to a Dorchester reception where Charles K Feldman would introduce his newly signed director, Val Guest. As this was the first I'd heard of the event I concluded they had either forgotten to tell me or didn't dare in case he changed his mind. Anyway, it seemed he hadn't, so off I went to the Dorchester to meet me. Thus began my unforgettable assignment on *Casino Royale*.

For the screenplay Charlie K had signed prestigious double-Oscar winner Ben Hecht who, sadly, had passed away in the middle of writing it. But not, as some unkind people suggested, because of it. Whereupon our unpredictable producer had engaged novelist-screenwriter Terry Southern to write another one before deciding to call in even more writers, including my old friend and collaborator Wolf Mankowitz. So, when I arrived on the scene I was handed a gaggle of scripts, none of which had much to do with the Ian Fleming book but from which, I was told, I might get some ideas.

'What happened to the original story?' I asked naïvely.

'Can't use it,' said Charlie. 'The other Bonds have stolen everything except the title and the casino.'

Somehow we began shooting on the scheduled dates with each of us four directors, John Huston, Ken Hughes, Joe McGrath and myself, managing to pull our rewritten segments together and cope with Charlie's overnight inspirations as well as those early morning phone calls telling us who to write into whatever sequence was coming up. When he told me to dream up a scene for Brigitte Bardot by next Thursday I sat up late and did it, only to be called the following night and told, 'Forget Bardot. Too many conditions. But Bill Holden's in town and he'll do it, change it to him.'

I first met William Holden that weekend when Charlie invited both of us to lunch at his Mayfair apartment the day before shooting. 'Hullo,' smiled Bill as we shook hands. 'Charlie asked me to break it to you gently. He wants this segment rewritten so that I turn out to be the next James Bond.' Seeing my ashen face he gripped my shoulder and grinned. 'Only kidding. I'm just your extra crowd tomorrow.'

Then there was George Raft, whose memorable performance as the coin-flipping Guido Rinaldo in the 1932 classic *Scarface* had elevated him to the position of Hollywood's quintessential movie gangster. Raft was in town to become the celebrity manager of London's new glitzy gambling spot, the Colony Club in Berkeley Square. 'Fit him in somewhere,' was the Feldman order when he brought him onto our casino set and introduced us.

'Christ, don't give me a lot of lines,' pleaded Raft.

'No lines,' I promised, 'just an old familiar scene. I want the camera to pan slowly across the roulette tables and find you leaning against that pillar flipping a coin – cut – and you're away.'

'Flipping a coin?' His head had come up sharply. 'Shit, that was 30 years ago – don't even know if I can still do it!' But he could and did. It was lucky we shot it that day because not long afterwards he was refused re-entry into Britain when they discovered that filmdom's quintessential gangster had too many close connections with the real ones in America.

Yet another brief appearance in *Casino* was made by a newcomer, a 19-year-old photographic model named Jackie Bisset, cast in the tiny part of Fleming's Miss Goodthighs. Not quite a beginner's dream but Jackie carried it off with all the panache and good humour that would eventually launch her into international stardom as Jacqueline Bisset.

Our other film newcomer was Woody Allen who had only just finished acting in his very first one, also for Feldman, a comedy called *What's New Pussycat?* Having also co-written that screenplay Woody had already encountered some of the Charlie K hazards. 'The man's a murderer. A script murderer,' said Woody one morning at Peartree Cottage, where we were working together on his segment of the *Casino* script, trying to write some comedic sense into the last few reels of the picture. One of our routines had just come back with Charlie's pencilled notes and 'Too long' scribbled at the top of the page, marked with his own suggested cuts. Most of which were the funny tag lines, leaving all the unfunny ones intact. I well remember one of Woody's scenes in which he's facing a firing squad. Tied to a post with his eyes blindfolded, he is offered a last cigarette. 'No thanks,' he says, 'it's bad for my health.' To me a funny, typical Woodyism, but not to Charlie. Back came our typescript marked GOOD SCENE, but with the line deleted. Woody was ready to set up his own firing squad until I promised the line would go back in when we shot.

On that first script-grumbling morning Yolande had invited Woody to stay for lunch. And not just any old lunch, because Yo, being Yo, had planned it scrupulously and wanted to surprise him with his first typically British meal. In conference with Edwards, our wonderful Welsh cook, she had gone through the gamut of staunchly British dishes. Tripe and onions? Too specialised. Bangers and mash? Too ordinary. Roast beef and Yorkshire pud? Too obvious. Irish stew, shepherd's pie...? 'Why not steak and kidney pie?' suggested Edwards. Fantastic, we chorused, fondly remembering his steak and kidney which was worthy of a Michelin rating.

So there we were, Woody and I, slogging away in the living room trying to keep our minds on the Feldman script instead of the heady aroma of lunch wafting in from the Peartree kitchen. Not a moment too soon Yo appeared in the doorway. 'Lunch is served,' she announced cheerfully and never was an order obeyed with more alacrity. How can I best describe that memorable moment when Edwards placed those plates of his succulent pie in front of us.

'Smells delicious,' said Woody as he peered under his piecrust. 'What is it?'

'English steak and kidney pie, sir,' beamed Edwards and there was a brief silence before Woody lowered his crust back onto the plate.

'Oh dear,' he sighed apologetically. 'I can't eat kidneys.'

A deathly hiatus. As he hadn't said if his problem was gastric or ethnic it was simply no good just offering to fork out the kidneys. But the unflappable Edwards took it in his stride, shot back into the kitchen, reappearing in no time at all with a four-star British omelette and the rest of Woody's first British banquet proceeded flaplessly.

Not so with the shooting of *Casino* when, too often, a flap a day kept filming at bay. Such as the morning Charlie decided green was the wrong colour-motif for the next day's set, so the art department repainted all night. Which also meant no sleep for a desperate wardrobe department, trying to change the co-ordinating colours of everything Ursula wore on that set, ending with the Third Assistant having to wake Orson Welles at 5.00 am to ask if he'd please come in and do a sequence that as yet he hadn't even learned. Or the week poor manic-depressive Pete Sellers had a sudden hate-everyone bout, causing Charlie K to remove director Joe McGrath, leaving the Sellers/Welles segment helmless, until replacement director Robert Parrish was conscripted into our army. And how can I forget the day John Huston grinned at me coming out of the projection room, saying, 'This could easily turn into a load of crap, couldn't it?'

'Easily,' I grinned back. 'That's why they engaged people like you to see it doesn't.'

'Hey, don't try passing the buck,' laughed John. 'We're all in this together, except that I'm about to get out.' His contract was up, he explained, his segment was all but complete and he couldn't wait to fly home to Ireland and play some drama-free poker on his Galway estate. 'Only a couple of Deborah Kerr bits left and you won't find them a problem. Or her,' he added. Then, seeing my blank look, 'Christ, didn't Charlie ask you?'

'Ask me what?'

'If you'd take care of those for me? They're only tie-ups and you'll love Deborah. Would you mind?'

No, I wouldn't mind and yes, I did love Deborah, a delightful, fun lady with a sense of humour to match. By then my own eight-week contract was up but Charlie asked me to stay on and help figure out the best way to tie the various directors' segments together. Normally, of course, this should have been done before we began, but as nothing seemed normal on *Casino* I agreed to write some linking sequences, provided I could use Niven and Andress as the links. At least that way I knew I'd have two chums around to giggle with and help keep my sanity for the rest of the picture.

However, nobody did much giggling the day a crowd of 300 dress-extras waited on the casino set for Peter Sellers to show up and he never did. An apologetic call from his home explained that, amongst other ailments, Pete was suffering from exhaustion and on doctor's advice was taking a short rest, whereupon he had flown to Spain, promising to be back next week. 'I don't want the sonofabitch back,' stormed an irate Feldman when told the news. 'If we can get by with the footage we have of him I'll terminate his contract right now!' And that's exactly what happened after Bob Parrish and editor Bill Lenny found that with clever manoeuvring and judicious cutting they had enough of Peter to complete his segment. The only shot missing would be one of him in the finale when all our 007s were to be shown as winged angels up in Heaven. 'Forget it,' barked Charlie, 'cut him out of Heaven!'

'Instead of cutting him out,' I ventured tentatively, 'you could cut him in with a lifesize cut-out. Just blow up a still and use that.' Which they did, placing it knee-deep in clouds at the back of the Heaven set. So, if you happen to catch a TV re-run, see if you can spot it.

Sooner or later all things come to an end, even the filming of *Casino Royale*, and, unless our mecurial producer had another brainwave, it looked like we could actually be finished by Christmas 1966. I had only one location left for some pick-up shots in Cap Ferrat, using doubles for Niven and Andress. And what joy to leave London in a below-freezing October and touch down in a sunny South of France.

But my joy was short-lived. After our first day's shooting I received an unexpected call from home. It was Yolande, to tell me that Vi, that treasured mother-figure of my youth, had died that morning in her nursing home. It was a shock, but not as great as it might have been because she'd been getting so frail since the death of husband Bill that we had arranged for her to go into a small, private nursing home in nearby Hampstead, close enough for Yo to visit while I was away. It was shortly after one of Yolande's visits that the indomitable, seemingly indestructible guardian of my formative years had finally left us forever. With a great deal of luck and a unit working above and beyond the call of duty I was able to finish our Riviera location and be home in time for her funeral. My ever-capable Yo having organised everything at the Golders Green Crematorium, it was there we said goodbye to that very dear lady, without whose early help and understanding I would probably have disintegrated long before I plucked up the courage to leave home.

By then my eight-week contract was in its seventh month and our home life almost non-existent. So can you wonder that my darling, helpful, patient wife, tired of waiting for a husband free enough to join her for a family holiday, finally decided to go it alone.

'You'll be on this epic forever,' she said one night, 'and I'm dying to go to Russia.'

'Dying to go where?'

'Soviet Union,' she explained patiently, as though to a backward child. 'I'm curious to see what all this Iron Curtain stuff is about and while you've been busy I've been taking Russian lessons, just to surprise you.'

Up until then I had learned to cease being surprised at anything the gregarious Yolande assayed in her thirst for travel, but this did rather shake me. Not least because at that time we were still at the height of the Cold War. However, trivialities like this never daunted Yo, who went ahead, booked herself onto a Russian boat, the MS Krupskaja, leaving Tilbury for Stockholm before disembarking at Leningrad where she took the train to Moscow, arriving in Red Square just in time to help celebrate their October Revolution parade. Just thinking about it left me speechless with admiration!

We were very near the end of production when Feldman invited me to dinner with his live-in French lady friend, Monique, plus Bill Holden on his last day in London. With Yo still in Red Square I accepted with alacrity and also because I found it impossible not to like this predictably unpredictable producer, with his classic gift for somehow managing to stay endearing even when he was driving you up the wall.

'And now for the good news,' smiled Charlie K over coffee and liqueurs. 'Val, in appreciation of your help in all this, I've decided to give you an extra screen credit. As Coordinating Director.'

It was a moment before I smiled back at him. 'Charlie, I love you for your generous thought, but if you do that I'll sue you.'

He gaped at me blankly. 'Sue me?'

'Yes, sue you. People are going to watch it and say, "This picture was *co-ordinated*?"' Both Monique and Bill Holden burst out laughing and, to his credit, so did Charlie.

'I know, I know, you think I'm a crazy sonofabitch, right?'

'Nobody answer that question,' warned the laughing Holden.

Many months later, when *Casino* had opened in the US, our Peartree Cottage telephone woke us at 4.00 am one morning. There was an only-too-familiar voice on the transatlantic line. 'Thought you'd like to know,' it said, 'we're now playing 18 theatres in and around New York. Want to hear the first week takes...?' He rattled off some mind-bending figures followed by a chuckle. 'Now who's a crazy sonofabitch?' asked Charles K Feldman.

For the film's London première at the Leicester Square Odeon, Columbia invited all our stars and every other 'name' they could think of. I remember sitting in the front row of the Royal Circle, which was lined with well-known faces, one of them being John Huston. As we took our seats John gave me a wicked wink, leaned across his partner and whispered, 'D'you think we're wise to be here?'

Thus ended one of the most unique assignments of my kaleidoscopic career. During which, I might add, I had also been trying to write the screenplay of a spy thriller for Columbia, *Assignment K*, with Stephen Boyd, Camilla Sparv and Michael Redgrave, which I was contracted to start shooting in Munich on 30 January. 'Exhausted' is possibly the wrong word for the way I felt with Christmas only a few weeks away; 'drained' would be a better adjective. 'What you need is a rest,' prescribed Dr Donlan, dropping a brochure in my lap. It was for a ten-day Christmas cruise on the SS *France*, at that time probably the most famous luxury liner afloat. Leaving Southampton 23 December with Christmas Day in Tenerife, then on to Dakar, Freetown, Sierra Leone and the Canary Isles with New Year's Eve in Lisbon, sailing home on 2 January. It read like a dream trip but getting back on the 2nd would give me scarcely three weeks before I was due in Munich and as yet I hadn't finished the final screenplay. 'Okay, so you write it on the cruise,' sighed Yo in her talking-to-an-idiot voice. 'What could be better? No interruptions, just get on with it.'

It was certainly a tempting temptation, even more so because our next visit from Terry, Yo's mom, was not until February, plus the fact that our Christopher was also far away in Washington DC being a hardworking scholar in Georgetown University, which meant a family-less Yuletide in Peartree Cottage. Decisions, decisions. I didn't even stop to flip a coin, simply flung a dozen scribble pads, a ream of typing paper and my portable Olivetti into a suitcase and off we sped, my fingers crossed, praying for no less than immediate inspiration and instant genius en voyage.

CHAPTER
EIGHTEEN

The SS *France* was everything it was cracked up to be, the acme of elegant affluence. In fact, director Jean Negulesco had chosen to put Marilyn Monroe, Lauren Bacall and Betty Grable aboard it to shoot their own luxury scenes for *How to Marry a Millionaire*. That turned into a stroke of luck for us because Negulesco's location manager later became my location manager and by that time he knew the right French words to whisper into the right French ears so that when Yolande and I stepped aboard we were given a VIP welcome.

As for Yo's scripting advice – 'No interruptions, just get on with it' – apart from the ship's Christmas revels, four movie theatres, two dance floors, a nightly buffet stretching the length of the longest promenade deck in maritime history and laden with everything from boars' heads down to hot dogs, as well as the midnight soupe a l'oignon Noctambule bar and the New Year's Eve costume ball, there were no interruptions. Somehow I managed to finish my script, even mailing back batches of it from every port at which we docked.

The making of *Assignment K* gave us no insurmountable problems producer-wise, production-wise or location-wise, although shooting one of the film's death-defying ski chases down the Austrian Alps, with a star who could barely stand up on skis, had us all hoping for inspiration. Our star, Stephen Boyd, was a non-skier and knew we'd be using stunt doubles for the hairier bits but also that he and co-star Camilla Sparv would at least have to do the basics for closer shots. Whereas Camilla, born and bred in Sweden, had practically grown up on skis and couldn't wait to do it all even without a double. Which is why Stephen decided to take a ski-ing course in Aspen, Colorado, before flying over to join us in Kitzbühel. So how come he was here now and still couldn't ski? What had gone wrong?

'Aspen went wrong,' said Stephen wryly. 'As I drove in I passed three ambulances driving out. Shook me a bit. Then when I reached the car park at the bottom of the learning slopes there were four more of them standing by with stretchers. I'm afraid I made a quick U-turn home. But don't worry, now I'm here I'll learn real quick...'

But he didn't, even with the help of Traudi Hochfilzer, the town's ace ski instructor. There just wasn't time and since necessity is the mother of invention we devised another way to shoot our intrepid hero pursuing villains down the mountains. And had someone only filmed us shooting it they might have made the comedy short of the year. First, we selected two stretchers and four of Kitzbuhel's husky Mountain Rescue team, men who had spent most of their lives on skis bringing down stretchers full of breaks and fractures. Then, placing the two stretchers side by side, they strapped our camera and operator onto the first one before getting Stephen to kneel on the second one where they fastened him securely, ski poles in hand. We were now ready for countdown. 'Okay, here we go. Stand by. Three... Two... One... Lift off... Action!' And away they went, side by side, gliding down the slopes with our star miraculously keeping his balance and the camera framing him only from the waist up as he wielded his ski poles like an Olympic veteran. Happily it worked. So well, in fact, that soon after the film premièred a laughing Stephen called me to say that not only had he received invitations to judge several ski fests but to enter them as well!

Strangely enough, while location filming is invariably full of the unexpected, sometimes the ones you expect to be the trickiest turn out to be the easiest and vice versa. I well remember one of the latter which happened in Venice. David Niven Jr, who was then handling my business at the William Morris office, had just arranged for me to direct my first and only TV commercial. It was for Buitoni and, although I knew nothing about making TV commercials, I had agreed when I heard I was to shoot it from a storyboard in Venice and Rome. Furthermore, it would be photographed by my old Bette Davis film friend, Oscar-winning Robert Krasker. The product turned out to be a new line Buitoni were marketing called 'Instant Pizza', which one simply dropped into a toaster and in not so many moments, bingo!, up it popped, cooked. Only an American giant like Buitoni would have had the nerve to try selling Instant Pizza to the Italians.

At least it got me to Venice. The storyboard called for a small boy to be seated at a table in a deserted St Mark's Square, putting an uncooked pizza into an electric toaster. This to be followed by shots of every statue in the square watching in frozen suspense as the moments tick by. Then a final whip-pan back to the boy as the finished pizza pops up. What could be easier? The Polizia had agreed to let us have an empty St Mark's provided we shot it at daybreak. Still no problem when Bobby Krasker and I rehearsed all the camera angles, lamp positions and action before retiring to our Hotel Danieli for peaceful dreams.

Came the dawn and someone was tapping on the door of my room. It turned out to be one of the hotel porters. 'Buon giorno, signore,' he smiled. 'When you are ready I am here to help you out.' I thanked him kindly but told him I already knew my way to San Marco. 'No, no, signore, out of the *hotel.* The floor is under water. I am here to carry you.' And at the bottom of the lobby stairs that's exactly what he did because the whole of the Danieli entrance was under a foot of canal water. It was also full of other guests being piggy-backed out and lowered onto hastily positioned duck-boards leading them to the gondola landing stages. Needless to say there were no popping pizzas in St Mark's that day but luckily we were able to fly to Rome and have their first pop-up in the Coliseum.

Then there was a film called *When Dinosaurs Ruled the Earth*, the very title just crying out for location problems. At least, that's how it sounded to me one hot day in June 1968 when Hammer producer Aida Young flew over to our Malta holiday pad to ask me if I'd like to direct it. I'd never made a prehistoric film before although I dimly recalled seeing Conan Doyle's classic movie *The Lost World* and thinking it might be fun to have a go at one sometime. And now, here it was. 'Could be interesting,' I said. 'How soon can I see a script?' Whereupon Aida burst out laughing. 'You've got to be joking,' she said between bursts. 'The answer is: as soon as you finish writing it.'

It appeared the incorrigible Jimmy Carreras had been at it again. Having made a box-office bonanza out of *One Million Years B.C.* with Raquel Welch, he decided it was time for a sequel. Summoning his art department, he told them to dream up a poster showing a rampant dinosaur with a writhing blonde in its mouth. Which they did, and Jimmy loved it. 'Perfect,' he enthused, 'now there's our sequel.' And there was Guest, in the middle of a Maltese vacation, agreeing to sit down and write it. Which meant no more swimming and lazing with Yolande on the Tigne beach, or watching the water polo matches in the pool below our penthouse terrace. From here on it would just be me and my Olivetti.

And as it happened I had barely finished typing FADE-IN before there was a long-distance telephone call for Yo. It was from our friend, producer-director Lewis Gilbert, and he was phoning from Rome. 'Yo, I'm over here making *The Adventurer* – the Harold Robbins book,' he told her, 'and I have two sequences in which I'd like to use a guest star appearance. Olivia de Havilland has agreed to do one of them and I'd love you to do the other.'

'Would I be shooting in Rome?' she asked tentatively.

'Yes, and we'd also need you here ahead of that for some fittings. Look, why don't I send you a script...'

'Never mind the script,' cut in my joyful wife, 'just send me the ticket!'

Which is pretty much the way Yolande came to join Bekim Fehmiu, Candice Bergen, Ernest Borgnine and Olivia de Havilland in Harold Robbins' sexy saga of an international playboy. It would be some 30 years later before I, too, would come face to face with the prolific Robbins. In fact Harold and I came face to face at least once a week because he turned out to be one of our neighbours when Yolande and I moved to Palm Springs.

'How's the autobiog coming along?' he asked me one night over one of Yo's famous home-cooked dinners.

'Slowly,' I had to admit.

'Well, if you need some help I'll always write a couple of chapters for you,' offered the magnanimous Harold Robbins. Maybe I should have taken him up on it.

However, back during that hot Mediterranean summer while Yolande was busy in Rome having costume fittings and fun, I was still in our Malta penthouse battling an Olivetti full of dinosaurs. As a matter of fact, I seem to remember I had just learned how to spell and type my first pterodactyl when another long distance call rang through my prehistoric world. This time it was London – Yo's agent, Aubrey Blackburn at the Christopher Mann office, asking me to tell her that Harold Fielding was planning to stage the hit Broadway musical *Mame* at Drury Lane with Ginger Rogers playing Mame, and how would Yolande like to join her and play Mame's best girlfriend? Needless to say, Yolande, who in her early Hollywood days had once been the youngest contract dancer on the MGM lot, would have liked it very much. But sadly her current commitments would plough through so many of their rehearsal dates that it was an impossible no-go from the start. I say 'sadly' because I'm sure she would have had fun teaming up with the ultra-talented Ginger who, as some shrewd person once remarked, could not only do everything Astaire did but was able to do it backwards and in high heels as well.

It was October that year before *Dinosaurs* went into production and for our locations we went to the Canary Islands. Mostly on the sparsely inhabited island of Fuerteventura, which looked ideally prehistoric with all its volcanic rock, sand dunes and waterfalls. Location problems? Yes, but not nearly as many as I expected. There was, of course, the moment when lighting cameraman Dick Bush, production manager Malcolm Christopher and myself first arrived at Las Palmas airport for a location recce and saw the plane that would fly us to Fuerteventura was an old World War II Fokker-Wolfe machine with its original German roundels still faintly visible under the new fuselage paintwork. As true Brits we climbed aboard with stiff upper lips and sat between a Monseigneur and two nuns. Somehow we felt a mite safer in their spiritual company. Until the pilot switched on his motors and our portside engine belched smoke and flames. He switched them off and on again with the same result. After his third attempt we sat in a seemingly endless silence. 'Problems?' I asked the passing stewardess.

'Pilot is not happy with the engines,' she shrugged. I stopped myself replying 'Neither are we', glanced through the porthole and saw a jeepful of four uniforms speeding across the tarmac towards us. As they surged aboard in a flood of Spanish our pilot emerged, led them onto his flight deck and closed the door. Once more the engines were revved, with the same fireworks before switch-off. Moments later our pilot came out and without a word marched down the aisle, the gangway steps and into the jeep, followed shortly by three other uniforms, leaving the fourth one in the cockpit. 'What's happening?' I asked the stewardess.

Another shrug. 'He is still not happy with them. But not to worry, we have a new pilot who is.' Even as she spoke the happy new one throttled up his engines, taxi-ing our smoke and bursts of flame down the runway for take-off, while Monseigneur and the two nuns closed their eyes and crossed themselves. Maybe that's why we landed safely in Fuerteventura. So it could hardly be called a location problem, just an emotional one. Especially when circling the tiny island airport we flew low enough to spot the rusting remains of a couple of earlier machines.

Most of the unit and cast stayed in the large but isolated hotel perched on the edge of an endless beach with rolling sand dunes as far as the eye could see along the Jandia Peninsular. German-owned, it had the only telephone in a 20-mile radius, and when it broke down, which it sometimes did, it was a long, bumpy jeep ride to our next point of communication because that was in olden times, before cellular phones. Malcolm Christopher had been clever enough to get us the best location caterer in Las Palmas, with the impressive name of Jesús Santos Del Bosque. I remember our first call sheet, at the bottom of which the production office had simply typed 'Catering by Jesus'. To which one of our 'sparks' had queried, 'Blimey, what's it going to be, bleeding loaves and fishes?'

The most important thing a director needs on a location of this complexity is a solid, dependable unit and luckily I had several of my long-time regulars with me. Not least of which was my First Assistant, John Stoneman. John had already been through many thick-and-thins with me, from the endurance tests of *Casino Royale* to the snowy traumas of *Assignment K* and would survive even more with me over the years. Today, however, I doubt if I could afford him because he has his own successful production company in Ontario. But back in Fuerteventura BC he was still successfully handling all my cavemen, monsters and sacrificial handmaidens.

We had near-perfect location weather, except for the occasional Sahara sandstorms on the African mainland which could sometimes trigger almost hurricane force winds towards the Canary Isles. In fact, on one of these days, just before the lunch break, we were shooting an idyllic love scene on our prehistoric raft drifting lazily on a ripple-free ocean when a sudden burst from the Sahara changed everything. Within minutes Atlantic breakers were thundering ashore and my two lovemakers were clinging for dear life to their dangerously rocking raft. Before I realised it four of my courageous technicians plunged fully clothed into the breakers, swam out and miraculously were able to pull the raft ashore. Heroes indeed, and that night at the hotel we threw a beer and champagne party in their honour. Later a smiling John Stoneman joined me at the swimming pool. 'You're going to love this, Guv,' he grinned, 'but all four have put in chits for 'no lunch break' money.' And you know what? Budget or no budget I was ready to suggest the accountants tripled it.

As for my two leading players, I'm not sure you'll know the names of Robin Hawdon and Victoria Vetri. Robin was a young, talented, up-and-coming juvenile whom I'd previously cast in the small part of Ronnie, the *Daily Express* office boy in *The Day the Earth Caught Fire*. He also wrote plays in his spare time. Now what can I say about Victoria Vetri? That she'd been a successful model, glamour girl, pin-up and centrefold, all of which hadn't given her much time to take up acting? So how come she was being star-billed in our epic? Well, it seems she had a big admirer in the American distributor's camp who persuaded Jimmy Carreras to cast her in *Dinosaurs* and become the new Raquel Welch. Anyway, she looked great in her leather thong bikini and animal-skin bra. Could Sarah Bernhardt have done that?

One of the main problems for actors in this kind of picture is having to react and play scenes with prehistoric monsters that aren't there until the special effects boys put them in later. For instance, when Robin and Victoria met up with a prowling dinosaur they had to react in horror to a sun hat, representing the monster's head, tied to the top of a 15-foot pole held by a T-shirted prop man. Which calls for a certain amount of talent and imagination. Likewise in the scene where Robin perches precariously atop a mountain crag, fighting off an attacking pterodactyl that wants to carry him off for its lunch but won't really be there until a couple of months later. Try it some time, it isn't easy.

And how lucky we were to get such a superb special effects animator as James Danforth turned out to be. Up until then Jimmy had always worked alongside Hollywood's king of special effects, Ray Harryhausen. *Dinosaurs* was to be his first solo effort and what a job he made of it. For once all the monsters had certain human characteristics, such as feelings. For example, watching the shot when Robin spears the pterodactyl, one can actually see it wince. And it was thanks to Danforth's groundbreaking genius on all the prehistoric creatures that when our picture received an Academy Award nomination that year it was for Best Special Effects.

Blowing the dust off my records I find it almost unbelievable that we commenced shooting at Shepperton Studios on 14 October and less than three weeks later, on 4 November, I was filming in the Canaries for 12 concentrated days before flying back to Shepperton, filming through Christmas and New Year to wrap up the whole production, excepting special effects, by 8 January! Today the mere thought of it has me searching for the valium.

Meanwhile Yolande, too, had been working flat out, rehearsing and recording for the BBC who had asked her to do another of Garson Kanin's hit plays, *The Rat Race*. And whom did she pick as her co-player? None other than the young newcomer we had first used in *Miss Pilgrim's Progress*, Arthur Hill. An Arthur who couldn't have envisioned that this BBC production would bring him into Gar Kanin's orbit, after which he'd be whipped off to Broadway to appear opposite Gar's wife Ruth Gordon in the Thornton Wilder classic, *The Matchmaker*. Thus was another award-winning career well and truly boosted. As for Yo and I, we were well and truly pooped.

'I feel Malta calling,' announced my lady wife one morning as I opened the mail. Agreeing wholeheartedly, I was about to call Air Malta for tickets when I noticed an envelope postmarked Rio de Janeiro. Puzzlement. Who did we know in Rio? Maybe it was a fan letter. Wrong. It was from the Rio Film Festival inviting us to their upcoming opening on 15 March, along with a European contingent consisting of the Ingmar Bergman star Ingrid Thulin, Roman Polanski and film legend Josef von Sternberg. I didn't need Einstein to tell me this meant goodbye Malta, hullo Brazil.

Rio was all we expected it to be and yet, in a strange way, less. The magnificent amphitheatre of mountains around the harbour and the majestically dominating figure of Christ on the Corcovado peak were more breathtaking than any of the picture postcards we'd seen of them. But as for the much-photographed, much-advertised Copacabana beach, I preferred the postcards. In those days it was a mess, disfigured beyond belief by dozens of volley ball posts embedded all over the golden sand, so braving the beach meant braving the flying balls. Then again, much of their architecture, streets and beautifully tiled pavements were so eyecatching one wondered why nobody had felt it worthwhile to replace all the missing tiles and fill in some of the potholes over which our Festival limousines bumped. And only in Lebanon had I see such a disturbing gap between the very rich and the desperate poverty of Rio's shanty towns, some of them built out of cardboard boxes and packing cases.

Otherwise it was a great festival. The luxurious Copacabana Palace Hotel, where we all stayed, happened to be the place our friend Thornton Freeland had filmed Fred Astaire and Ginger Rogers in *Flying Down to Rio*. It also boasted the largest swimming pool in Rio, even a tennis court on the roof and everything else you could wish for – except air-conditioning. 'And it's no good opening the windows,' said Ingrid Thulin, 'because it's even hotter air coming in!'

Maybe housekeeping could find us an electric fan for the bedroom? There were grovelling apologies, but all fans were currently in use. So Guest, like mad dogs and Englishmen, went out in the midday sun, armed himself with a Portuguese phrasebook, invaded downtown Rio and bought a fan of our own. I seem to remember that when we finally checked out of the Copacabana Palace we gave it to the maid as an extra tip.

One of the other interesting sights in Rio that month was, of course, Josef von Sternberg. The *World Film Encyclopedia* describes him as 'one of the most mysterious and enigmatic of Hollywood's directors'. He has also been characterised as a volatile man of mystery and contradiction, although the only contradiction I perceived was when a *Life* photographer lined us up around the pool and wanted to change Sternberg's position in the group. 'I'd like Joe in the middle, please,' he suggested. '*Josef*, if you please,' contradicted the icon firmly, but at least he did as he was told.

Enigmatic? Well, if wearing riding boots and sometimes a turban-like sun hat made him that, so be it, but with me he was surprisingly down to earth and I found him the most fascinating part of the whole festival. Born in Vienna of poor Jewish parents, Josef Sternberg didn't have a Von to his name until he came to America when his first Hollywood producer thought it would look more intriguing that way on the marquees. Over the years Joe – oops – Josef had held all manner of jobs throughout Europe; in fact there's an oft-told story that he once worked at Elstree's BIP studios in the carpenters' shop where he was known to one and all as plain old Joe Stern, the chippie. 'Is bullshit,' contradicted Josef when I mentioned it at the pool one day. 'Big bullshit. Walter Winchell dreamed this bullshit.' And yet there are still old Elstree-ites around who swear... But who cares, bullshit or not he later made movie history directing Emil Jannings' first talkie, *The Blue Angel*, for which he'd spotted a plumpish but attractive young fräulein on the Berlin stage, ordered her to lose weight and cast her opposite Jannings. Then, in true Svengali fashion he groomed her, planned her future and took her to Hollywood, thereby carving his name and that of Marlene Dietrich into motion picture immortality.

The last memorable incident of that Rio Film Festival was the night Roman Polanski returned to his room to find his passport had been stolen. Polanski panic. He was Polish, he moaned, had a special passport and without it he was a displaced person, how would he get to Rome where he had to be in two days' time? As we were all flying back via Rome the festival top brass pulled every Brazilian string to allow Roman to join us on the plane without a passport. But what about Rome? 'They won't let me in,' wailed Roman. We tried to reassure him that maybe the Rio police would find it and call the airport. They didn't. But somehow, by the time we touched down in Rome, cables, telegrams and diplomatic phone calls had done the trick and our displaced director was met by an embassy official who steered him through Immigration as we waved a collective arrivederci.

On the flight back to London Yolande and I had but a single thought: we now needed a holiday to get over our Rio holiday, which meant 'Hullo Air Malta, two tickets please.' That was before I listened to our Ansafone messages, one of which was from the Morris office – my friend and agent John Mather telling me that Harry Saltzman wanted to talk about a new film project. 'Sounds like there's another Bond coming up,' I told Yo, 'so for the moment you fly on ahead.'

'Okay,' she agreed, 'you can join me when you have to script it.'

Saltzman's greeting was typical mogul speak. 'You could have made a lot of dough from the last picture of mine you didn't do,' he grinned, 'so don't make another mistake now.' Which was exactly what I was about to do, but this time in a different way.

As it turned out this wasn't another Bond movie but something much wilder. 'How would you like to make the first outer space musical?' smiled Harry.

It took a moment to sink in. 'Wait a minute, you mean science fiction space?'

'Only partly,' he enlarged. 'We have this story about a pop group who are vacuumed up by a UFO to teach other aliens how to make music.'

Well of course, I should have fled there and then before he pushed a draft script across his desk. But my innate curiosity held me transfixed as he enlarged on the project. Apparently his long-time partner Cubby Broccoli was not involved in this one and co-producer would be one of New York's leading A&R recording managers, Don Kirshner. The story, by novelist David Benedictus, was called *Toomorrow*, spelt with a double-O. Trying to follow his Double-O Seven luck? The newly formed group, consisting of three guys and a girl, would also be called Toomorrow. The girl, he enthused, was a knockout New Zealander who also played the guitar in her own cabaret act. At present she had an unmarketable name but that could be changed. And the guys were three great all-American kids and he was convinced the film would launch the group into fame and fortune.

'Want to meet them?' he asked and without pausing for my yea or nay pressed an intercom button. 'Send them in,' he ordered. And in they came, the newly formed Toomorrow group. There was Karl Chambers, an instantly likeable six-foot African-American with a smile almost the same size; Ben Thomas, not as tall but perfect casting for any film's 'love interest', and Vic Cooper, sedately cheerful and perfect for the group's 'straight man'. But the one who really lit up Harry Saltzman's rather gloomy office was his 'adorable New Zealander'. If she could sing as well as she looked, I thought, nothing could hold her back. And nothing did, not even the name Harry wanted to change, which was Olivia Newton-John.

I won't bore either you or me with the making of this lighthearted piece of sci-fi for Saltzman's newly formed Swiss-based company Sweet Music Productions; let's just say we had a mixture of fun and fiascos shooting it. Fun with 'Livvy' Newton-John and the rest of the group, plus working with one of the most underrated actors on the London stage, Roy Dotrice, who was then appearing in his own one-man production as John Aubrey in *Brief Lives*. I was also lucky enough to have some of my old production stalwarts helping me, like cameraman Dick Bush, First Assistant John Stoneman and, having long since finished riding camels across those Lawrence-of-Arabian deserts with David Lean, that doyen of production managers, John Palmer.

The fiascos? First there was Harry Saltzman's late decision that he didn't like the Benedict script and would I do a quick rewrite? Followed by the almost daily lists arriving from co-producer Don Kirshner in New York to Harry Saltzman in Lowndes Square suggesting new story additions and deletions, all of which Harry dispatched to Peartree Cottage with instructions for me to call Don and talk him out of them. With the production date not far from countdown, I flew to New York for a face-to-face with music master Kirshner and came back with the feeling that apart from the music and Newton-John he didn't really think much of anything to do with the picture, including Harry Saltzman. Ah well, I sighed philosophically, hey-ho and lackaday, press on.

Miraculously we finished our shooting on schedule and Harry decided to extend my contract to cover the editing stages and music recording with Hugo Montenegro. A lot of hard work but fun — until the Morris office told me Sweet Music were no longer sending my cheques. After eight weeks of no pay they advised me to quit work and take Saltzman to the High Court. I did both and found that not only was Sweet Music in trouble with me but with its own Swiss bank. We were told that Harry had put up part of his share in the Bond films as collateral for a picture loan, a deal that was forbidden by his partnership with Cubby Broccoli, which stipulated there could be no other partner in James Bond's Eon Productions. I think that was the beginning of the end for their lucrative partnership which they dissolved not long after.

I won the lawsuit but not the money and although I allowed *Toomorrow* to have its première at the London Pavilion, I slapped a writ on Sweet Music to prevent any further public showings until the money was forthcoming. It never was, which is probably why all you lucky people never see re-runs on late night television. But *Toomorrow* also had some good results. At least it had launched Livvy on to the silver screen and into public awareness and after that she notched up at least one Top 10 hit a year for over a dozen years, as well as a string of records, Grammy Awards and co-starring with John Travolta in *Grease*.

There was another happy ending to *Toomorrow*. To play Karl Chambers' girlfriend I cast a very attractive model who had once been a Miss Guyana. Known professionally as Shella, her real name was Shakirah Baksh. One day between takes, she told me her British work permit was about to expire and she was afraid the Home Office wouldn't renew it again. Since she was an attractive asset and seemed to be a particularly nice person I thought it might help to write her a letter on company notepaper saying that we would employ her in our next production if she was able to get a work permit. It did the trick and they renewed it, which brought her yet another stroke of luck because had she returned to Guyana she might never have met, dated and married her future husband who was, and still is, our talented friend Michael Caine.

I'm afraid *Toomorrow* never made history but in the middle of shooting, 21 July to be exact, something else did. A man named Neil Armstrong made a giant leap for mankind and landed on the moon. An awe-inspiring feat made even more impressive for us filmmakers because he did it without the help of Jimmy Danforth, Ray Harryhausen or any of our special effects boys. I looked upon this as one of life's gentle reminders that none of us is indispensable.

Somehow during all this Yolande found time in her equally busy life to fly off to Los Angeles and spend a couple of weeks with mother Terry, returning in time for Noël Coward's pre-70th birthday cocktail party at the Savoy's River Room restaurant. Only Noël could have thought of a pre-birthday party and it was just for close friends. He did this knowing that at his real birthday bash, same hotel only three days later, there would be hundreds of guests, as well as BBC Television cameras recording the occasion with all its celebrity speeches, so he wouldn't have much chance to talk to any of us. Which was thoughtful, especially as he'd been through a rough time healthwise and was still a little frail. But even a frail Noël was better company than many of the great unfrail and he survived both events with his usual wit and humour, although there were only four short years left before the Master finally departed us for good.

But even in death he was able to leave us a last chuckle. 'The only thing that really saddens me over my demise,' he wrote in his diary, 'is that I shall not be there to read the nonsense that will be written about me ... There will be lists of apocryphal jokes I never made. What a pity I shan't be here to enjoy them.'

CHAPTER
NINETEEN

The new year, 1970, brought us another memorable moment. And it wasn't that the first Boeing 747 Jumbo jet went into transatlantic service, getting us there and back a little quicker. Nor the fact that Ted Heath had finally ousted the Labour Party and become Prime Minister. For Yolande and I, more momentous than any of that was the news that a recently issued recording was already way up in the charts. It was the first LP of *Jesus Christ Superstar* and Andrew brought us a copy when Yo organised a celebration dinner for us all at Peartree. The little boy who had wanted to grow up and write musicals was well on his way.

Another unexpected event was about to burst with scary suddenness. John Mather had arranged an appointment for me at Pinewood Studios to lunch with producer Robert Baker, who said he wanted to talk to me. Since Bob was the man responsible for the incredibly popular TV series *The Saint* with Roger Moore, I was intrigued by the thought that maybe he now wanted to launch it onto the big screen. He didn't.

'I'm about to do a new series with Roger,' said Bob over lunch. 'It's called *The Persuaders!* and this time we've got Tony Curtis with him. Like to have a go?' To say I was surprised would be using the wrong word; stunned would be closer. A TV series – me? Until that moment in the Pinewood restaurant, television was something that enabled us to watch Wimbledon when we hadn't bought tickets, catch up with the day's news, see an occasional play or even spend a merry evening laughing at the new BBC series, *Monty Python's Flying Circus* with newcomer John Cleese. So I had nothing against TV, unlike dear Noël whose non-apocryphal advice was, 'Television is for appearing in, not looking at.' Neither did I embrace the dictum of CP Scott, editor of the *Manchester Guardian*, who told us, 'The word is half Greek, half Latin. No good can come of it.' It was simply that to me it was unknown territory.

'You can also write some of the episodes for us,' added Bob, probably wondering if my pole-axed expression meant I had been hoping for a better offer. I tried to explain it was only because it wasn't my medium and, flattered as I was to be asked, he'd be much better off with a good, solid TV director. Bob shrugged, said he didn't agree but to give it a thought anyway and let him know. Driving home I tried to convince myself I'd done the right thing and not just won the Idiot of the Year Award.

It was two days later that a couple of unexpected visitors turned up at Peartree Cottage during my morning coffee break. They were Roger Moore and Tony Curtis. 'So you don't want to direct us,' was Roger's opening line. 'Is it our personalities or lack of experience?' asked a straightfaced Tony. When they'd finished sending me up I tried to explain that I was a film man with no TV experience. 'So, what's the difference?' shrugged Tony. 'Just shoot it the same way you'd shoot a film and cut out the long shots.' I can't say whether any text book on How To Direct for TV has put it quite as basically as Professor Curtis, but I can say that before the end of my coffee break he had pulled me into television.

Directing and writing some of *The Persuaders!* was a lot of fun and even more hard work, shooting as we did on locations in Cannes, Nice, Monte Carlo and Rome. Even more so when schedules required six to ten minutes' screentime a day with a ten-day maximum to film an entire episode. It was most heartening when it eventually won an award in London for 'TV Series of the Year' followed by heaven knows how many similar citations in France and the rest of Europe. It is also interesting to note that even as I write this, 20 years later, I have just finished chatting on the phone with Bob Baker who tells me that to this day *The Persuaders!* is still being re-run in France where it has become cult viewing.

So why didn't they make a follow-up series? Some uncharitable people said it was because no one could face the prospect of another year's work with Bernie Schwartz, alias Tony Curtis. Untrue and unkind. The reason can be summed up in two words: James Bond. Cubby Broccoli had asked Roger to take over James Bond from Sean Connery, and Bob Baker, being the true British gent that he is, felt he couldn't stand in the way of such an offer. Neither did he feel like doing the series with anyone else. So I hope that dispels the nasty rumours.

Not that Tony couldn't be a problem at times, but at least he had a sense of humour about it. Often, when he was arguing or complaining about this or that, Roger would amble over and ask, 'What seems to be the problem, Bernie?' Whereupon the skirmishes usually ended in laughter. Apropos of which, I have an indelible recollection of the morning Tony arrived on the Cannes Croisette in a state of hostility towards the wardrobe people who had or had not done something or other. As the Curtis anger echoed across the Carlton plage, a quietly unruffled Roger walked over, gently took hold of Tony's lapels, looked him straight in the face and said, 'To think those lips once kissed Piper Laurie.' There was a beat of silence before our angry co-star collapsed in a paroxysm of laughter, as did the entire unit. It was at least ten minutes before Tony Curtis could pull himself together enough to resume shooting.

We could have done with Roger's lighthearted approach the day we were working just outside Nice in a dried-up, boulder-strewn river bed. It was a long shot of a pickup truck hidden under a small bridge. In the driver's cab were Tony and the episode's leading lady, Joan Collins. I can't recall why or from whom they were hiding, only that they had just been 'miked' up for their dialogue. While we were positioning sun reflectors and waiting for the clouds to move into place, Joan and Tony were talking in the driver's cab, unaware that their dialogue was still coming through the unit speakers. Joan was wondering if she should take another look at her script which was somewhere out there on her chair. Tony was in one of his let's-get-this-over-and-have-a-smoke moods and said something like, 'Christ, it's only a few lines.' But Joan, not unreasonably, felt she'd like a quick look at the preceding scene. Whereupon Tony swung around and snapped, 'Why don't you just say the fucking lines!' His words ricocheted off the boulders, reverberating down the valley as an outraged Joan wrestled with the cab door, jumped out and clambered over the rocks to put as much distance between her and the truck as possible.

Faced with this kind of production hiccup, the wise director usually says 'All right, take ten' and has them roll out the tea and coffee urns. As it happened Joanie, being the pro she is, rose above it in less time than I would have done and was back in that driver's cab playing the scene so well that no one would ever suspect she wasn't exactly a member of the Tony Curtis fan club.

Back in London, knowing I hoped to film one of our episodes at Woburn Abbey, home of the

Duke and Duchess of Bedford, the Duke invited us to look around the estate and the Duchess, that wonderful Parisienne who had already made a guest appearance for me in *The Beauty Jungle*, arranged a lunch for us in their ancestral dining hall. The table was awash with crested silver and monogrammed glassware, the walls panelled with Old Masters and a gracious Duchess was asking, 'Now, would you care to sit facing the garden or the Canalettos?'

Decisions, decisions, which my practical Yolande solved by answering, 'Well, Val loves Canalettos so I'll face the garden.'

All in all I enjoyed almost every minute of my hardworking television début and there must have been something contagious about it because over the next couple of years I was to become involved in the birth of several series, the next invitation coming from Monty Berman who was about to launch a series called *The Adventurer*, not to be confused with Harold Robbins' *The Adventurers*. Berman's series was to star the popular American actor Gene Barry and one would think that, having shot the series all over Elstree, Antwerp, Düsseldorf and heaven knows where else, I'd have a fileful of memories. Oddly enough I have only two lasting ones.

The first, when our art director was instructed that wherever possible all our set doors should be built to open right to left, so that our star could enter showing the left side of his face, which, we were informed, was his best. How's that for the ultimate in star clout? The only other actor I worked with who ever discussed his face was Forrest Tucker when he came over to make *The Abominable Snowman* with me in 1957. 'Just so you know,' he told me casually on one of our first meetings, 'this side of my face I'm the good guy, that side of my face I'm the shit.' Either side he seemed to do all right.

My other recallable moment on *The Adventurer*, and my favourite, was when we were shooting on a quayside in Antwerp docks, where we had been given permission to use a barge for one hour before it put to sea. All our hero had to do was run across the quayside and jump aboard. For matching purposes it had to be shot in full sunlight, and although we had sun there were little balls of fluffy clouds that kept drifting across it just as we were ready to shoot. After several aborted takes ruined by a recalcitrant cloud, we had only 15 minutes left before we lost the barge forever. That was when my frustrated lighting cameraman, the incomparable Frank Watts, stepped forward and stretched his arms to the sky with the heartfelt plea, 'Come on, God, do you want to fuck about or make movies?' Surely worth including in any book of film quotations.

When a director has made too many films, as have I, there are bound to be a few highly forgettable ones. At least you hope they're forgettable until some TV busybody unearths them for screening on the archive movie channels. Which is why I sometimes scan the weekly TV guides to see what others they've excavated in case it might be wiser to leave town for a while until they're forgotten again.

However, one film I made was highly unforgettable. Not because it was an epic of any kind, but due to the drama-filled days of filming it in Johannesburg and the Namibian desert at the height of South Africa's fanatical apartheid era. Worldwide, the film was known as *The Diamond Mercenaries* but in America, which is addicted to title changing, it was renamed *Killer Force*, and it was about a renegade group of mercenaries planning to rob South Africa's largest diamond mine in the Namibian desert.

For our mercenaries we had Telly 'Kojak' Savalas, Peter 'Easy Rider' Fonda, Christopher 'Dracula' Lee, Hugh 'Wyatt Earp' O'Brian and last but not least, OJ Simpson. Woa back, hold your horses! This was many moons before his infamous murder trial but even way back then we were to have other 'OJ' problems. Not least of which was our delectable leading lady, Swedish actress Maud Adams, who had recently finished the latest Bond movie, *The Man with the Golden Gun*, and was soon to find herself as co-star in one of our own off-screen dramas as well.

Let's take it from the top. To begin with, the picture almost never got made at all because of the

Association of Cine Technicians. To our utter surprise we found the ACT had put a complete ban on any of their technicians working in South Africa. I asked them to convene a special meeting to let me know what problems they were having with South Africa and at that meeting their head man, Alan Sapper, answered me in one sentence: 'We don't like their government.'

'Is that all?'

'Isn't that enough?' asked Alan Sapper.

I tried hard not to smile and answered, 'Look, I don't like *our* government but it doesn't stop me making films here.' This was followed by a lot of mumble-mumble, whisper-whisper before reason saw the light of day and the ban on *Mercenaries* was lifted, albeit grudgingly.

It was Steven Pallos who had invited me to join him in this venture, having met up with an American gentleman named Nat Wachsberger who claimed to have considerable South African finance at his disposal for a possible adventure film to be made in that country from a story written by one Michael Winder and called *The Diamond Mercenaries*. None of us knew much about Wachsberger except that he'd been part of several small Hollywood productions, but an adventure film in South Africa sounded intriguing. So Guest went into instant labour to help give birth to a draft shooting script. Armed with which, Nat had flown back to LA and talked Jack Gilardi of ICM into an imposing line-up of some of their stars.

My first recce flight to Johannesburg was made more fun finding myself sitting next to actress Liz Frazer, on her way there to do a commercial. After landing at Jan Smuts Airport we stood together in the middle of 200 other passengers in that vast arrival hall, waiting to go through Immigration, when the tannoys began blaring messages. It seemed London had contacted Johannesburg's Killarney Studios to locate me on arrival and help me through the mob. Obviously that message had been passed on in Afrikaans to an airport attendant and she did her hurried best to translate it into English. What came through the booming tannoys was: 'Would Mr Val Guest, passenger from London, please expose himself.' After a moment's hush the entire arrival hall exploded with laughter, during which Liz Frazer nudged me and said, 'Well, go on, I dare you.' Thus was my official entry into the Republic of South Africa.

But life wasn't quite as lighthearted once I passed through the barriers. Wherever one looked there were signs proclaiming WHITES ONLY. Outside rest rooms, cafés, even on waiting room benches and in Johannesburg itself many stores used similar announcements. Even more disturbing, there seemed to be a tacit understanding that whites had right of way on all sidewalks. I found it quite a lot to digest in one gulp.

Then came the day when John Pellat, our production administrator, was booking everyone into Johannesburg's Carlton Hotel only to be told that, much as they welcomed us all staying there, unfortunately they were unable to accommodate OJ Simpson. Why not? 'Well sir... you see, sir...' Whereupon we started the daddy of all rows – threatening to withdraw stars, unit, everybody – and finally were able to muster enough clout to have OJ granted special VIP and consular privileges, establishing a precedent that would shortly benefit Sammy Davis Jr on his upcoming South African tour, when he would have faced the same problem had he not been a VIP.

But we almost went back to square one the night an elated OJ did triumphant pirouettes in the Carlton foyer to celebrate being the first black man to reside there. It never dawned on the likeable but highly unpredictable OJ that in those days, in spite of all his football fame in America, the rest of the world had barely heard of him. He had supreme confidence that just being OJ would get him through anything. And most of the time it did. But don't think we didn't have all our fingers and legs crossed on our first South West African location in Swakopmund, staying at a small hotel called the Hansa on the edge of the Namibian desert. It was here that OJ defied the then arbitary apartheid death sentence for black men found with white women by romancing my leading lady, Maud Adams, and driving off with her into the desert for 'picnics' between filming.

'OJ, for God's sake be careful,' I warned him.

'Aw man, relax,' he grinned. 'I can take care of myself.'

Then there were our unit helicopters, which deposited us every morning in the middle of the desert, near the Angolan border, so we could shoot on virgin dunes inaccessible to people or vehicles. We found it a trifle nervewracking because the South African air force was holding armed manoeuvres in the same area for possible guerrilla warfare with Angola. Making sure our 'copters weren't mistaken for marauding Angolans was also tricky. Especially the chopper that hovered every now and then, around 4.00 pm, over our tented HQ in the sand dunes and always landed the same passenger. It was Yolande, who had been able to join us briefly between plays and decided to make herself useful by flying in tea-time treats from a German bakery next to our hotel. I'm sure I don't have to tell you what a morale booster that was for an English unit so far from home, in the middle of a blazing desert.

Then there was the day she brought us more than just teacakes in the form of a message from ICM's Jack Gilardi in Hollywood, telling producer Nat Wachsberger: 'If Peter Fonda's cheque isn't on my desk within 48 hours I'll send my men after you.' Those cheques were delivered on time but it wasn't long before other money problems were coming in from all points of the compass and passed to Wachsberger in his Johannesburg bunker, while we waited with bated breath for him to wriggle in or out of them. Inevitably it became my turn for money troubles with Nat but having no 'men' at my disposal, I settled for top LA attorney, Gerald Lipsky. But how do you serve a summons on someone who has just left the country on a world cruise? Need any more problems? Like one of our stars flying into Smuts Airport with a gun in his luggage, to say nothing of sundry other smokeable items.

Apart from all this, I still have pleasurable Namibian moments etched in my sands of time. For instance, who could forget the sight of big, bald-headed Telly Savalas during a sun-blazing lunch break, stripped to his boxer shorts, doing a soft-shoe shuffle in the desert, rehearsing his upcoming Las Vegas cabaret act with the choreographer he'd flown in from California? Or even Hugh O'Brian, also during his lunch break, trying to work out the most dramatic way to get shot in the back and roll down a sand dune to die, which was to be his first scene after lunch. Six rolls...? Seven...? On Hugh's eighth roll Peter Fonda grunted and sauntered away with his mug of coffee. Twenty minutes later, returning for his own scene, the first thing Peter asked me was, 'Has Brando died yet?'

Only tiny vignettes but fine shading for the portraits of my star players. I mean, who would suspect that the scholarly, immensely popular Christopher Lee seemed to have but one worry on his professional mind, that he would only be remembered as Dracula. And when OJ, who happened be a great fan of his, greeted him every morning with 'Hi, Drac,' Chris was always consummate actor enough to smile as though he enjoyed it.

Perhaps my most personal memory of that location was the sight of Yolande, in the cool of the evening, sitting on a sand dune thumbing through the pages of a contract from Hodder & Stoughton, who were publishing her autobiography, *Shake the Stars Down*. Peter Fonda was also intrigued by the sight.

'If it's a contract, sign it,' joked practical Peter.

'I can't,' laughed Yo, 'not without a witness.'

'You're talking to a professional one.'

So there and then it was signed and witnessed in the Namibian desert. I doubt if Hodder & Stoughton ever noticed who the witness was but it must have brought her luck because when *Shake the Stars Down* came out it was listed in the top four autobiographies of the year. It was even Number One in Ireland. Oh, and I almost forgot, the American publishers changed the title to *Third Time Lucky*. Okay, so it's an old American custom and I should be so lucky.

June the 2nd 1975 was the momentous day we finally finished our desert filming and just to make things more eventful it was also Yolande's birthday. To celebrate it Nat Wachsberger, who had now joined us in Swakopmund, had organised a surprise party for her at our hotel and invited all the cast. Knowing that Yo was then on a high protein diet, he had even flown in lobsters for the occasion. Nat was fond of Yo because of the help she'd been, keeping the various actors' problems under control. Many times if Telly, Chris, Hugh, or any of them had some special worry or suggestion to make they'd take it to her, knowing that in all the chaos of desert filming she was probably the best way to get it to me. Nat was aware of this and was sincerely grateful. So much so that one day, out of the blue, he told her, 'As a present I'm going to give you a mink coat.'

Yo had laughed and replied, 'Thanks, but I already have a mink coat.'

'Not like the one I'll give you,' he said magnanimously. 'I have a furrier friend in New York and when you get home I'll fly him to London and fit you.'

Needless to say, that was the last she heard of it. Anyway, the day after the party found us back in Johannesburg with three more shooting weeks ahead and somehow or other we managed to do it with five days still in hand to complete our location wrap-up. On 28 June the early morning plane would fly us all back to London and our South African adventures would be over.

We thought. Until the night before our departure when John Pellat hurried into our hotel suite to warn us that Nat Wachsberger had flown back to LA, leaving some angry unpaid bills baying at the production office doors. In fact, John warned us, at that very moment there was a plan afoot to hold back the entire unit's return plane tickets next morning, including ours, as a temporary form of collateral. 'Well, well,' I sighed, 'so what now?' He took two tickets from his briefcase and pressed them on me. 'There's a Rome plane out of here at midnight and I suggest you're on it,' he said and was gone like the Scarlet Pimpernel. They seek John here, they seek John there... I'm sure people have been decorated for less valour than John Pellat's.

Without the help of undercranked cameras I doubt if anyone has packed as quickly as Yo and I did that night and, thanks to the valiant John Pellat, midnight saw us safely aboard the Rome flight. From Rome we'd catch a plane home to rain, rain, glorious rain. At least, I did. Yo simply said, 'I can't be in Rome and not see Florence,' disembarked, got on a train and did just that. But then Yolande always had this driving ambition to see the world whilst she and it are still there.

Eventually, in spite of all, *The Diamond Mercenaries*, or *Killer Force*, premièred in New York and was lucky enough to end up in *Variety*'s Top Five box-office grossers. Not in the same league, of course, as that quintissential desert film called... called... ah yes, *Lawrence of Arabia*, compared to which ours was a puny offering. And to think how I carried on about working in sand for a month while dear David had spent nearly two years of his life up to his knees in it. For that achievement alone he deserved to go down in cinema history.

Meanwhile my life had many more unexpected surprises up its sleeve. Such as the day I returned to Peartree after a three-day trip to Los Angeles for some *Killer Force* promotions to find Yolande busy packing her suitcases.

'Oh, goody,' I chirped, 'are we off to Malta?'

'No, I'm off to Tokyo.'

'To where?' I asked, dimly aware I'd been through this routine before.

'Tokyo, Japan,' she clarified with a smile.

'Don't tell me you've been learning Japanese.'

'Not yet, but you never know,' she laughed, then sat me down to explain that Lewis Gilbert was about to make his new film there, *Seven Nights in Japan* with Michael York, and had invited her to fly over and be in it. Knowing my travel-thirsty Yo, I was pretty sure the answer had been 'Just send the ticket.'

Two days later she was off on Thai Airways and I settled down for a period of what is known in the profession as 'resting'. A gentleman named Gerry Anderson soon put a stop to that. Gerry was the creative genius who, amongst other things, had dreamed up the wildly successful TV series *Thunderbirds*. His new brainchild was called *Space: 1999* for which he had signed the two *Mission: Impossible* stars Martin Landau and his then-wife, Barbara Bain.

'Are you still strong enough to join us in outer space?' he had quipped one day in the Pinewood bar. Well, before you could say 'We have lift-off' I was back into TV. My memories of that series? Only warm ones. Lovely time, lovely people and as for Martin Landau, it didn't matter to him if the doors, even spaceships, opened right to left or left to right, his talent and charm still came through them. Incidentally, the gods or whoever controls our destinies must have been laughing when 20 years later, in those very 1990s about which we were all trying to be so prophetic, Martin would win his first Academy Award for playing Bela Lugosi in the movie *Ed Wood*.

It would be another three years of see-sawing between TV and films before I happened into my most intriguing TV experience of all. It began the day after I'd returned from the Cannes Film Festival, at which Yolande and I had been a part of the official British delegation, when I received a call from André Previn's brother, Steve. 'You standing or sitting?' he began. I told him at the moment I was standing. 'Well sit,' he instructed, and then, 'Now, how would you like to make a Sherlock Holmes and Doctor Watson TV series in Warsaw?'

For a moment I wondered if I'd heard right. Warsaw in Poland? That was the same as Yo going to Russia, it was still behind the Iron Curtain, full of KGB and all the menacing things we made films about. So what in heaven's name would the Poles be wanting with Sherlock Holmes? 'It's a matter of foreign currency,' Steve explained. 'They need foreign currency desperately and this is one way they can get it.'

This whole incredible deal had been engineered by Sheldon Reynolds, American radio and TV writer who had previously produced and directed a couple of films including *Foreign Intrigue* with Robert Mitchum. Sheldon, or Shelley as he was called, had arranged that in return for a piece of the action the Poles would give him their Poltel Studios with all building and production staff. For his part he would supply the actors and key technicians. It seemed that Steve Previn, one of the top luminaries in Sam Arkoff's American International Pictures (who had been involved in the US distribution of *The Diamond Mercenaries*), had suggested me to Reynolds who said he would like me to do it. 'But I have to warn you,' Steve went on jokingly, 'that if you say yes you may never speak to me again.' The inference being that he had no idea what trying to make a TV series behind the Iron Curtain might entail. 'Anyway,' he went on, 'they want to start next month. Sheldon's already written some of the scripts. Think it over and give their London office a call. The production manager is George Fowler, maybe you know him.'

I knew him well, having given George his first Assistant Director job on *Just William's Luck*, and he'd stayed with us through several of Yolande's films, from *Miss Pilgrim's Progress* to *Mr Drake's Duck* and onwards. Be that as it may, the whole thing had begun to sound so fascinating I was almost prepared to do a Yolande and say, 'Just send the ticket!' Instead I did the next best thing, called the Morris office and asked John Mather to fix the deal. And by a lucky coincidence Yolande had just taken some time off from films and theatre to finish a writing contract for Charles Wintour, editor of the London *Evening Standard*, so we were able to plunge into James Bond territory together.

Warsaw turned out to be an impressive city full of surprises. So did Communism. To begin with, it had allowed a splendid, capitalistic Inter-Continental hotel called the Victoria to operate smack on its main square, and it was here that Shelley Reynolds and his wife Andrea welcomed us into a comfortable suite that was to be my on-and-off home over the next four months. The impeccably dressed Andrea Reynolds, they explained, would be in charge of the wardrobe department and I have to record that in all my studio years this was the only time when I knew that if I dropped into that department at 7.00 am before shooting I would inevitably be greeted by a wardrobe mistress looking like a fashion spread from *Vogue*. Years later, of course, parted from Sheldon, Andrea would become world famous as the much-photographed lady friend of Claus von Bulow, on trial for the alleged murder of his wife. But that's another story. In fact, they turned it into a film called *Reversal of Fortune* in which our own Jeremy Irons won an Academy Award for his portrayal of that very same Claus von Bulow.

Meanwhile, before leaving London we had all been warned that just because our Warsaw hotel was American-owned didn't mean the rooms wouldn't still be 'bugged' in true KGB fashion. So if there was anything you didn't want heard, save it for the streets or the parks. Furthermore, don't think that turning up the room radio or flushing the toilet would drown your words because extra sound only turned up extra mikes. I must say we had some fun trying to guess where our mikes were hidden. Behind the pictures? Inside the air vents? There was also a large built-in mirror taking up most of our sitting room wall and I kidded Yo it was probably a two-way one with camera and cameraman behind it. Every dawn, on my way down to the hotel café where we all met for our pre-shooting breakfast, I would bid our mirror 'Good morning'.

Apropos of which, during our first few meals those of us who ordered toast were informed sorry, no toast, toasters were being serviced, replaced or were in some way out of operation. One morning as I left our room I waved at the mirror and asked, 'Why can't we ever get any bloody toast?' Down in the café the boys laughed when I told them the story. I gave my usual order to the waitress adding, 'I suppose it's still useless asking for toast.' 'Oh no, sir,' she chirped, 'what kind of bread would you like?' Coincidence? Of course, but what if...?

My next Polish surprise was at the Poltel Studios where the whole of their vast lot had been transformed into an enormous section of Sherlock Holmes' Baker Street. Working with Shelley's art director and an album full of old photographs, they had created an incredibly authentic set complete with hansom cabs and gaslight. I spent most of the first week's shooting on it with probably the largest unit anyone had ever seen since the original *Ben-Hur*. This, I was informed gently, was Communism. No one was allowed to be out of work, so they were drafted in to any going operation. The fact that most of them slipped away to sleep in the fields or hidden doorways meant nothing to the studio. They were not out of work, and that justified the system, a system that also seemed to turn a blind eye to one of the most flourishing businesses in Warsaw, the black market. On the set, on locations or in the streets people would nip out of alleyways offering everything from caviar to currency. The caviar was Russian and, along with antiques, was strictly forbidden to be taken out of Poland. Currency was another matter. Smooth-talking operators would accost you with fistfuls of Polish szlotes to exchange for pounds, dollars, francs or whatever. It was even rumoured that our Sherlock Holmes series was being shot on black market film stock.

However, it was Yolande who stumbled on the biggest surprise of all, having bought a ticket at the Warsaw Opera House to see the opening night of a visiting German opera company singing their version of the classic *Ages of Man*. The overture finished, the curtain rose on a striking set depicting the Garden of Eden, over which could be heard the melodious off-stage voices of the star baritone and diva playing Adam and Eve. Moments later the singing Adam and Eve made their entrance. And they were both stark naked with only a transparent net holding things together. The portly baritone and well-endowed diva sang the whole of the first scene bouncing their essentials around Eden while the

Poles watched po-faced. But all in all, Yolande reported, it was an enjoyable evening and had given opera what one might call new dimensions.

It was after completing my first two episodes that I came to the conclusion that directing another 11 of them under existing pressures would be a lot easier if only I had another director with me shooting them back to back, and I suggested Roy Ward Baker. The same Roy Baker from those olden days together at Gainsborough, since when he had carved a reputation for himself as a hardworking and respected director in his own right. So, almost before the next 'Elementary, my dear Watson', Roy was sealed, signed and over in Warsaw being bugged with the rest of us.

With National Theatre actor Geoffrey Whitehead playing Holmes and the equally talented Donald Pickering as Watson it could have been a great series but sadly, somewhere along the line, Sheldon Reynolds landed in some currency-changing fraças with the Polish authorities. Andrea was even incarcerated briefly while Shelley had all his film negatives confiscated, leaving him with nothing but a cutting copy to try and sell to the world. To the best of my knowledge he never did and I don't think the series was ever screened in its entirety, except maybe behind the Iron Curtain.

Nevertheless, it was an unforgettable experience and as our new Polish friends came to the Okecie Airport to wave goodbye they also crossed their fingers for us, knowing that my brave Yolande had slipped a kilo tin of illegal Russian caviar into her luggage.

'Anything to declare?' asked the stern-faced Polish customs officer.

'Nothing,' said innocent-faced Yo.

'Not taking out any antiques?' he probed.

'Only me,' she answered promptly. Slowly the stern face broke into a grin, then a laugh as he chalked our cases through and we were off back to jolly old Capitalism and a Russian caviar party.

CHAPTER
TWENTY

It was now into the 1980s with me not far behind, into my seventies, when something I read in the press one day made me sit up with a jolt and sit back with a gasp. And it wasn't the two-inch newspaper banners announcing that Prince Charles had chosen that year to marry Lady Diana Spencer, nor the showbiz headlines that America's ABC Television had topped all other viewing figures with their New Year launch of a series called *Dynasty* – two of the writer-producers of which, Mike and Bob Pollock, would become our friends and neighbours years later in far-away Palm Springs. No, it was nothing as newsworthy as Prince Charles or ABC starting a new dynasty, it was merely a jokey little squib in Peter Noble's *Screen International* column stating that, according to their records, I had now chalked up more film credits than I'd had birthdays.

Just an inch of funny ha-ha time for Peter but sheer disbelief time for me, until a hurried delve into my files proved that, incredibly, he was right. I was a trifle shaken to find the tally was so high and for the first time lapsed into a serious ponder as to whether or not I should be thinking of slowing down with a little more tennis-in-the-sun time.

Yolande, who had just come out of the hard work and hassle of filming *I Thought they Died Years Ago*, a thriller for London Weekend Television with co-stars Nicole Maurey, Maxine Audley and Faith Brook, thought it was one of my rare brilliant ideas. The question was where? Sadly, our Malta paradise had lost a lot of its charm since Colonel Gaddafi's buddy, the leftist Dom Mintoff, had become its new Prime Minister. Sometimes referred to as 'Little Stalin', he had changed the whole feel of that sunny island and even Frankie Howerd had sold up his holiday home and got out. Although, in fairness to Mintoff, I found him pleasant enough in person when he visited London during the shooting of *Space: 1999*. He had summoned me to the Royal Garden Hotel in Kensington to ask if I would help them build up the Maltese film industry. Knowing that Yo had already decided to get rid of our penthouse there while we still could, I thanked the PM for the compliment but regretted to say I was already over-committed. Who knows, I might have become the Mediterranean's Sam Goldwyn.

Anyway, with Malta 'out' we had mulled over a sunny, tennis-filled semi-retirement home in two other places, the South of France or California. If, after a few more reels, we were about to become 'the folks who live on the hill', Yolande would prefer it was a French hill. However, since we already knew the French hills pretty well, we decided to case California's Pacific coastline before taking any big leap. The first moment we were both clear of commitments we winged our way to San Francisco, hired a car and coasted along the Pacific Coast Highway to spend our first night in Carmel-by-the-sea.

Carmel had been a bohemian artists' village where the streets didn't even need numbers and was hailed by many people as an adorable place to live. Not least of those many people being Clint 'make my day' Eastwood who went as far as saying, 'It's the nearest you'll get to paradise without dying.' But then, Clint was also the mayor of Carmel as well as owning a restaurant there called the Hog's Breath, so he would, wouldn't he? Nonetheless, it was a delightful resort except for its winter weather, with all the clouds and rain we were trying to leave behind in London. Which meant 'hullo and goodbye Carmel,' but we felt the least we could do before leaving was lunch at Clint's own restaurant. It turned out to be a cosy enough place where the ambience, the food and the service were fine, topped only by the surprise 'Today's Special': Mayor Eastwood himself at the cash desk, checking up on the takings.

That afternoon, back on the coast road, we skipped San Simeon where someone had already overdone the retirement-home-on-the-hill bit. His name, of course, was William Randolph Hearst and Hearst Castle had every one of its 100-plus rooms filled with priceless art and antiques, as well as its surrounding acres strewn with a treasure trove of sculptures and statuary. Fabled also for its many celebrity house guests, from film stars to Winston Churchill and George Bernard Shaw. It was GBS who summed it up so neatly after his first visit: 'This is the way God would have done it if he had the money.'

After several more fruitless forays it was clear the Pacific coast wouldn't give us the weather we needed and there was nothing left but to head inland and spend the remainder of our holiday in the spot we knew had almost perennial sunshine. Where else but Palm Springs and where better to stay than at one of Hollywood's favourite playgrounds, Charles Farrell's Racquet Club. MGM used to boast it had 'More stars than there are in Heaven', but on any given weekend the Palm Springs Racquet Club could boast of more stars than there were in MGM. And this club, now part of film folklore, came into being quite by chance when stage and screen matinée idol Charles Farrell and tennis chum, actor Ralph Bellamy, bought the land in a defiant moment and on a passing whim. 'We created the Racquet Club because we were tennis nuts,' was how Charlie put it.

But the full story is more intriguing. In those days Palm Springs was little more than a collection of dirt roads, miles of sand, sagebrush and cactus with, according to Ralph, less than 200 permanent residents, excluding the Indians. At weekends, as soon as they left the studios Charlie and Ralph drove down to a couple of rented homes in the desert and spent their weekends playing tennis at the El Mirador Hotel, which boasted some of the few courts in Palm Springs. But as they weren't staying at the hotel they could only do this because El Mirador's owner, one Warren Pinney, had given the two young movie stars a special dispensation to use the courts when none of his hotel residents wanted them. But tennis nuts being tennis nuts it wasn't long before Pinny's office was flooded with guests complaining the courts were always full of Farrell and Bellamy.

One day, at the end of their game, the two stars were summoned to Pinney's office where he told them politely but firmly never to darken his courts again. To work off their surprised shock they hired a couple of horses and it was while they rode down a sand trail, that would one day be called Indian Canyon Avenue, they spied a solitary LAND FOR SALE sign stuck in a barren piece of desert. Neither Ralph nor Charlie could remember who had the idea but it was, 'Why not buy it and build our own damned courts?' Which they did, all 53 acres, for which, Ralph said, they paid $3,500. But simply building a couple of courts cost them double that, which in those days was a lot of outlay for some weekend tennis. The courts were finally finished by Christmas Day 1933 and to help defray expenses our two tennis nuts charged their friends a dollar a day to drive down and play on them.

'It started in a haphazard way,' was how Charlie explained it, 'and grew in the same crazy, mixed-up fashion.' As the news spread it brought the elite of Tinseltown lining up for courts, which was when Charlie nudged his partner with another idea. What if they turned it into a club? That evening they sat down, made a list of 175 of their tennis-loving friends, asked them if they'd pay $50 to join the new Racquet Club of Palm Springs and it was the birth of a legend. From then on you could have watched Clark Gable and Carole Lombard having a warm-up with Errol Flynn and wife Lilly Damita, Spencer Tracy and Katie Hepburn game-and-setting William Powell and girlfriend Jean Harlow, or been there on the memorable day that Ginger Rogers actually won the club's Pimms Cup tournament. Cary Grant and Barbara Hutton even spent part of their honeymoon there, followed by such steady weekenders as Monroe, Grable, Hayworth, Bogart and Bacall.

Then came more courts, a restaurant and a bar, behind which Bing Crosby would often play bartender and sing at the same time. Through the years it had remained one of the movie colony's favourites, gathering new weekender friends such as my old Columbia boss Mike Frankovich, Patrick *Avengers* Macnee, Shelley Winters, Olivia Newton-John, Howard Keel, even our new London neighbour, George Hamilton. They were all there and, oh yes, so were Yolande Donlan and Val Guest. Not that we were steady weekenders but since the demise of our Malta abode we'd made frequent getaways to Palm Springs, joined the club and rented one of their condominiums, where we met so many old friends as well as lots of new ones. It soon began to feel like a home from home, especially when they actually conscripted me onto the Racquet Club committee. And what a chuckle that would have given those two bowler-hatted, umbrella-furled chaps with whom this long-ago *Hollywood Reporter* columnist had walked around Hyde Park's Rotten Row one Sunday morning in olden day London.

It was a telephone call from present day London that jolted my 'retirement' holiday. It came from producer Greg Smith, asking me one of the most unexpected questions I'd ever been asked. What did I think of the idea of remaking my old Will Hay film *Ask a Policeman* and rewriting it for the currently very popular double act of Tommy Cannon and Bobby Ball? I took a deep breath. Rewrite a 45-year-old script, even if they could find a copy? 'What do you have to lose?' asked the practical Yo. The answer was SLEEP, of which I lost quite a bit once I'd said yes and launched myself into the almost impossible task of striving to achieve something that wouldn't have the late Bill Hay turning in his grave.

I had first met Greg Smith several years back at Twickenham Studios when I had lunch with him and his then co-producer Michael Klinger. They were planning to make a light-hearted comedy romp called *Au Pair Girls* and was I free? I was, and it turned out to be a happy partnership in which Greg and I seemed to hit the right buttons. Greg was a bright, highly ambitious young producer, and Yolande always referred to him as Irving Thalberg Jr. After *Au Pair Girls* we worked on several productions together, the first when Greg gave me a paperback novel called *Confessions of a Window Cleaner*, one of an amusing series of *Confessions* books by Timothy Lea. After Yo read it she threw up her hands in despair. 'The whole subject is just nonsensical sex rubbish,' she declared, and stopped calling Greg 'Thalberg'.

So, to do or not to do *Confessions*, that was the problem. In Yo's eyes, had it been a play, Olivier would never have put it on at the National. However, Greg was so sure it could be a huge commercial success and make us all a fortune that Yo, who'd always had a dream of buying a villa for our retirement, said maybe she'd just have to push her integrity aside for the dough. 'Okay,' she sighed. 'So you make a sex comedy.'

Some time later she pointed out to me that times change and even the eminent Lord Olivier had since been seen on the screen bonking away in the sexy Harold Robbins film *The Betsy*. 'And that,' she added, 'wasn't even funny.' Today they tell me *Confessions of a Window Cleaner* has become a cult film around the world. Which only goes to show that making films is a constant surprise. 'And look at all those Hammer horror movies,' said Yo. 'Same thing. Had I known they were going to become a cult I might have had fun doing one.'

My next adventure with Greg was *The Shillingbury Blowers*, starring the incomparable Trevor Howard. Greg and television's Francis Essex came to Peartree one day with a delightful script Francis had written about a small village called Shillingbury and their brass band, conducted by the local odd-job man, to be played by Trevor, and how they suddenly found themselves in the National Brass Band Contest.

We had great fun shooting *The Shillingbury Blowers* and two memorable moments have remained with me over the years. The first occurred before Greg had signed up Trevor Howard. There had been a barrage of warnings that, good as he was, Trevor had a drinking problem which could play havoc with our tight schedule. I decided the only way to handle the dilemma was to meet it face to face. I invited Trevor to Peartree, told him there was nobody I would rather direct in the part, but if I disregarded all those warnings it would be my head that was on the block. Trev stared at me for a moment before his craggy face broke into a grin. 'I couldn't work with a decapitated director,' he said and raised his right hand. 'So I hereby give my word of honour there'll be no tots on any shooting day, so help me God.' And the delightful Trevor kept his word, turned in his usual endearing performance and at the end-of-picture party spent the evening toasting every member of the cast and crew until an understanding Greg organised a chauffeur-driven limousine to help him get home.

My other recall is shorter, sweeter and funnier. When the first print for the American market was flown into Los Angeles airport it was immediately siezed and impounded by Customs, convinced that with a title like *The Shillingbury Blowers* it could only be a porno film. After a private screening to a roomful of top echelon, who I'm sure were disappointed to find the blowers were only a brass band, the dust settled and the film was allowed into the country for American release. But only after the title was changed to *And the Band Played On*. Happily, both titles turned out to be popular enough for us to follow up with a six-part series called *Shillingbury Tales*.

Back to the drawing board and the re-scripting of *Ask a Policeman*, now called *The Boys in Blue*. Trying to accomplish this before the end of 1981 found me continually hunched over a hot typewriter until Yolande, tired of looking at the back of my head, decided to fly off to Spain and play tennis with Bjorn Borg. That's always a great party-stopping line until I add that it was a tennis clinic which Bjorn was holding at the Puente Romano hotel in Marbella. We have a treasured photograph of a smiling Bjorn and Yo shaking hands across the net and I often kid people that it was after this game he decided to quit tennis. And as if that wasn't enough, the new year had barely begun, with me up to my ears in pre-production nonsense, before Yolande flew her tennis racquet to Florida. This time invading Amelia Island to be Chris Evert's doubles partner in a tennis match. True it was only at Chrissie's own tennis clinic but for Yo it was no less of an achievement. It also went to show that Charlie Farrell and Ralph Bellamy weren't the only tennis nuts. Incidentally, less than a month later Maggie Thatcher decided to invade another island, but this wasn't for tennis, it was to liberate the Falklands.

As for me, the year finished with the completion of *The Boys in Blue*, hopefully without anyone turning in their graves, except perhaps me. After a spell of night location shooting, battling the October winds and rain, for the first time in my gnarled career I did an unpardonable thing and collapsed with pneumonia. But every cloud has a silver lining and this one revealed that you can't have pneumonia and still smoke. As soon as that cloud had passed my guru of a wife proclaimed: 'As you've already stopped, why start again?' Confucius couldn't have put it better and thus ended the habit of a lifetime.

For my recuperative break Yolande took the helm and this time, instead of renting a Racquet Club condo, lashed out and bought one. It was a perfect place to relax for a couple of weeks, play some tennis and ponder whether that executive producer in the sky had really been trying to tell me something. Retirement has to be one of life's tougher decisions. Some achieve retirement, others have retirement thrust upon them but semi-retirement is somewhere in the middle and even trickier. Which is why a long-distance call from Roy Skeggs at Elstree, asking if I'd like to get involved in his new *Hammer House of Mystery and Suspense* series, had this old circus horse smelling the sawdust again and prancing back into the ring.

I thoroughly enjoyed the whole assignment as well as meeting and working with an array of new talent such as Jenny Seagrove, US TV's Dirk Benedict, Hollywood's Carol Lynley, *Dynasty*'s English heart-throb, Chris Cazenove, and the immortal Bing's lovely daughter, Mary Crosby, who had gained her own piece of TV immortality as the person who shot JR in *Dallas*. Meanwhile Yolande, adept at springing surprises, had gone ahead and bought the Racquet Club condo next to ours so that mother Terry could spend her September days there in the California sun she'd missed so much since coming to live with us in London. A kindly, loving plan that went awry. One shattering evening at Peartree, going upstairs to tell Terry that Yo was dishing up dinner, I found the dear self-sufficient lady who, at the grand old age of 94 still couldn't bear the thought of anyone having to help her do anything, had fainted in her bath and drowned.

After her flower-decked funeral we returned to an empty Peartree Cottage which suddenly seemed larger because of it. By now Christopher had moved out to lead his own life as a language professor at Richmond College, while son David Guest had long ago bought his own home and become nothing less than admin manager of the British Safety Council. So now we were two, living in a three-storey house with 14 rooms. Was it time to think the unthinkable and maybe buy a smaller town house?

Eventually, after two more years of indecision, we relinquished our beloved Peartree and bought a small but delightful little mews cottage tucked away on a cobbled cul-de-sac in Belgravia. It had what American estate agents call 'location, location', being halfway between Buckingham Palace and Harrods, as well as almost next door to the Lloyd-Webber town residence. In fact, on the day we moved in, 7 October to be exact, Andrew was having tizzies about the dress rehearsals of a new little opus he'd dreamed up and was due to open two days later at Her Majesty's Theatre. They were wasted tizzies because it opened to rapturous applause and he'd entered onto yet another page of theatrical history with *The Phantom of the Opera*.

He also made a bit of mews history when, quite apart from buying up half of it, he seldom used the obligatory shiny limousine one might expect of one of the world's richest composers. Instead, he could be seen being driven back and forth in an old, upright London taxicab. Why? Because Andrew had figured out that a London taxi is allowed to pull up and park practically anywhere in town, so why not buy his own cab and take advantage of it? But then we always knew Andrew was a genius.

Our other location-location neighbours were George Hamilton a few doors down from us, Roger Moore in the house on the corner and composer Leslie Bricusse with a place almost opposite, both of them a stone's throw from Joan Collins' London pad. Around the other corner we had our favourite violinist, Yehudi Menuhin, as well as Anthony Hopkins to open the village fair when he wasn't filming. It was almost a Royal Command cast list and word of it must have got around because shortly after Maggie Thatcher left Downing Street she decided to move into our location-location, making herself the undisputed top of the bill.

We still had our Racquet Club pied-à-terre in the sun, using it whenever work permitted, and as the eighties drew to a close we seemed to find more excuses to use it for longer stretches. It soon became obvious another decision was looming and shortly after New Year's we flew there for six weeks, sold the condos and bought another house before returning home to prepare for our next changeover. I found an amusing reminder scribbled in my 1989 diary: EIGHT WEEKS TO TAKE-OFF – 25 PACKING DAYS LEFT. On the 23rd of those days there is another nostalgic diary note which reads simply: WESTMINSTER ABBEY – OLIVIER REMEMBRANCE THANKSGIVING SERVICE.

It was the last event we attended before leaving for California and what a moving yet somehow exhilarating experience it was. In a typically thoughtful gesture Larry's widow, the talented Joan Plowright, had invited Yolande and the rest of his leading ladies to attend. From where I sat it was moving enough to watch Yolande and Maggie Smith listening to the eulogies read by John Gielgud and Alec Guinness, but when a line of actors and actresses, who had worked with Larry, walked slowly down the aisle carrying some of the props he had used in his plays, a sword, a crown, a goblet, a dagger... it was breath-catching.

Today we still have our cosy, cobbled mews cottage but now spend most of the year in Palm Springs luxuriating in our comfortable, cloistered hacienda on the edge of the Canyon Country Club golf course. There we can sometimes glance out of the window and watch history in the making as ex-President Gerald Ford tries to putt his ball into the 14th hole. And what else do I do in my retirement? Perhaps the best answer is to quote from 'My Diary of a Day' which I wrote for *World Cinema*.

'Beautiful Palm Springs morning and all's well with the world. After months of labour pains the screenplay for the Fox remake of *The Day the Earth Caught Fire* completed and delivered yesterday. Dived into the pool and out again for a London call from my agent, Dennis Selinger, to say the company who plan to remake *Expresso Bongo* have agreed to the contract terms. Two remakes in one year? Wow. What can go wrong on such a day? Plenty. And it does around noon.

'A call from someone at Fox. "Thought you'd like to know the new boss has read the script and had a brilliant idea. What if the male lead, the hard-drinking, self-destructive reporter, was a woman? Keep up with the times." Are they serious? Very. "Of course," he goes on, "this means the leading lady will now have to be a man." After my first shock I come back with my brilliant idea. Why does the leading lady have to be a man? Why isn't the hard-drinking, self-destructive woman reporter in love with another woman? Keep up with the times. Fox calls a hasty conference.

Which shows that in a writer's life there's no such thing as a perfect day. Or a perfect life? Of course not, but give or take a reel or two I've had an incredibly lucky one. Here we are into a new millennium and I'm amazingly still standing, What's more I have an adorable, unpredictable wife who, deciding there were still too many things she didn't know, enrolled in California's College of the Desert. In 2000 she not only graduated with highest honours but was also their Valedictorian! Which started me wondering if all those years ago they were right casting me as the Village Idiot.

What's more, I still have two lovely homes, sons, grandchildren and a snuggly toy poodle, Mischa, an Animal Samaritan therapy dog Yo takes around hospitals to help cheer and cure the patients.

It all happened one life, and looking back I'm amazed at just how much happened. I'm also eternally grateful to all those people along the way who helped to make it happen.

As for my end of term report, I think it might read: 'Worked hard, tried hard, could have done better.' Anyway, as my old workmate Woody Allen once said, he didn't want to achieve immortality through his work, he wanted to achieve it by not dying.

I think I'll drink to that. God bless and, as our neighbour Bob Hope would say, thanks for the memories.

FILMOGRAPHY

s: screenplay   d: director   p: producer   lp: leading players

Titles in **bold** indicate Val Guest as director. All other films and television episodes listed have screenplays written, or co-written, by Val Guest.

All titles are listed under the year in which production began.

1932
The Maid of the Mountains
(British International Pictures)
d: Lupino Lane
p: Walter Mycroft
lp: Harry Welchman, Pat Patterson

The Innocents of Chicago
(British International Pictures)
p/d: Lupino Lane
lp: Henry Kendall, Bernard Nedell,
Margot Grahame

1935
No Monkey Business
(Radius Productions)
d: Marcel Varnel
lp: June Clyde, Gene Gerrard,
Richard Hearne, Renee Houston

1936
Public Nuisance No 1 (Cecil Films)
d: Marcel Varnel
p: Hermann Fellner, Max Schach
lp: Frances Day, Arthur Riscoe,
Muriel Aked, Claude Dampier

All In (Gainsborough Pictures)
d: Marcel Varnel
p: Edward Black
lp: Ralph Lynn, Gina Malo,
Jack Barty, Claude Dampier

Good Morning, Boys!
(Gainsborough Pictures)

d: Marcel Varnel
p: Edward Black
lp: Will Hay, Graham Moffatt, Lilli
Palmer, Martita Hunt, Charles Hawtrey

1937
O-kay for Sound
(Gainsborough Pictures)
d: Marcel Varnel
p: Edward Black
lp: Bud Flanagan, Chesney Allen,
Jimmy Nervo, Teddy Knox,
Charlie Naughton, Jimmy Gold,
Graham Moffatt

Oh, Mr Porter!
(Gainsborough Pictures)
d: Marcel Varnel
p: Edward Black
lp: Will Hay, Moore Marriott,
Graham Moffatt, Sebastian Smith,
Agnes Lauchlan

1938
Convict 99
(Gainsborough/Gaumont-British)
d: Marcel Varnel
p: Edward Black
lp: Will Hay, Graham Moffatt,
Moore Marriott, Googie Withers,
Peter Gawthorne, Basil Radford,
Kathleen Harrison

Alf's Button Afloat
(Gainsborough Pictures)

d: Marcel Varnel
p: Edward Black
lp: Bud Flanagan, Chesney Allen,
Jimmy Nervo, Teddy Knox, Charlie
Naughton, Jimmy Gold, Alastair Sim

Hey! Hey! USA!
(Gainsborough/Gaumont-British)
d: Marcel Varnel
p: Edward Black
lp: Will Hay, Edgar Kennedy, Fred
Duprez, David Burns, Edward Ryan

Old Bones of the River
(Gainsborough Pictures)
d: Marcel Varnel
p: Edward Black
lp: Will Hay, Moore Marriott,
Graham Moffatt, Robert Adams,
Jack Livesey

1939
Ask a Policeman
(Gainsborough Pictures)
d: Marcel Varnel
p: Edward Black
lp: Will Hay, Moore Marriott,
Graham Moffatt, Glennis Lorrimer,
Peter Gawthorne

Where's That Fire?
(Gainsborough Pictures)
d: Marcel Varnel
p: Edward Black
lp: Will Hay, Moore Marriott,
Graham Moffat, Peter Gawthorne,

Eric Clavering, Charles Hawtrey

The Frozen Limits
(Gainsborough Pictures)
d: Marcel Varnel
p: Edward Black
lp: Bud Flanagan, Chesney Allen,
Jimmy Nervo, Teddy Knox, Charlie
Naughton, Jimmy Gold, Moore
Marriott, Eileen Bell

Charley's Big-Hearted Aunt
(Gainsborough Pictures)
d: Walter Forde
p: Edward Black
lp: Arthur Askey, Richard Murdoch,
Graham Moffat, Moore Marriott,
Phyllis Calvert, Felix Aylmer

1940
Band Waggon (Gainsborough Pictures)
d: Marcel Varnel
p: Edward Black
lp: Arthur Askey, Jack Hylton,
Richard Murdoch, Patricia
Kirkwood, Moore Marriott

Goofer Trouble
(Ministry of Information)
d: Maurice Elvey
s: JOC Orton, Val Guest
lp: Fred Emney, David Farrar,
Edward Chapman, Robert Beatty

Gasbags
(Gainsborough Pictures)
d: Marcel Varnel
p: Edward Black
lp: Bud Flanagan, Chesney Allen,
Jimmy Nervo, Teddy Knox, Charlie
Naughton, Jimmy Gold, Moore
Marriott, Peter Gawthorne

1941
Inspector Hornleigh Goes To It
(Gainsborough Pictures)
d: Walter Forde
p: Edward Black
lp: Gordon Harker, Alastair Sim,
Phyllis Calvert, Edward Chapman,
Charles Oliver, Raymond Huntley

The Ghost Train
(Gainsborough Pictures)
d: Walter Forde
p: Edward Black
lp: Arthur Askey, Richard Murdoch,
Kathleen Harrison, Morland
Graham, Herbert Lomas

I Thank You (Gaumont-British)
d: Marcel Varnel
p: Edward Black
lp: Arthur Askey, Richard Murdoch,
Lily Morris, Moore Marriott,
Graham Moffatt, Kathleen Harrison

Hi, Gang! (Gainsborough Pictures)
d: Marcel Varnel
p: Edward Black
lp: Bebe Daniels, Ben Lyon, Vic
Oliver, Moore Marriott, Graham
Moffatt, Felix Aylmer

1942
Back-Room Boy
(Gainsborough Pictures)
d: Herbert Mason
p: Edward Black
lp: Arthur Askey, Moore Marriott,
Graham Moffatt, Googie Withers,
Vera Francis

The Nose Has It!
(Ministry of Information)
s: Val Guest
lp: Arthur Askey

King Arthur Was A Gentleman
(Gainsborough Pictures)
d: Marcel Varnel
p: Edward Black
lp: Arthur Askey, Evelyn Dall, Anne
Shelton, Max Bacon, Al Burnett,
Vera Francis, Ronald Shiner

1943
Miss London Ltd
(Gainsborough Pictures)
s: Marriott Edgar, Val Guest
p: Edward Black
lp: Arthur Askey, Max Bacon, Sheila
Bligh, Noni Brooke, Evelyne, Dall,
Peter Graves, Richard Hearne

1944
Bees in Paradise
(Gainsborough Pictures)
s: Marriott Edgar, Val Guest
p: Edward Black
lp: Arthur Askey, Anne Shelton,
Peter Graves, Ronald Shiner, Jean
Kent, Max Bacon, Antoinette Cellier

Give Us the Moon
(Gainsborough Pictures)
s: Val Guest p: Edward Black
lp: Margaret Lockwood, Vic Oliver,
Peter Graves, Roland Culver, Max
Bacon, Frank Cellier, Jean Simmons

1945
I'll Be Your Sweetheart
(Gainsborough Pictures)
s: Val Guest, Val Valentine
p: Louis Levy
lp: Margaret Lockwood, Michael
Rennie, Vic Oliver, Peter Graves,
Moore Marriott, Frederick Burtwell

1946
London Town
(General Film Distributors)
d/p: Wesley Ruggles
lp: Sid Field, Greta Gynt, Kay Kendall,
Tessie O'Shea, Claude Hulbert, Sonnie
Hale, Mary Clare, Petula Clark

Paper Orchid (Columbia British)
d: Roy Baker p: William Collier
lp: Hugh Williams, Hy Hazell,
Sidney James, Garry Marsh, Andrew
Cruickshank, Ivor Barnard

1947
Just William's Luck
(Alliance Communications)
s: Val Guest p: William Collier Jr
lp: William Graham, Garry Marsh,
Jane Welsh, Hugh Cross, Kathleen
Stuart, Leslie Bradley, AE Matthews

Once Upon A Dream
(Rank Film Productions)
d: Ralph Thomas
p: Anthony Darnborough

s: Victor Katona, Patrick Kirwan
(story Val Guest)
lp: Googie Withers, Griffith Jones,
Guy Middleton, Raymond Lovell,
Hubert Gregg, Dora Bryan

1948
William Comes To Town
(Alliance Communications)
s: Val Guest p: William Collier Jr
lp: William Graham, Garry Marsh,
Jane Welsh, AE Matthews, Muriel
Aked, Hugh Cross, Kathleen Stuart,
Michael Medwin, Jon Pertwee

1949
Murder at the Windmill
(Associated British Films)
s: Val Guest p: Daniel M Angel,
Nat Cohen
lp: Garry Marsh, Jon Pertwee, Jack
Livesey, Eliot Makeham, Jimmy
Edwards, Diana Decker

Miss Pilgrim's Progress
(Angel Productions)
s: Val Guest p: Daniel M Angel,
Nat Cohen
lp: Michael Rennie, Yolande Donlan,
Garry Marsh, Emrys Jones, Reginald
Beckwith, Helena Pickard, Jon Pertwee

1950
The Body Said No
(New World Angel)
s: Val Guest p: Daniel M Angel
lp: Michael Rennie, Yolande Donlan,
Hy Hazell, Jon Pertwee, Valentine
Dyall, Reginald Beckwith

Mr Drake's Duck (Eros Films)
s: Val Guest p: Daniel M Angel
lp: Douglas Fairbanks Jr, Yolande
Donlan, Jon Pertwee, Wilfrid Hyde
White, Reginald Beckwith, Howard
Marion-Crawford, Peter Butterworth

1951
Another Man's Poison (Eros Films)
d: Irving Rapper p: Douglas

Fairbanks Jr, Daniel M Angel
lp: Bette Davis, Anthony Steel, Gary
Merrill, Emlyn Williams, Barbara
Murray, Reginald Beckwith

Happy-Go-Lovely (Exelsior Films)
d: Bruce Humberstone
p: Marcel Hellman
lp: David Niven, Vera-Ellen, Cesar
Romero, Bobby Howes, Diane Hart,
Gordon Jackson, Barbara Couper

1952
Penny Princess
(Conquest Productions)
s/p: Val Guest
lp: Dirk Bogarde, Yolande Donlan,
AE Matthews, Anthony Oliver,
Edwin Styles, Kynaston Reeves,
Peter Butterworth

1953
Life with the Lyons
(Exclusive/Hammer Film Productions)
s: Val Guest, Robert Dunbar
p: Robert Dunbar
lp: Ben Lyon, Bebe Daniels, Barbara
Lyon, Richard Lyon, Hugh Morton,
Horace Percival, Molly Weir

The Runaway Bus
(Eros/Conquest Productions)
s/p: Val Guest
lp: Frankie Howerd, Margaret
Rutherford, Petula Clark, George
Coulouris, Terence Alexander,
Belinda Lee

1954
Dance Little Lady (Renown Pictures)
s: Val Guest, Doreen Montgomery
p: George Minter
lp: Terence Alexander, Mai
Zetterling, Guy Rolfe, Mandy Miller,
Eunice Gayson, Reginald Beckwith

The Men of Sherwood Forest
(Exclusive/Hammer Film Productions)
s: Allan MacKinnon
p: Michael Carreras
lp: Don Taylor, Reginald Beckwith,

Eileen Moore, David King Wood,
Douglas Wilmer, Harold Lang

The Lyons in Paris
(Exclusive/Hammer Film Productions)
s: Val Guest p: Robert Dunbar
lp: Ben Lyon, Bebe Daniels, Barbara
Lyon, Richard Lyon, Horace
Percival, Molly Weir

Break in the Circle
(Exclusive/Hammer Film Productions)
s: Val Guest p: Michael Carreras
lp: Forrest Tucker, Eva Bartok,
Marius Goring, Reginald Beckwith,
Eric Pohlmann, Guy Middleton,
Arnold Marle, Fred Johnson,
David King Wood

The Quatermass Xperiment
(Exclusive/Hammer Film Productions)
s: Val Guest, Richard Landau
p: Anthony Hinds
lp: Brian Donlevy, Jack Warner,
Margia Dean, Richard Wordsworth,
Thora Hird, Gordon Jackson,
David King Wood

1955
They Can't Hang Me
(Vandyke Picture Corporation)
s: Val Guest, Val Valentine
p: Roger Proudlock
lp: Terence Morgan, Yolande
Donlan, André Morell, Ursula
Howells, Anthony Oliver, Guido
Lorraine, Reginald Beckwith

Women Without Men
(Exclusive/Hammer Film Productions)
d: Elmo Williams
p: Anthony Hinds
s: Val Guest, Richard Landau
lp: Beverly Michaels, Joan Rice,
Avril Angers, Thora Hird, Hermione
Baddeley, Gordon Jackson

It's a Wonderful World
(British International Pictures)
s: Val Guest p: Dennis O'Dell
lp: Terence Morgan, George Cole,
Kathleen Harrison, Mylene
Demongeot, James Hayter, Harold

Lang, Maurice Kaufmann, Richard Wattis

1956
The Weapon (Periclean Films)
s: Hal E Chester, Fred Freiberger
p: Frank Bevis
lp: Lizabeth Scott, Steve Cochran, George Cole, Herbert Marshall, Nicole Maurey, Jon Whiteley, Laurence Naismith

Quatermass 2
(Hammer Film Productions)
s: Nigel Kneale, Val Guest
p: Anthony Hinds
lp: Brian Donlevy, John Longden, Sidney James, Bryan Forbes, William Franklyn, Vera Day

1957
The Abominable Snowman
(Hammer Film Productions)
s: Nigel Kneale p: Aubrey Baring
lp: Forrest Tucker, Peter Cushing, Maureen Connell, Richard Wattis, Robert Brown, Michael Brill

The Camp on Blood Island
(Hammer Film Productions)
s: Jon Manchip White, Val Guest
p: Anthony Hinds
lp: André Morell, Carl Mohner, Edward Underdown, Barbara Shelley, Phil Brown, Michael Goodliffe, Michael Gwynn, Richard Wordsworth

Carry On Admiral (Renown Pictures)
s: Val Guest p: George Minter
lp: David Tomlinson, Peggy Cummins, Brian Reece, Eunice Gayson, AE Matthews, Joan Sims, Lionel Murton, Reginald Beckwith

Up the Creek
(Hammer Film Productions/ Byron Film Productions)
s: Val Guest, John Warren, Len Heath p: Henry Halsted
lp: David Tomlinson, Peter Sellers, Wilfrid Hyde White, Vera Day, Liliane Sottane, Tom Gill, Michael

Goodliffe, Reginald Beckwith

1958
Further up the Creek
(Hammer Film Productions/ Byron Film Productions)
s: John Warren, Len Heath, Val Guest p: Henry Halsted
lp: David Tomlinson, Frankie Howerd, Shirley Eaton, Thora Hird, Lionel Jeffries, Lionel Murton, Sam Kydd, John Warren, David Lodge

Life is a Circus
(Vale Film Productions)
s: Val Guest, Len Heath, John Warren p: EM Smedley-Aston
lp: Bud Flanagan, Chesney Allen, Jimmy Nervo, Teddy Knox, Charlie Naughton, Jimmy Gold, Eddie Grey, Shirley Eaton

1959
Yesterday's Enemy
(Hammer Film Productions)
s: Peter R Newman
p: Michael Carreras
lp: Stanley Baker, Guy Rolfe, Leo McKern, Gordon Jackson, David Oxley, Richard Pasco, Russell Waters, Philip Ahn, Bryan Forbes, Wolfe Morris

Expresso Bongo
(Val Guest Productions)
s: Wolf Mankowitz p: Val Guest
lp: Laurence Harvey, Sylvia Syms, Yolande Donlan, Cliff Richard, Meier Tzelniker, Ambrosine Phillpotts

Hell is a City
(Hammer Film Productions)
s: Val Guest p: Michael Carreras
lp: Stanley Baker, John Crawford, Donald Pleasence, Maxine Audley, Billie Whitelaw, Joseph Tomilty, Vanda Godsell

1960
Dentist in the Chair (Briand Films)
d: Don Chaffey

p: Bertram Ostrer
lp: Bob Monkhouse, Peggy Cummins, Kenneth Connor, Eric Barker, Ronnie Stevens, Vincent Ball, Eleanor Summerfield, Reginald Beckwith

The Full Treatment
(Hammer Film Productions)
s/p: Val Guest
lp: Claude Dauphin, Diane Cilento, Ronald Lewis, Francoise Rosay, Bernard Braden, Katya Douglas, Barbara Chilcott, Anne Tirard

1961
The Day the Earth Caught Fire
(Melina Productions)
s: Wolf Mankowitz, Val Guest
p: Val Guest
lp: Janet Munro, Leo McKern, Edward Judd, Michael Goodliffe, Bernard Braden, Reginald Beckwith, Gene Anderson, Renée Asherson, Arthur Christiansen

1962
Jigsaw (Val Guest Productions)
s/p: Val Guest
lp: Jack Warner, Ronald Lewis, Yolande Donlan, Michael Goodliffe, John Le Mesurier, Moira Redmond, Christine Bocca, Brian Oulton

1963
80,000 Suspects
(Val Guest Productions)
s/p: Val Guest
lp: Claire Bloom, Richard Johnson, Yolande Donlan, Cyril Cusack, Michael Goodliffe, Mervyn Johns, Arthur Christiansen

The Beauty Jungle
(Rank Film Productions)
s/p: Val Guest
lp: Ian Hendry, Janette Scott, Ronald Fraser, Edmund Purdom, Jean Claudio, Kay Walsh, Norman Bird, Janina Faye

1964
Where the Spies Are
(Val Guest Productions)
s: Wolf Mankowitz, Val Guest
p: Val Guest, Steven Pallos
lp: David Niven, Françoise Dorléac,
John Le Mesurier, Cyril Cusack, Eric
Pohlmann, Richard Marner

1966
Casino Royale
(Famous Artists Productions)
d: John Huston, Kenneth Hughes,
Val Guest, Robert Parrish,
Joseph McGrath
s: Wolf Mankowitz, John Law,
Michael Sayers, Val Guest
p: Charles K Feldman, Jerry Bresler
lp: Peter Sellers, Ursula Andress, David
Niven, Orson Welles, Joanna Pettet,
Daliah Lavi, Woody Allen, Deborah
Kerr, William Holden, Charles Boyer,
John Huston, Kurt Kasznar, George
Raft, Jean-Paul Belmondo, Terence
Cooper, Barbara Bouchet

1967
Assignment K (Gildor Productions/
Mazurka Productions)
s: Val Guest, Bill Strutton, Maurice
Foster p: Ben Arbeid, Maurice Foster
lp: Stephen Boyd, Michael Redgrave,
Carmilla Sparv, Leo McKern,
Robert Hoffman, Jeremy Kemp

1968
When Dinosaurs Ruled the Earth
(Hammer Film Productions)
s: Val Guest p: Aida Young
lp: Victoria Vetri, Robin Hawdon,
Patrick Holt, Patrick Allen,
Imogen Hassall

1969
Toomorrow (Lowndes Productions)
s: Val Guest p: Don Kirshner,
Harry Saltzman
lp: Olivia Newton-John, Ben Thomas,
Vic Cooper, Karl Chambers, Roy
Dotrice, Imogen Hassall

1972
Au Pair Girls (Tigon Pictures)
s: David Adnopoz, Val Guest
p: Guido Coen
lp: Astrid Frank, Johnny Briggs,
Gabrielle Drake, Me Me Lai, Nancie
Wait, Joyce Heron, Daphne
Anderson, Ferdy Mayne

1974
Confessions of a Window Cleaner
(Columbia Pictures)
s: Christopher Wood, Val Guest
p: Greg Smith
lp: Robin Asquith, Anthony Booth,
Sheila White, Dandy Nichols, Bill
Maynard, Linda Hayden, John Le
Mesurier, Joan Hickson

1975
The Diamond Mercenaries
(Michelangelo Productions)
s: Val Guest, Gerald Sanford,
Michael Winder p: Nat Wachsberger,
Patrick Wachsberger
lp: Telly Savalas, Peter Fonda, Hugh
O'Brian, Christopher Lee, OJ
Simpson, Maud Adams

1982
The Boys in Blue (Apollo Leisure)
s: Sid Colin, Sidney Green,
Val Guest p: Greg Smith
lp: Tommy Cannon, Bobby Ball,
Suzanne Danielle, Roy Kinnear, Eric
Sykes, Jack Douglas, Edward Judd,
Jon Pertwee, Arthur English

TELEVISION

1971
The Persuaders! (Television Reporters/
International Tribune/ITC)
p: Robert S Baker
lp: Tony Curtis, Roger Moore,
Laurence Naismith

The Gold Napoleon
d: Roy Ward Baker, Val Guest

s: Val Guest
guest cast: Susan George, Alfred
Marks, Harold Goldblatt, Michael
McStay, Hugh Manning

Angie … Angie
s: Milton S Gelman
guest cast: Larry Storch, Lionel
Murton, Kirsten Lindholm, John
Alderton, Anna Brett

Five Miles To Midnight
s: Terry Nation
guest cast: Joan Collins, Robert
Hutton, Robert Rietty, Ferdy
Mayne, Jean Marsh

1972
The Adventurer (Scoton/ITC)
p: Monty Berman
lp: Gene Barry, Barry Morse, Catherine
Schell, Garrick Hagon, Dennis Price

The Bradley Way
s: Gerald Kelsey
guest cast: Richard Marner, Janet
Kay, Anthony Ainley

Has Anyone Here Seen Kelly?
s: Tony Williamson
guest cast: Sandor Eles, Anouska
Hempel, Eric Pohlmann,
Lionel Murton

Deadlock
s: Donald James
guest cast: Wolfe Morris, Mervyn
Johns, Jennie Linden, Burt Kwouk,
Robert Rietty

I'll Get There Sometime
s: Tony Williamson
guest cast: Patrick Jordan, Pippa
Steel, Frank Barrie, John Levene

The Solid Gold Hearse
s: Tony Williamson
guest cast: Sydney Tafler, Kevin
Stoney, David Weston, Janos Kurucz

To the Lowest Bidder
s: Donald James
guest cast: Anthony Nicholls, Jane

Asher, Sheila Gish, Carl Rigg,
Gillian Bailey

Full Fathom Five
s: Donald James
guest cast: André Morell, Prunella
Ransome, Peter Jeffrey, Michael Gwynn

Going, Going...
s: Gerald Kelsey
guest cast: Arnold Diamond,
Burt Kwouk, Norman Bird,
Bridget Armstrong

1975
Space: 1999
(Group Three/RAI/ITC)
p: Fred Freiberger
lp: Martin Landau, Barbara Bain,
Nick Tate, Zienia Merton, Tony
Anholt, Catherine Schell

The Rules of Luton
s: Charles Woodgrove
guest cast: David Jackson, Godfrey
James, Roy Marsden

The A-B Chrysalis
s: Tony Barwick
guest cast: Ina Skriver, Sarah Douglas

Dorzak
s: Christopher Penfold
guest cast: Lee Montague,
Jill Townsend

1979
The Shillingbury Blowers (ITC)
s: Francis Essex p: Greg Smith
lp: Trevor Howard, Robin Nedwell,
Diane Keen, Jack Douglas,
John Le Mesurier

**Sherlock Holmes and Doctor
Watson** (Polish Television)
lp: Geoffrey Whitehead,
Donald Pickering, Patrick Newell,
Kay Walsh

The Shillingbury Tales (ITC)
p: Greg Smith
lp: Robin Nedwell, Diane Keen,
Lionel Jeffries, Bernard Cribbins,
Jack Douglas, Joe Black, Linda
Hayden

1980
**Dangerous Davies –
The Last Detective** (ITC)
s: Leslie Thomas, Val Guest
p: Greg Smith
lp: Bernard Cribbins, Bill Maynard, Joss
Ackland, Bernard Lee, Frank Windsor,
John Leyton, Maureen Lipman

1983–4
Hammer House of Mystery
and Suspense
(Hammer/Twentieth Century Fox)
p: Roy Skeggs

In Possession
s: Michael J Bird
lp: Carol Lynley, Christopher
Cazenove, David Healy, Judy Loe

Mark of the Devil
s: Brian Clemens
lp: Dirk Benedict, Jenny Seagrove,
George Sewell, John Paul

Child's Play
s: Graham Wassell
lp: Mary Crosby, Nicholas Clay,
Debbie Chasen

INDEX